Jonathan Holmes has produced in indispensable manual for marriage counseling. This excellent volume will prove a well-used resource for counselors. Highly recommended.

TEDD TRIPP, author, pastor, conference speaker

Counsel for Couples is rich with well-rounded, mature, biblical wisdom stemming from years of loving, pastoral ministry. I know of nothing else like it.

PAUL TAUTGES, author; senior pastor, Cornerstone Community Church, Mayfield Heights, Ohio; founder, Counseling One Another

Jonathan writes honestly about the realities of helping couples and points out hidden gospel opportunities to share true hope found in Christ, wisdom in Scripture, and our lives with others. Highly recommended.

LILLY PARK, PhD, assistant professor of Biblical Counseling, Southern Baptist Theological Seminary

Counsel for Couples is a great read for those who want to grow in their ability to care for marriages in trouble. It will help you counsel marriages better!

GARRETT HIGBEE, president, Twelve Stones Ministries; director of pastoral care, Great Commission Collective

What a unique and helpful trove Jonathan has labored to give us! From the concrete and practical elements of couples work to one personal story after another, here we have a rich reference that runs the gamut of marital counseling.

AARON SIRONI, LCPC, faculty member, Christian Counseling & Educational Foundation

As I look back on my pastoral and counseling ministry, I wish I'd had this book to guide me. I look forward to using it in my ministry and in training future biblical counselors.

DAVID MURRAY, professor of Old Testament and Practical Theology, Puritan Reformed Seminary

I've read many books on marriage, but Jonathan Holmes filled practical gaps and provided new strategies I now use to serve my church family. Read it and sharpen both your understanding of marriage and your wisdom in counseling.

P. J. TIBAYAN, pastor-theologian, Bethany Baptist Church, Bellflower, California; blogger at gospelize.me

Much sage wisdom can be found in this helpful and practical guide for biblical counselors.

ERIC L. JOHNSON, PhD, senior research professor of Pastoral Care, Southern Baptist Theological Seminary

From helping couples navigate the arduous paths created by things such as adultery, abuse, and pornography to guiding husbands and wives with rich wisdom to help cultivate marriages that reflect the beauty of God, *Counsel for Couples* is a must-read for anyone desiring to serve those who have entered the sacred covenant of marriage.

JEREMY LELEK, PhD, LPC-S, president, Association of Biblical Counselors

A wise, Scripturally-saturated primer on marriage counseling. If you're a pastor in search of biblically-based counseling resources, this should become a well-worn guidebook on your desk.

MICHAEL R. EMLET, MDiv, MD, faculty and counselor, Christian Counseling & Educational Foundation

Jonathan Holmes is a rare kind of counselor—thoroughly biblical and attentive to the delicate dynamics of how people actually experience marriage. This book is a needed guide to addressing those dynamics with wisdom and skill.

JEREMY PIERRE, PhD, Lawrence & Charlotte Hoover associate professor of Biblical Counseling; chair, Department of Biblical Counseling & Family Ministry

A tremendous gift to the church! This book is anchored in the truth of God's Word, saturated with the sufficiency of God's grace, and written for the equipping of God's people. Easily accessible to young and mature believers alike.

DR. SCOTTY WARD SMITH, pastor emeritus, Christ Community Church, Franklin, Tennessee; teacher in residence, West End Community Church, Nashville, Tennessee

My heart was thrilled to sense Jonathan's kind eyes, gentle voice, and gospel of hope on every page of this book. If you often find yourself on the steep and thorny path of marriage counseling, this weathered map will help you find God's way forward.

DAVID "GUNNER" GUNDERSEN, PhD, BridgePoint Bible Church, Houston, Texas

This book is abundantly practical, thoroughly biblical, and deeply refreshing. Here is real help for those called to shepherd the flock of God among them.

J. J. SHERWOOD, lead pastor, Five Points Community Church

This book is an excellent basic primer in Christian marital counseling. Biblical, comprehensive, and realistic—the best marriage counseling resource available now to pastors and biblical counselors.

SAM R. WILLIAMS, PhD, professor of Counseling, Southeastern Baptist Theological Seminary, Wake Forest, North Carolina

A helpful, thoughtful, practical, comprehensive, and edifying book on marriage counseling. Jonathan equips counselors with truth from God's Word and encourages them to communicate it in love.

Loving, biblical counseling with individuals is complex. Loving, biblical counseling with couples is exponentially complex. Jonathan Holmes has done the biblical counseling movement a great service.

I've been waiting for this book my entire ministry. This book is a treasure trove of wisdom for marriage counseling in the church. If you minister among married couples, you need to buy this book right now. Read it and keep it handy on your shelf for quick consultation.

Rather than candy-coat the challenges of counseling couples, Jonathan faces them head-on. He offers real gospel-anchored hope for the counselor and the counselee. This book is well-researched, founded on a rich biblical theology, filled with practical examples, and informed by experience. It's a must-have for pastors, counselors, and church leaders.

A delightful guide for those seeking to help married partners, and a much-needed reference for every biblical counselor's library. The "One Couple's Story" sections are gold mines of practical wisdom for everyday life.

This book is not only a must-read but a must-reference. The most comprehensive and scripturally-faithful work on couples counseling I have ever read.

A superb contribution to the field of marriage counseling! This should be required reading for anyone involved in pastoral ministry.

Read this book cover to cover—it is useful immediately. Then keep it close by as a handy reference tool. It is filled with Jonathan's pastoral experience, to which he adds many other wise, reliable voices and resources.

EDWARD T. WELCH, counselor and faculty, Christian
Counseling & Educational Foundation

Whether you're a pastor, a counselor, or a layperson who wants to help marriages flourish, this book will help you help others. It's a resource you'll come back to again and again.

BOB LEPINE, senior vice president, FamilyLife

Marital counseling presents some of the most difficult challenges of ministry. This book walks us through a labyrinth of marital issues by providing wisdom from the gospel of Christ and practical insights from the Bible.

TIM SAVAGE, PhD, council member, The Gospel
Coalition, Cambridge, England

What makes this book stand out is how it walks the pastor/counselor through the process of couples counseling with key points to cover, sample questions for counselees, and brief scripts for counseling. And it covers important topics that are rarely addressed in marriage books, including in-law relations, infertility, and miscarriage.

JIM NEWHEISER, director, Christian Counseling Program;
associate professor of Practical Theology, Reformed Theological
Seminary, Charlotte, North Carolina; executive director,
The Institute for Biblical Counseling and Discipleship

Counsel for Couples is an excellent introduction to the basic skills of marriage counseling and an overview of key challenges addressed in marriage counseling. Jonathan brings together best practices and leading voices in an extremely practical book.

BRAD HAMBRICK, pastor of counseling, The Summit Church,
Durham, North Carolina; author, *Creating a Gospel-Centered
Marriage* mentoring series (bradhambrick.com/gcm)

This is a new must-have resource for pastors. I'll be taking all our pastors through the first part together for group discussion and encourage all of them to have the book on their shelf for when they need to refer to the second part before difficult counseling appointments.

SCOTT ZELLER, executive pastor, Redeemer Dubai

COUNSEL
for
COUPLES

COUNSEL

for

COUPLES

A Biblical
and Practical Guide *for*
Marriage
Counseling

JONATHAN D. HOLMES

ZONDERVAN REFLECTIVE

Counsel for Couples
Copyright © 2019 by Jonathan Holmes

Published in Grand Rapids, Michigan, by Zondervan. Zondervan is a registered trademark of The Zondervan Corporation, L.L.C., a wholly owned subsidary of HarperCollins Christian Publishing, Inc.

Requests for information should be addressed to customercare@harpercollins.com.

Zondervan titles may be purchased in bulk for educational, business, fundraising, or sales promotional use. For information, please email SpecialMarkets@Zondervan.com.

ISBN 978-0-310-63639-7 (audio)
ISBN 978-0-310-57738-6 (ebook)

Library of Congress Cataloging-in-Publication Data

Names: Holmes, Jonathan D., author.
Title: Counsel for couples : a biblical and practical guide for marriage counseling / Jonathan D. Holmes.
Description: Grand Rapids, Michigan : Zondervan, [2019] | Includes bibliographical references.
Identifiers: LCCN 2019000985 | ISBN 9780310576273 (hardcover)
Subjects: LCSH: Marriage counseling. | Church work with married people. | Marriage—Religious aspects—Christianity. | Pastoral counseling.
Classification: LCC BV4012.27 .H65 2019 | DDC 259/.14—dc23 LC record available at https://lccn.loc.gov/2019000985

Art direction: Tammy Johnson
Interior design: Kait Lamphere

Printed in the United States of America

24 25 26 27 28 29 30 31 32 33 34 /TRM/ 16 15 14 13 12 11 10 9 8 7 6 5 4 3 2

To Jennifer

Many people get the joy of calling you friend, a few others call you aunt, and an even smaller amount call you sister, mother, and daughter. I'm beyond amazed and humbled, though, that I'm the only one who can call you wife. I love you to the moon and back.

To the lay counselors at Parkside Church and the counselors at Fieldstone Counseling, this book is dedicated to you. You labor quietly, wisely, and compassionately without acclaim; you speak words of life and truth into couples' lives and offer yourself as an instrument in the Redeemer's hands. Thank you.

CONTENTS

PART 1:
The Basics of Counseling Couples

PART 2:
Specific Issues You Will Face
in Marriage Counseling

PART 3:
Conclusion

FOREWORD

The writer of Hebrews encourages his readers to submit to their leaders: "For they are keeping watch over your souls, as those who will have to give an account" (Heb. 13:17 ESV). Such is the staggering responsibility we have as pastors in loving and caring for the people entrusted to us. We are all out of our depth in pastoral work. We cannot rely on our own expertise or training or experience but must trust in God's ability to use frail instruments filled with his Spirit. And let us not move too quickly to instruct others in these matters, or we may lose sight of the fact that we ourselves are also in need of the material we teach.

We must avoid the snare of professionalism. Speaking about sexual immorality in the church, the apostle Paul issued a warning: "Let anyone who thinks he stands take heed lest he fall" (1 Cor. 10:12 ESV). As I write this, yet another high profile evangelical pastor has failed to heed these words, and sadly, this is not an isolated incident. It is all too easy for us to urge those under our care to live lives of practical godliness while failing to address our own struggles. Yet we dare not neglect our own vineyard while busy tending the vines of others.

In the 1700s, the godly minister Richard Baxter, vicar in Kidderminster, wrote four massive volumes providing an outline in practical Christianity. My own copy of the fourth volume runs 1,047 pages! Few of us have the time or the patience to wade through this material, but be not alarmed. Holmes to the rescue! The book you hold is far shorter and more accessible. And even though they are separated by more than three centuries and an ocean, both authors have this in common: they are convinced of the sufficiency and power of God's Word to address the most difficult and challenging marital issues. In the sorest of trials you face in counseling others, you will be encouraged to find the comfort and grace and forgiving mercy we have in him who is touched with our infirmities.

Unlike some books that are overly complex and leave us feeling inadequate, this book provides help for the "ordinary pastor." As pastors, we need not pretend to be marriage counselors or sex therapists, for Holmes directs us to the Bible as the source of our wisdom. He reminds us that in teaching the Bible we are not simply trying to prevent people from divorcing; we are seeking to get people into heaven.

In the 1970s, British journalist Jill Tweedie wrote an article entitled, "When Marriage Is Just a Cage" in which she expressed her hope that "outside the bonds of Christian marriage we will discover what love is all about."[1] Forty years later there is no evidence that her hope has been fulfilled. Yet marriage as God established, between one man and one woman, is still under severe attack.

Today we need wise pastors who are trained and equipped to address the challenge of failing marriages. To help people navigate these troubled seas, we must be deeply convinced of the absolute authority and reliability of the Bible while displaying the kind compassion found in the Lord Jesus. We must not apply biblical principles in a ruthless, unfeeling, and unthinking way. When people know that we love them, they will accept what we say, even when we must offer a rebuke or a word of challenge. "Love me," said Augustine, "and then say anything to me and about me you like." Richard Baxter's flock used to say, "We take all things well from one who always and wholly loves us."[2]

It is a great privilege to be invited to write this foreword and to commend the work of my friend and colleague, Jonathan Holmes. There is nothing abstract or merely theoretical in these pages. I have seen how this thoroughly biblical and eminently practical material has worked in our own congregation, and I have been greatly helped and challenged in reading this book. I pray that it will receive a wide readership, and I hope that it will be used to strengthen marriages, even as we are directed to the One who loves us with an everlasting love.

Alistair Begg
Parkside Church

1. Jill Tweedie, "When Marriage Is Just a Cage," *Guardian*, 1976.
2. Richard Baxter, *The Reformed Pastor* (Carlisle, PA: Banner of Truth Trust, 2007), 118.

ACKNOWLEDGMENTS

A book of this magnitude would not be possible without the prayers and support of so many individuals. In many ways, this book is the fruit of men and women, past and present, who have discipled and taught me through their teaching, books, and personal conversation. This book is also the fruit of the husbands and wives I've had the honor and privilege of counseling.

Thank you to Deepak Reju for having the conversation with me about writing on this topic and getting the project off the ground. Thank you to Bob Kellemen for introducing me to Ryan Pazdur and the wonderful team at Zondervan. Over ten years ago, you reached out to me to participate in the first meeting of the Biblical Counseling Coalition. Since then your investment, mentorship, and pursuit have been blessings in my life.

Thank you to Ryan Pazdur and your team at Zondervan. The attention to detail and way you have ushered this project from start to finish have been a most enjoyable experience. Thank you to Josh Blunt and Kim Tanner for working with me on each round of edits. Your feedback and comments have made this a stronger book with greater clarity.

To my colleagues at Parkside Church, I thank you for your ongoing support and encouragement. Along the way you have asked questions, provided feedback, and been an overall cheerleader for this project. I cannot think of a better pastoral team to serve with. I want to especially thank Adam Romans, who I've had the joy of serving with at Parkside Green for over a decade. Not only are you family, but you have been a supporter of biblical counseling and Fieldstone from day one. No one at Parkside has been a bigger encourager or supporter of me and this project than you.

To the staff of Fieldstone Counseling, thank you for reading through the manuscript and offering feedback. A special thank you to Sue Moroney, who read through one of the earlier drafts and provided critical feedback. Thank you to Joy King who spent time helping me in the final stages of editing. Thank you to Colleen Metzger for copying and binding multiple drafts of this book for me to read. Thank you to many others who read drafts of individual chapters and provided feedback: Chris Moles, Brad Hambrick, Marsha Raymond, Karen Wilkinson, Steve Moroney, and Adam Bryant Marshall.

To my colleagues and fellow colaborers in the biblical counseling movement, I pray this book helps us further the conversation and development of a robust, biblical, compassionate model of care for couples. Thank you to Brad Hambrick, Joe Keller, Deepak Reju, and others who have had conversations with me and helped shape the content of this book. Thank you to Aaron Sironi, who, at an early stage of the project, shared his wisdom and insight on the often overwhelming task of marriage counseling. While we didn't end up getting to carry out the project how we had hoped, I look forward to writing with you at some point. To Ed Welch, thank you for the encouragement to write the book in such a way that it could also be used by couples. Your writing, friendship, and investment in Parkside and Fieldstone's counseling ministries will never be forgotten.

To the many couples who have invited me into the most intimate areas of their lives, I say through tears: thank you. I believe David Powlison describes being invited into people's lives as akin to handling the "fine china" of their hearts. I feel this deeply, and I am so thankful for any small role I have been able to play. Your stories have impacted me greatly, and this book is a culmination of what I have learned in the office with you all.

This project would not have been completed on time except for the generosity and patience of my wife, Jennifer. Jen, thank you for allowing me to take valuable family time over Thanksgiving and Christmas break to complete the final draft of this book. I've said time and time again that one of the reasons I do marriage counseling is because it helps me in my marriage! I am not perfect by any stretch of the imagination, and yet you have shown great love and forbearing patience with me over the past thirteen years of our marriage.

To my four daughters—Ava, Riley, Ruby, and Emma—I pray that if God has marriage in store for you, that you will marry godly men who treasure our Savior, Jesus Christ and who will love you faithfully, compassionately, and graciously. Most of all I pray and hope that you will come to know Jesus Christ personally as your Lord and Savior. I love you so much.

Lastly, thanks be to God for giving us the gift of marriage, which tells the story of your covenant love to us in Christ. May this book serve the purpose of helping couples embody this most precious story.

INTRODUCTION

The book you are holding in your hand is the book I wish I had when I started off in pastoral ministry over ten years ago. It is a book written by an ordinary pastor for other ordinary pastors and counselors who are faithfully seeking to love and shepherd the people God has entrusted to them.

I'll never forget my first marital counseling session: Julie's husband had recently confessed to an extra-marital affair, and I was put in the awkward position of having to break the news to his wife. I was absolutely terrified. Talk about getting thrown into the deep end of the pool (and I don't swim by the way)! Here I was, two months into the job, and the elders of my church were asking me to meet this woman who was about to hear earthshaking news that would change the course of her life.

Somehow I made it through the session by God's grace. By the end, there was a mountain of tissues rivaling the height of my nearby trash can. The feeling I had in that moment was one of complete and total helplessness. I felt lost. Needless to say, I was woefully unprepared.

I suspect that, like me, you're not a licensed marriage and family therapist and you didn't do a doctoral dissertation on pastoral counseling. Yet I know that the majority of pastors meet and counsel couples on a weekly basis.

Before I began the process of writing this book, I put together a survey and sent it to pastors to gain a sense of how equipped they felt to do marriage counseling. The responses were encouraging in many ways, but also showed that many pastors and lay leaders felt inadequately trained to do marriage counseling. One person wrote, "I feel ill-equipped to create an overall plan (how many times to meet, what tools are needed, etc.) and then carry it out. I often feel like I just have an appointment and fly by the seat of my pants."

Another person remarked that marriage counseling feels like "managing disintegration by going from trouble to trouble." Response after response from pastors, counselors, and lay leaders alike showed that the myriad of issues that come in marriage counseling can feel overwhelming. Despite the obstacles that seem to make marriage counseling difficult, many of the respondents wrote about their encouragement when marriages began to grow in Christ. One pastor replied, "I enjoy watching the two individuals grow in their relationship with Christ, as well as with each other. To see them experience peace, joy, contentment, and encouragement in a way they had not previously done."

What I realized as I went through these responses is that most pastors and counselors do enjoy marriage counseling, but they don't know *how* to do marriage counseling. Friend, that is what this book is designed to address.

Here is my goal for this book: I want to leave you with a solid, biblical theology and methodology to help you navigate through the world of marriage counseling. My conviction is this: God's Word is sufficient and powerful enough to address the deepest of marital issues and robust enough to assess the everyday issues you will encounter in marriage counseling. I believe the Bible gives us the most comprehensive understanding of who we are, what we were made for, why life is hard, and what makes it better. Scripture does not come to us in the form of a textbook on marriage counseling methodology, but it does contain for us the Story of stories, which I believe can transform and fundamentally re-story marriages for his glory.

With that being said, let me tell you a little about the format of the book and how it might best serve you in your ministry. In the first six chapters of the book, it is my hope to lay out some of the basics when it comes to marriage counseling—and counseling in general. Whatever your level of competency when it comes to counseling, these chapters lay out a basic understanding of biblical counseling for marriages.

Chapters seven through sixteen address individual issues most pastors, counselors, and lay leaders will encounter in marriage counseling. Each of the chapters will include a biblical understanding of the issue and steps to practically counsel the couple. At the end of every chapter, I've tried to compile a list of resources that address that chapter's content. One of the most frequent inquiries I receive from pastors and counselors is, "Can you recommend a resource for me on the issue of _____?" Now you'll have that list for yourself.

Along the way, you'll read testimonies of other well-known voices in the biblical counseling movement who will share their own stories of how God can change marriages for the better. Their testimonies are meant to *equip* you. You'll also hear real-life testimonies of couples who have benefitted from biblical marriage counseling; their stories are meant to *encourage* you.

There is another audience and group of people who also might benefit from this book: couples in crisis. While the primary audience of this book is pastors, elders, counselors, and lay leaders, you might be a husband or wife in need of marital encouragement or perhaps marital correction. The content in each chapter will provide principles you can take to heart and apply to your marriage.

I'll leave you with two of my favorite passages when it comes to counseling because for me they address two aspects of my counseling ministry: (1) my only hope in counseling is in the power of the Word of God, and (2) my profound sense of inadequacy apart from the person and work of Jesus Christ. May we as pastors and counselors never forget either truth.

> For the word of God is alive and active. Sharper than any double-edged sword, it penetrates even to dividing soul and spirit, joints and marrow; it judges the thoughts and attitudes of the heart.
>
> HEBREWS 4:12

> Such confidence we have through Christ before God. Not that we are competent in ourselves to claim anything for ourselves, but our competence comes from God. He has made us competent as ministers of a new covenant—not of the letter but of the Spirit; for the letter kills, but the Spirit gives life.
>
> 2 CORINTHIANS 3:4–6

PART 1

THE BASICS OF COUNSELING COUPLES

Chapter 1

GETTING THE LAY
OF THE LAND

Be shepherds of God's flock that is under your care, watching over them—not because you must, but because you are willing, as God wants you to be.

1 PETER 5:2

We keep bringing in mechanics when what we need are gardeners.

PETER SENGE

Jeff and Jennifer Jones have been married for twenty years. Currently, they're preparing to send their first daughter, Riley, off to college and get their twin sons, Carson and Connor, adjusted to high school. Four years earlier, though, Jeff and Jen had just received the surprise of their life: they found out they were pregnant.

Since they had thought they would be empty nesters soon, Jeff and Jen felt torn between being excited to welcome little Chloe into the family and realizing their dreams of worldwide travel would need to be postponed for eighteen more years.

Jennifer admits she is not doing well. The past twenty years with Jeff have been fine, almost uneventful. Yet in many respects she wonders where those years have gone. Why haven't she and Jeff grown and connected in deeper ways? The only connection they seem to have is communicating pick-up and drop-off times for the boys' basketball practice and Chloe's pick-up from preschool.

From the outside looking in, the Joneses look great. They're happy, they're together . . . but both Jennifer and Jeff instinctively know things aren't right. After a particularly hectic day, Jennifer snaps at Jeff, which initiates a long, drawn-out fight. (The fights used to be more sporadic but have lately come with increasing frequency and heightened emotion.) Jeff tells Jennifer they need to talk to someone at church—and so they reach out to you.

Jeff and Jennifer come in and sit down. You're nervous (but hope they don't see it) and they're nervous. In twenty years of marriage they've never needed "counseling." After giving you some basic background of what brought them in, Jennifer says, "Things are just off. I don't feel connected to Jeff anymore, and frankly, I'm worn out."

So, what's your next move? What do you do? What do you say? Closing in prayer and dismissing them isn't an option at this point. There's no time to excuse yourself for a few hours to go and do research and preparation. You don't have a phone-a-friend. What's your initial goal? How do you spend the next thirty to forty-five minutes?

These types of scenarios can be scary. Most churches cannot afford to have a staff counselor or resident therapist, much less a pastor of counseling. Most of the counseling is either referred out to a local Christian counseling center or is hopefully taken care of in a couple of meetings with the pastor. But Jeff and Jennifer obviously have some trust in you to address their issues. How do you move forward? Are you equipped to help them in these moments?

Doing marriage counseling can be a daunting task even for those who have years of experience and are licensed for such work. Well-known marriage therapists Drs. John and Julie Gottman describe the work as facing "two dragons trying to immolate each other. We . . . feel scared sometimes, and we've been doing this work for decades."[1]

Counselor and author Everett Worthington quips, "Most counselors dread dealing with troubled marriages even though troubled marriages often form the majority of their caseload."[2] If this is how licensed professionals feel about marriage counseling, then what hope do people like you or I have when it comes to helping couples in crisis?

PASTOR, YOU ARE A COUNSELOR

I readily acknowledge that many of you are already laboring faithfully to help couples who are struggling and hurting. Many of you spend hours—many late in

---

1. Julie Schwartz Gottman and John M. Gottman, *10 Principles for Doing Effective Couples Therapy* (New York: W. W. Norton, 2015), 23.
2. Everett Worthington, *Hope-Focused Marriage Counseling: A Guide to Brief Therapy* (Downers Grove, IL: InterVarsity Press, 1999), 20. Dr. Worthington comes from a different perspective and school of counseling (integration), but his observation is worth mentioning.

the evening—offering wise counsel to those in need. Sometimes you see repentance, growth, and change, and sometimes you don't. Marriage counseling can be a long, arduous journey for both the counselor and the couple, and yet despite these obstacles, I'm convinced that pastors[3] are well positioned to meet marriages in crisis with the hope of the gospel. Gregory the Great called pastoral care and counseling the "art of arts."[4] While some pastors may not view themselves as counselors, all pastors counsel. In fact, William Clebsch makes a point that many church attendees view their pastors as counselors: "Gauged both by consumer demand and by the clergyman's self-evaluation, the chief business of religion in the United States is now—as it probably has long been—the cure of souls."[5]

Author and counselor David Powlison states it bluntly: "Pastor, you are a counselor. Perhaps you don't think of yourself that way. (And perhaps your people don't think of you that way, either.) Perhaps you don't want to be a counselor. But you are one."[6] This might surprise some of us. We attended seminary to preach, not counsel—right?

But why do we pastors separate *preaching* the Word from *counseling* the Word? Paul Tripp explains the similarity between the two pastoral duties: "From a biblical perspective, both public and personal ministries base their hope for change on the Word of God. They are simply different methods of bringing the Word to people in different contexts."[7] This is not to say pastors should seek to turn their Sunday morning sermons into group counseling sessions. E. Brooks Holifield notes the error in going toward that extreme: "Despite some excessive enthusiasm, Protestant clergy have profited vastly from the new sensitivity to pastoral counseling. The problem is that our era has evidenced a singular preoccupation with psychological modes of thinking—modes which have tended to refashion the entire religious life of Protestants in the image of the therapeutic. When Harry Emerson Fosdick

---

3. Throughout the book I will refer to pastors as the primary audience, but the principles apply to any doing ministry in the church (e.g., elders, deacons, lay counselors, life group leaders, Bible study facilitators, etc.). David Powlison writes on an expanded audience in addition to pastors as counselors, "All human beings are counselors, whether wise, foolish, or mixed. *All* Christians are meant to become wiser counselors. God intends that every word you ever say to anyone is actively constructive in content, intention, tone, and appropriateness. That's Ephesians 4:29. Those who face *any* affliction should find you a source of tangible, life-renewing comfort. That's 2 Corinthians 1:4. Wisdom sets the bar high. We are to become a community in which substantial conversations predominate. You who are not pastors will grow in wisdom by considering how pastoral work particularizes the wisdom of Christ in the cure of souls whenever the body of Christ is working well." "The Pastor as Counselor," *Journal of Biblical Counseling* 26, no. 1 (2012): 25.

4. Gregory the Great, *Regula Pastoralis* (New York: Newman, 1950), 21.

5. E. Brooks Holifield, *A History of Pastoral Care in America: From Salvation to Self-Realization* (Eugene, OR: Wipf & Stock, 1983), 307.

6. Powlison, "The Pastor as Counselor," 23.

7. Paul David Tripp, *Instruments in the Redeemer's Hands* (Phillipsburg, NJ: P&R, 2002), 21.

referred to the sermon as counseling on a large scale, he forgot that Protestant sermons, at their best, have interpreted an ancient text that resists reduction to the psychological."[8]

And what does the Bible say about the pastor's role as a counselor? In his letter to the Ephesians, Paul recounts the glories of being *in Christ*; for three chapters, he layers truth upon truth about who we are in Christ and the resulting privileges of that relationship. In chapter four, however, Paul makes a transition, urging those in Christ to live a certain way: "I urge you to live a life worthy of the calling you have received. Be completely humble and gentle; be patient, bearing with one another in love. Make every effort to keep the unity of the Spirit through the bond of peace" (Eph. 4:1–3).

Our union with Christ has direct pastoral and ethical implications on how we live and how we treat others. And Paul goes on in Ephesians four to describe the way God has equipped the church to help us deal with those implications. When Jesus ascended on high, he "gave gifts to his people" (4:8). These gifts include the ministries of apostles, prophets, evangelists, shepherds, and teachers. Paul tells us that the purpose of these gifts is to equip God's people for works of service so that ultimately the entire body of Christ can be edified and built up.

We might be tempted to end our reading there. Some might read Ephesians 4:12 and say, "See! That's it. I'm a pastor/teacher who preaches and builds up the body of Christ. There's nothing in there about *counseling* people." If we read further, though, we see Paul continuing his outworking of the believer's calling by exhorting *all* the members of the body of Christ to be growing and maturing in their faith (Eph. 4:13). And he describes in detail how this will work out: "*Speaking the truth in love*, we will grow to become in every respect the mature body of him who is the head, that is, Christ" (Eph. 4:15, emphasis mine).

There you have it. This is counseling in its simplest formulation: *speaking truth in love*. Paul tells us this is for every believer! Every pastor, every evangelist, every minister of mercy—all of us who are a part of the body of Christ—are called to speak the truth in love. This is at the very heart of what it means for every pastor to be counseling. Counseling is one of the many ways we can *take the truths of God's Word and speak them in love in the context of a personal relationship with the goal of growing in godliness.*

This definition of counseling embraces constituent elements that naturally fall within the ministry of a pastor. Powlison writes, "Counseling is not essentially a technical enterprise calling for technical expertise. It is a relational and

---

8. Holifield, *A History of Pastoral Care in America,* 356.

pastoral enterprise engaging in care and cure of the soul. Both psychotherapy and psychiatry attempt pastoral work, engaging in 'care and cure of the soul' as their etymologies accurately signify. Sigmund Freud rightly defined therapists as 'secular pastoral workers.'"[9]

Pastor, you are called to publicly proclaim the truth of God's Word in public, but you are also called to privately minister the truth of God's Word interpersonally. Every pastor is a counselor. Paul is not alone in calling pastors to this task either. Peter reminds us to "Be shepherds of God's flock that is under your care, watching over them—not because you must, but because you are willing, as God wants you to be; not pursuing dishonest gain, but eager to serve; not lording it over those entrusted to you, but being examples to the flock" (1 Pet. 5:2–3). Shepherds shepherd by being among their people, leading and guiding them—not by keeping them at arm's length.

In one of the most intimate and moving letters to a church, Paul recounts with sincere fondness the time he spent among the people of Thessalonica: "Instead, we were like young children among you. Just as a nursing mother cares for her children, so we cared for you. Because we loved you so much, we were delighted to share with you not only the gospel of God but our lives as well. Surely you remember, brothers and sisters, our toil and hardship; we worked night and day in order not to be a burden to anyone while we preached the gospel of God to you" (1 Thess. 2:7–9).

This is not a letter from a detached pastor who has a "Sunday-only" mentality. No, Paul is a gentle, affectionate leader who embraces his calling as a pastor and shepherd. His proclamation of the gospel was not limited to pulpit ministry alone. Powlison notes that Paul's relationship here with the Thessalonians is decidedly "emotionally involved."[10] He goes on to write, "If Jesus had entered into purely consultative, professional relationships, he'd have had to stop being a pastor."[11]

As Dr. Martyn Lloyd-Jones wrote perceptively in *Preaching and Preachers*, "To love to preach is one thing, to love those to whom we preach quite another."[12] We should resist the temptation to equate our love of preaching with a love for people. Lloyd-Jones insisted that the latter does not necessarily follow from the former. Rather, as ministers of God's Word, we realize that part of the joy and happiness

---

9. Powlison, "The Pastor as Counselor," 26. This does not mean there is not a role for mental health professionals but rather notes that their ultimate concerns are inherently religious in nature and can only be addressed by the truth of Scripture.

10. Powlison, "The Pastor as Counselor," 27.

11. Ibid.

12. Erik Raymond, "Preaching and Preachers," December 26, 2007. *The Gospel Coalition*: https://www.thegospelcoalition.org/blogs/erik-raymond/preaching-and-preachers.

that comes from preaching and pastoral ministry arises out of our love for those whom God has entrusted to us. This is what counseling is all about, and it is a part of your vocational calling to care for people whom God has entrusted to you.

WHY PASTORS AS COUNSELORS?

Pastors are often well positioned to be a good counselor for a variety of reasons. In fact, many pastors are already doing the *work* of counseling without naming it as such.

- *Weekly or at least regular contact.* Pastors have the opportunity for regular contact with couples. Whether a Sunday service or a midweek Bible study, a pastor has the opportunity to run into husbands and wives with more frequency than a professional counselor.[13]
- *Theological training and education.* Not all pastors complete a seminary/graduate degree, but many do. Recently, there has been a healthy discussion about the lack of pastoral care courses in the typical MDiv program. That being said, many pastors leave seminary with a level of theological training that enables them to understand Scripture and a desire to shepherd those in their care.
- *Opportunity to network and create continuity of care.* The church is full of people with varying gifts and callings. Often a pastor will have at their disposal a wide range of people that can be asked for help. Relationships with medical and mental health professionals both inside and outside the church become an opportunity to seek additional help and counsel on complex cases.
- *Ability to provide long-term care.* The church is well suited for long-term care. As we look at the storyline of Scripture, we understand that all of God's people will be gathered together to spend eternity with him. The church is God's ordained institution to inaugurate this reality, and as such, functions as a place where people can grow together in Christ. Counseling is often a short-term relationship, but one which naturally dovetails with ongoing discipleship, service, and involvement in the church.

---

13. You can help make contact outside a marriage counseling session less awkward or embarrassing for couples by having a discussion with them regarding how best to approach and interact with them. Some couples do not mind mixing conversation about their marriage and counseling with other topics of conversation. Others might prefer to keep that aspect of your relationship confined to the office. Either way, you can help alleviate any concerns at the outset of a relationship by assuring couples that you will treat the counseling relationship with confidentiality and wisdom.

- *Body of knowledge about the couple.* Another benefit a pastor brings to marriage counseling is typically some sort of background knowledge or context of the couple. This is especially true for pastors who have been in their role for an extended season of ministry.[14]
- *Built-in trust.* Many people have some level of trust with their pastor and church leadership. When couples come in need of counsel, in some way their outreach to you is indicative of some sense of trustworthiness. While not always the case, many couples understand that pastors and elders function with spiritual authority and oversight for their lives.
- *Financial considerations.* I've seen several couples seek counseling in the church for financial considerations. While insurance coverage varies, many couples are still left with steep co-pays and a limited amount of marital therapy sessions. The church can often provide marriage counseling to couples at little to no cost.

HOW MUCH TIME SHOULD I SPEND COUNSELING?

You might think, "So there's a good argument for me to be doing counseling, but how much time should I put into this endeavor?" This is a good question and one that does not have an exact answer. Some pastors have a greater bandwidth for pastoral counseling, and thus are willing and able to dedicate a significant amount of time to it. Other pastors find themselves more interested in outreach ministry, discipleship, music, or administration. In smaller churches, lead pastors have to play multiple roles, which can often prevent them from seeing couples in counseling. In larger churches, pastors are not always expected to counsel if they have someone on their team dedicated to counseling ministry.

All things considered though, I believe a percentage of a pastor's load, regardless of church size, should be dedicated to coming alongside and caring for the needs of the people. David Powlison adds an important caveat on the *kind* of people you should endeavor to counsel, which I believe translates to marriage as well:

You should always be involved with a few people who are slow movers, with strugglers. The temptation is to counsel leader types, gifted people who

---

14. This dynamic can also cut the other way. When a pastor does not have a good history with a spouse it can predispose them from offering counsel because of the effort or difficulty involved. Every marriage counseling session offers the pastor to approach the couple with Christlike love and a desire to listen and be informed.

want to grow. People who are a quick study. People who get it. Educated, independent, competent people. Influential people. Such people often make for efficient counseling (though not necessarily). They might not need more than a consultation or two. It doesn't necessarily require you to deal with the confusion, willfulness, and suffering of the human heart. But sheep are often needy, confused, broken, harassed, stubborn, fearful, slow to grow, and forgetful. They are really just like pastors and other leaders, however much the ideas of our own competency can beguile us.[15]

Ouch! What David says is not only convicting, but also illuminating in terms of the type of people we tend to gravitate toward. We don't mind counseling couples—as long as they don't need *too* much help. We don't mind helping people—as long as they don't take up *too* much of our time.

There is something about the slowness of growth. There are hard-fought battles of sanctification one sees firsthand in counseling that enrich and deepen the substance of a pastor-counselor. Change is hard and tough. People don't change because they hear one good sermon on a Sunday. Couples don't magically transform their communication through a good book you recommend or a podcast you ask them to listen to.

In fact, the irony in ministry is that in the long run, the people to whom we are called to minister actually teach us far more than we teach them. Couples in need of help train and tutor the pastor in the hard but good realities of shepherding and overseeing. As we listen to their struggles and weaknesses, we actually find that we are far more like those we counsel than we are different. The author of Hebrews reminds us of this duality in the human minister: "He is able to deal gently with those who are ignorant and are going astray, since he himself is subject to weakness. This is why he has to offer sacrifices for his own sins, as well as for the sins of the people" (Heb. 5:2–3).

HOW DOES COUNSELING HELP US AS PASTORS?

You likely already know that your calling as a pastor includes not only the public ministry of the Word in preaching and teaching, but also the interpersonal ministry of the Word in counseling. But frankly, you admit, you just don't have the time or the skill to do this work.

Counseling doesn't just make us better pastors; it also makes us better teachers.

---

15. David Powlison, *Speaking Truth in Love* (Winston-Salem, NC: Punch, 2005), 130.

When pastors counsel their people, it also sharpens and helps us become better preachers of the Word in several ways.

First, counseling helps us take what we proclaim publicly and apply it personally. If one of the hallmarks of expository preaching is moving from the text of God's Word to the grit and grime of everyday life, then counseling ministry helps us simply by doing this in reverse. We should read and study the text, but we must also dedicate ourselves to the hard work of reading and understanding the people we lead.

Marriage counseling will bring you a host of practical issues which will force you to apply the truths of God's Word to everyday life. From conflict and communication to finances and family dynamics, marriage counseling is an excellent context for the pastor to show that the hope of the gospel has everyday implications.

Think of our couple, Jeff and Jennifer. What hope can you offer them in the midst of their marriage struggles? You know they can get counseling from a myriad of marriage and family therapists. But what they won't get is a living hope, a resurrected Christ who promises to complete the good work of grace he began in them. Pastor, you have something of immense and inestimable value to offer couples who need to see hope and light in the midst of despair and darkness.

Secondly, counseling enriches and expands your understanding of your people. Counseling your people will make your sermons come alive; indeed, counseling will likely have an animating influence on how you preach. As the great Puritan pastor Richard Baxter wrote, "It will furnish you with useful matter for your sermons, to talk an hour with an ignorant or obstinate sinner, as much as an hour's study will do, for you will learn what you have need to insist on and what objections of theirs to repel."[16] Baxter may not be advocating for a one-to-one ratio of study and counseling, but the point he is making is clear: spending time with people in their hurts and struggles should be a core component of our preparation for preaching and teaching.

Counseling brings you into contact with living, messy, wonderful, and complicated people. (Perhaps for some this is exactly why you do not like counseling!) It is much easier to preach against sin in the pulpit than to confront an abusive husband in a difficult marriage. It is easier to preach about the unity only Christ can bring than to help couples resolve chronic conflict in their marriages.

When you talk about examples of sin and suffering from the pulpit, are these illustrations mere abstractions and random anecdotes? Or are they real-life scenarios of ensnaring and entangling struggles that you know your people face?

---

16. Richard Baxter, *The Reformed Pastor* (Carlisle, PA: Banner of Truth Trust, 2007), 228.

Counseling provides real-life narratives of what is happening in your church body, which, in turn, helps your preaching to be relevant and personal in the best of ways.

A third benefit that comes when pastors embrace their calling as counselors of the Word is that it pushes us out of self-dependence and toward Christ. When I speak with pastors, counseling is the one ministry for which they often feel ill-equipped. Most seminary programs give a significant portion of time to hermeneutics, exegesis, and preaching, but offer few courses on counseling. Jeremy Pierre and Deepak Reju, in their excellent work for pastors, write: "Ultimately, your confidence does not rest on your skill set, no matter how developed. Instead, your confidence is in the power of the gospel of Jesus Christ through the proclamation of his Word. What goes for the pulpit goes for the counseling room."[17]

Many pastors enjoy preparing for the work of preaching and proclaiming God's Word each week. Yet the people to whom we preach come to us Monday through Saturday with problems, burdens, and difficulties that can't be handled by a sermon. This calls us to rely on the Holy Spirit in a profound way. When a couple is sitting across from you recounting their dilemma, there is no time to consult a commentary or look something up online. When faced with untangling the complexities of life, you realize you cannot do this task on your own. Like Paul, you cry out, "Who is equal to such a task?" (2 Cor. 2:16). Counseling ministry grounds the pastor in a fundamental realization that only the Spirit of God can open blind hearts and blind eyes.

A final benefit of counseling as a pastor is that it helps build the church and Christ's kingdom. As pastors, we desire that our churches are places where the gospel is proclaimed, people are saved, and the saints are equipped for the work of ministry. Paul gives us the vision for how this is accomplished in Ephesians 4. When you, alongside your people, are engaged in speaking the truth in love, the inevitable result is a church that resembles Jesus Christ.

When counseling ministry is a strong and vital part of your church, you will have a stronger, more compassionate, hope-filled congregation. Your church needs to see its pastor involved and engaged in its people's lives. They are watching you for cues on how to care for people. What an opportunity to teach through your actions! I'm not saying the pastor can counsel every marriage problem or individual that comes through the doors of the church, but each pastor should endeavor to include the work of counseling as a part of their ministry.

Counseling might not be near the top of your list as you think through your duties as a pastor, but it *is* a calling from God on every member of his body. Pastors

---

17. Jeremy Pierre and Deepak Reju, *The Pastor and Counseling: The Basics of Shepherding Members in Need* (Wheaton: Crossway, 2015), 33.

are uniquely positioned to carry out the work of counseling, and there are many ways it benefits his preaching. This hit home one Sunday after I finished preaching from the book of Job. In chapter nine, Job cries out, "When he passes me, I cannot see him; when he goes by, I cannot perceive him" (Job 9:11).

Earlier that week I had met a single young man who was struggling with depression, which in turn would often lead him to abuse alcohol. We had spoken at length about his faith, his situation, and his loneliness. When I would press him to describe his private life with God, he would often demur or offer Christian clichés with little specificity. After a bit more probing, he finally exclaimed, "I don't trust God! I don't really think he could care less about me!" Instantly, my mind went to Job. Here we have a man who is "blameless and upright, a man who fears God and shuns evil" (Job 1:8), and yet does not sense God's presence or power in his life.

I looked at the young man sitting across from me and told him he was not alone in this experience. I told him many godly men and women have wrestled with this issue. The following Sunday when I preached, this young man's face was firmly planted in my mind as I sought to recount Job's personal experience of abandonment by God. Connecting Job's experience with a previous counseling conversation greatly enriched my exposition. Through the work of the Holy Spirit, I was able to point not to myself or my own experience but to one in Scripture who also felt abandoned by God.

LAYING THE PROPER FOUNDATIONS

Recently, my wife and I decided to add a deck to our home. Possessing little (okay, zero) knowledge of how to construct a deck, we relied on our friend and the "deck guy" at Lowe's.

With the elevation of our home, the footers for the deck needed to be an additional twelve inches deeper than what is typically prescribed. The higher up we expected to build our deck, the deeper the foundation needed to be in order to support the structure. With great gusto we set out to dig multiple holes at a depth of thirty-six inches, only to realize this was no small task. Have you ever tried to dig a three-foot hole? It's not easy! There were times when I thought to myself, "Wouldn't it be easier if we just dug *two* feet down?"

Thankfully, my friend reminded me that the hard work was necessary if we wanted the deck to weather the elements and be a stable and safe structure. Preparing a proper foundation for our deck ensured our ability to construct a usable and enjoyable space for our family.

The same goes for counseling. We have covered the fact that pastors are called to the ministry of counseling. But as we embark on a journey of becoming better counselors, we also need a proper foundation to help us build a biblical methodology for marriage counseling in particular.

Let's revisit the definition of biblical counseling[18] we used earlier: *Biblical counseling is taking the truths of God's Word and speaking them in love in the context of a personal relationship with the goal of growing in godliness.*

If we take each of the constituent elements of this definition, we can build a solid foundation from which a biblical methodology can be developed.

Biblical counseling is utterly dependent on Scripture.

Biblical counseling is distinctive from other forms of counseling in that we believe Scripture is sufficient to address and speak to all of life's issues. Some might push back on the conviction that Scripture is sufficient by highlighting areas where Scripture is silent, and thus *not* sufficient (e.g., the Bible does not specifically mention issues like schizophrenia, bipolar, OCD, or personality disorders). When we say Scripture is sufficient, it means God comprehensively has revealed to us what we need to live a life that pleases him. Scripture forms and guides our understanding of who we are (embodied souls), why we were created (purpose) and why we do what we do (motivation). The Confessional Statement of the Biblical Counseling Coalition states it well:

> When we say that Scripture is comprehensive in wisdom, we mean that the Bible makes sense of all things, not that it contains all the information people could ever know about all topics. God's common grace brings many good things to human life. However, common grace cannot save us from our struggles with sin or from the troubles that beset us. Common grace cannot sanctify or cure the soul of all that ails the human condition. We affirm that numerous sources (such as scientific research, organized observations about human behavior, those we counsel, reflection on our own life experience, literature, film, and history) can contribute to our knowledge of people, and many sources can contribute some relief for the troubles of life. However, none can constitute a comprehensive system

---

18. Robert Cheong, pastor of care at Sojourn Church, has written an excellent article on using the word *care* instead of *counseling*. Depending on the culture of your church, this might be a more appropriate way to describe the ministry of counseling. Robert K. Cheong, "Why We 'Care' Instead of 'Counsel' Each Other," *Journal of Biblical Counseling* 30, no. 2 (2016): 2–6. https://www.ccef.org/wp/wp-content/uploads/2016/01/1-WhyWeCare-Cheong.pdf.

of counseling principles and practices. When systems of thought and practice claim to prescribe a cure for the human condition, they compete with Christ (Colossians 2:1–15). Scripture alone teaches a perspective and way of looking at life by which we can think biblically about and critically evaluate information and actions from any source (Colossians 2:2–10; 2 Timothy 3:16–17).[19]

Too often, methodology is based on what's pragmatic and efficient, and in turn, becomes disconnected from a biblically-informed theology. It can be easy to affirm the sufficiency[20] of Scripture in our preaching and teaching, but practically deny it in interpersonal ministry. As pastors, we must have a confidence that God's Word provides "that the servant of God may be thoroughly equipped for every good work" (2 Tim. 3:17).

Biblical counseling is concerned with speaking truth in love, within the context of relationships.

Because we believe biblical counseling should be based on the truth of Scripture, it is imperative that pastors know how to take the truth of God's Word and minister it in a counseling relationship. There are many counselors who would claim to speak truth, but it is not truth revealed from God's Word. Many counselors speak lovingly, but not the kind of love revealed in the person and work of Jesus Christ. This is a distinct hallmark of biblical counseling: counsel that is given *in love*.

The apostle John gives us a stunning definition of love in 1 John 4:10 which radically challenges our cultural understandings of love: "This is love: not that we have loved God, but that he loved us and sent his Son as an atoning sacrifice for our sins."

True biblical love, in other words, is not a feeling or an emotion; it's an action. Biblical love is sacrificial in nature and modeled after Jesus Christ. This kind of love calls you and me to a life of sacrifice. This should display itself in the way we counsel.

Paul Tripp writes, "We want ministry that doesn't demand love that is, well, so demanding! We don't want to serve others in a way that requires so much personal sacrifice. We would prefer to lob grenades of truth into people's lives rather than lay down our lives for them. But this is exactly what Christ did for us. Can we

---

19. http://biblicalcounselingcoalition.org/confessional-statement.
20. Not only the sufficiency of Scripture but also Scripture's inerrancy and infallibility.

expect to be called to do anything less?"[21] It is this kind of love that should mark biblical counselors. We labor and strive to show the sacrificial love of a Savior to couples who need to see love actualized in a true relationship.

This has radical implications for how you and I counsel. When we speak, we speak not out of fear, but from love (2 Tim. 1:7). We realize confrontation does not need to be divorced from love, but that confrontation can be an entirely legitimate expression of biblical love. We understand that when we speak truth in love, we are modeling godly communication that many couples need to see incarnated. When we speak truth in our counseling to couples, we show the practical benefit of God's Word in everyday life. When we really pause and consider how important and distinctive this element of biblical counseling is, the implications are endless.

Biblical counseling is oriented toward growth in godliness.

Mike and Amy were a young couple, married about five years, who were seeking counsel for chronic conflict in their marriage. Each of them came with weaknesses that in turn exposed the other's weaknesses: Mike was passive and shut down instantly at criticism; Amy was a verbal processor who felt Mike was shutting her out and hiding. When I asked Mike and Amy what they were hoping to receive out of marriage counseling, they both replied, "We want a happy marriage."

Don't get me wrong—that is a good goal for marriage counseling, but it will not be enough to get a couple through the ups and downs of married life. As a pastor, you know there is a higher calling for your time together. Here is your goal in marriage counseling: you desire the husband and wife to become more like Christ each and every day. This is a lofty-sounding goal at first, but Christlike change is particular, measurable, and observable. It's a change in the tone of voice when a wife responds to a husband's tardy arrival at dinner. It's the pausing for prayer before shooting off a mean-spirited text. It's the desire to share what you are learning from God's Word in your personal devotion time.

This does not mean we want to downplay other worthy goals such as increased communication, which focuses on active listening and gracious speech. I always want to keep the ultimate goal in view, which, in turn, should affect how the couple lives out their life together.

This growth in godliness will not happen overnight; there will be hills and valleys to traverse. Yet this goal must remain at the forefront of your counsel and direction. Anything less than gospel-centered transformation will ultimately fall short of God's plan for marriage.

---

21. Tripp, *Instruments in the Redeemer's Hands*, 118.

PUTTING IT ALL TOGETHER

Life comes at you quickly, and it is easy to feel overwhelmed and unprepared when it comes to the task of caring for your people. With good intention, we refer our people outside for counseling because we don't believe we are equipped for this work.[22] Scripture is clear: pastor, you are a counselor. You counsel each Sunday from the pulpit, and you counsel every time you have a conversation with a member from your church.

As pastors, we want to embrace our calling as preachers of the Word but also as counselors of God's Word. We realize as pastors that we have a profound privilege of bringing the "word of life" to couples in crisis (Phil. 2:16). When we seek to counsel from God's Word, we grow in our understanding of our people, our handling of the text, our dependence on the Spirit, and our congregation begins to look like a place where people are becoming more like Christ.

One Couple's Story

Dan and I often say we front-loaded the challenges of marriage during our years of dating. Although there's no shortage of counsel available for those who are engaged or married, when we decided to call off our engagement—but stay together—there appeared to be no blueprint for how to proceed.

Looking back, I still remember vividly the loneliness of that first year after we canceled our wedding. Well-meaning friends didn't want to address the issue directly because they feared making us uncomfortable. Others readily offered advice, but often without a full understanding of our situation. And because Dan was the youth pastor of our church at the time, neither of us felt free to speak openly about our relationship.

After a year of treading water relationally, we decided to pursue biblical counseling with Jonathan and Jen. Frankly, one of the immediate differences we both recognized was the power of being in community. It was a relief to finally process openly with good friends. In counseling us, Jonathan and Jen showed us, again and again, how those in the church can live out the call

---

22. I do not want to imply that pastors should not refer to trusted, professional counselors. There will be times when you *should* refer counselees out to a Christian counselor. I will seek to address that and provide some helpful criteria in the following chapters.

to bear one another's burdens. By asking us hard questions and nudging us to process difficult issues in new ways, we saw, in time, that one of the real gifts of the church is the promise that we weren't made to absorb life's challenges in isolation.

Biblical counseling also challenged my own myopia. Jonathan and his wife, Jennifer, regularly contextualized our particular situation in the broader, greater story unique to the gospel—the story of a loving, creative Father who is drawing his children to himself over the arc of redemptive history. While other counseling perspectives might focus on the challenges of the individual or couple, positing our own story within the overarching gospel narrative injected much-needed perspective. I could lift my eyes from my own circumstances and realize that the God who cared for the details of my life and "put my tears into [His] bottle" (Ps. 56:8 NKJV) was not circumscribed by my situation. I could make choices—freely and prayerfully—and entrust my life to a loving, sovereign God.

Dan and Olivia Southam

Counselor Fieldnotes

Marriage counseling is hard work. Anyone who sits across from a couple in distress knows this fact all too well. How do I inject hope into a hopeless marital situation? There are two confidences that serve as a platform for me, allowing me to help out in hard situations.

Confidence in God. If I'm honest, there are times when I don't know what to say or what to do. How often have I prayed, "Lord, what do I do here?" The Spirit never fails me. I don't get an explicit word from the Lord, "Your next step is . . ." What often happens is the counselee says something that we need to delve further into, or a Scripture text comes to mind, or words come to my mouth that I didn't expect, or something else. God moves us along in the process. If I rested all my confidence in myself, then I'd be undermining the One who reigns over what goes on in the counseling room. God's in charge, so don't be scared. He'll guide you through it, no matter how bad the marriage.

Confidence in God's Word. Scripture is really more than adequate to address people's problems. So the question is not in God's Word, but if you have confidence in God's Word. Do you really believe it is necessary, sufficient, powerful, and relevant for the moment? Do you know how I can tell if you (the reader) believe this? By watching you do counseling. How you use the Word shows me a lot about what you are putting your confidence in—worldly techniques, your own abilities, some unfounded hope, or God's all-sufficient Word.

Dr. Deepak Reju, Pastor of Counseling, Capitol Hill Baptist Church

RESOURCES

Jay E. Adams, *Competent to Counsel: Introduction to Nouthetic Counseling*
———, *Solving Marriage Problems: Biblical Solutions for Christian Counselors*
Richard Baxter, *The Reformed Pastor*
Robert W. Kellemen, *Gospel-Centered Counseling: How Christ Changes Lives*
———, *Gospel Conversations: How to Care Like Christ*
Robert W. Kellemen and Kevin Carson, ed., *Biblical Counseling and the Church: God's Care through God's People*
Heath Lambert, *A Theology of Biblical Counseling: The Doctrinal Foundations of Counseling Ministry*
Jeremy Lelek, *Biblical Counseling Basics: Roots, Beliefs and Future*
Jeremy Pierre and Deepak Reju, *The Pastor and Counseling: The Basics of Shepherding Members in Need*
David Powlison, "The Pastor as Counselor," *Journal of Biblical Counseling*, 26, no. 1 (2012): 23–39
———, *Speaking Truth in Love: Counsel in Community*
———, *Seeing with New Eyes: Counseling and the Human Condition Through the Lens of Scripture*
Paul David Tripp, *Instruments in the Redeemer's Hands: People in Need of Change Helping People in Need of Change*
Edward T. Welch, *Side by Side: Walking with Others in Wisdom and Love*

Chapter 2

GETTING TO THE HEART OF THE ISSUE

For as he thinks in his heart, so *is* he.
PROVERBS 23:7 NKJV

Batter my heart, three-person'd God, for you
As yet but knock, breathe, shine, and seek to mend;
That I may rise and stand, o'erthrow me, and bend
Your force to break, blow, burn, and make me new.
JOHN DONNE, HOLY SONNET 14

Hi, Pastor Holmes. Thanks for seeing David and I this afternoon. I want to start off by saying that my husband is not the problem that brings us to marriage counseling today—it's me. My heart is a deep well of desires and passions. Desires and passions that, when they go unfulfilled, lead me to get angry with him. Sure, we fight about a bunch of things—finances, his work schedule, how we never go on dates anymore—but I know these issues really stem from my fundamental lack of security in my relationship with God and, by extension, my relationship with David . . ."

. . . said no person in a counseling session ever! This scenario is too good to be true. People rarely come into counseling with biblical insight into their own heart. Most come in looking at their situation or their spouse as the biggest problem in their life. Drawing their gaze to examine their own heart is critical for biblical counseling; the heart is *the* place where authentic and genuine biblical change takes place. Paul Tripp writes, "Christ transforms people by radically changing their hearts. If the heart doesn't change, the person's word and behavior may change temporarily because of an external pressure or incentive. But when the pressure or incentive is removed, the changes will disappear."[1]

Getting those who come to you for counseling to examine their own hearts will be one of the most determinative aspects of your marriage counseling. Are they primarily victims of each other's sins? Are they destined to repeat the same patterns of conflict they saw in their respective childhoods? Perhaps they are simply a product of their environments and their circumstances.

Where do we find a comprehensive knowledge of human beings? All conversations about the constitution of human identity and motivation must come from Scripture. For it is in Scripture that God is revealed as Creator and man and woman as his creation. People made in the image and likeness of God. Born for purpose.

WHY AND HOW DID GOD CREATE US?

Every counseling system has an anthropology, and biblical marriage counseling is no different. Bob Kellemen explains the necessity of rooting our understanding of humanity in the narrative of Scripture by asking, "Are we part of a story where we're our own source of wisdom for living and where reality is the result of a chance evolutionary process? Or are we a part of a grand gospel story that is sovereignly and affectionately guided by a God who has a good heart and whose Word is our loving source of wisdom for living?"[2]

Before Scripture tells us what went wrong with God's creation of Adam and Eve, it tells us what was right about God's creation. Before we ask what went wrong, let us first see how God intended us to live.

An image-bearer

We were created to be image-bearers of a triune God. In Genesis 1:26–31, it is mentioned four times that we are made in God's image. This has significant implications for us as individuals. In the ancient Near East, rulers would erect images of themselves around the perimeter of their land to cue visitors and travelers that they ruled in this area. It was a sign to people of who reigned in that land.[3] God created human beings to point to his glory and majesty in creation. He created us in his image so that we could bear testimony and witness to who he is.

---

1. Paul David Tripp, *Instruments in the Redeemer's Hands* (Phillipsburg, NJ: P&R, 2002), 62.

2. Bob Kellemen, *Gospel-Centered Counseling: How Christ Changes Lives* (Grand Rapids: Zondervan, 2014), 97.

3. John W. Walton, *Genesis: The NIV Application Commentary* (Grand Rapids: Zondervan, 2001), 130.

Heath Lambert notes, "Being made in God's image does not mean that we are identical to God. It means that we are like him and portray his nature to the world."[4]

A relator

Part of being created in God's image means we have a built-in capacity for relationships. After the familiar cadence of "God said . . . created . . . saw that it was good" there was something that was not good about his creation (Gen. 2:18); that is, not good in the sense of not being fully completed. Adam was not able to fully image God on his own; he needed a helper suitable for such a task. God in his wisdom and love created Eve to help Adam come into his full capacity as an image-bearer. As Adam and Eve related to one another in the Garden of Eden, they displayed the divine community of God.

A worker and caretaker

An aspect of how God created us that often gets overlooked in the Creation account is the fact that God created us to work—he created us with responsibilities. Genesis 2:15 says, "The LORD God took the man and put him in the Garden of Eden to work it and take care of it."[5] God created Adam and Eve to work in the Garden of Eden. This was not a vacation without responsibilities; it was quite the opposite! God created Adam and Eve to "be fruitful and increase in number; fill the earth and subdue it. Rule over the fish in the sea and the birds in the sky and over every living creature that moves on the ground" (Gen. 1:28). This means that *work* is not a result of the fall, but rather a part of what it means to be a created being: we fulfill and obey the commands of our Creator. What he says, we do.

A lover-worshipper

We are created by God and like God. We have the capacity and responsibility to be in relationship with others and to care for God's creation. We are also created *for* God. Bob Kellemen and Sam Williams write, "One of the central components, perhaps the essence, of the *imago Dei* is the capacity for a particular type of relationship with God, characterized by love, worship, and obedience . . . We are

---

4. Heath Lambert, *A Theology of Biblical Counseling: The Doctrinal Foundations of Counseling Ministry* (Grand Rapids: Zondervan, 2016), 185. Later, Lambert explains this is the "most important reality about what it means to be a human being" (189).

5. Lambert notes that of all the descriptions of what it means to be made in the image of God, this aspect of our being is the most "textually obvious," and yet one that gets overlooked. He notes, "Human beings demonstrate this [dominion over creation] element of the image of God whenever we exercise stewardship in the world. . . . We legitimately image God when we steward the areas of responsibility he has given to us" (Lambert, *A Theology of Biblical Counseling,* 187).

not just responsible for ourselves—we are responsible to Someone."[6] This vertical aspect of our being is critical in counseling. Because we are created beings, we have responsibility to our Creator. We are not self-ruled individuals, but image-bearers of the living God. We are called to love and worship him.[7]

Knowing these aspects of our being helps us know what went wrong in the fall. Right after Genesis 1 and 2, we get Genesis 3. Human history forever changes in a moment of sin. Instead of seeking to be image-bearers of God, Adam and Eve hide from God. Instead of relating to one another as God designed, they move to blame-shifting and shame. Instead of enjoying work in a garden characterized by *shalom* or peace, they are now consigned to working in a hostile environment: "Cursed is the ground because of you; through painful toil you will eat food from it" (Gen. 3:17).

C. S. Lewis sums up the effects of the fall, "Fallen man is not simply an imperfect creature who needs improvement: he is a rebel who must lay down his arms."[8] This is where the Bible speaks to what goes wrong in marriage—and any relationship for that matter—in far greater depth than anything secular psychology offers us. The problem with humanity is not communication problems or a bad past; the problem with humanity is rebellion against God (Rom. 3:1–18). Therefore, any remedy to marriage difficulties must rightly begin with this understanding of humanity.

WHY DO WE DO WHAT WE DO?

My daughter Ruby recently has been getting angry and upset when things don't go her way. Only five years old, she is more than capable of articulating what is going wrong and what she wants. Typically, she and her older sister get into fights and quarrels. During this season of life, they are like oil and water. The other day, after another argument, Ruby put her hands on her hips, stared straight at Riley, and screamed, "You make me so angry right now." Part of me wants to laugh because

---

6. James MacDonald, Bob Kellemen, and Steve Viars, eds., *Christ-Centered Biblical Counseling* (Eugene, OR: Harvest House, 2013), 120.

7. James K. A. Smith in discussing discipleship makes the case that the way to do so is to "be attentive to and intentional about what you love" (*You Are What You Love*, [Grand Rapids: Brazos, 2016], 2). This aspect of being a lover-worshipper often fades into the background of humans being primarily thinking-cognitive beings. Smith explains that we often treat discipleship as a "didactic endeavor" or an "intellectual project, a matter of acquiring knowledge." I believe biblical counseling is a form of intensive discipleship, and Smith's critique here is on point. Biblical counseling at its core should not simply be an acquiring of more biblical knowledge but a fundamental reorientation of what we love and worship. Smith's writing is a helpful corrective on this dynamic and has been immensely helpful to me.

8. C. S. Lewis, *Mere Christianity* (New York: HarperCollins, 2001), 59.

at her age her anger is not all that destructive. Another part of me grieves because she has bought into the deceitfulness of sin.

In her world, her anger is caused and motivated by something *outside* herself, namely a bossy older sister. When I asked her later why she gets so upset, she replied with a similar answer, "Riley makes me so mad. She's not nice to me." Isn't this the same dynamic we find time and time again in marriage counseling? Sure, there are more sophisticated details, excuses, and rationalizations, but the essence is the same: you made me do it! You're responsible for my actions, not me. Such thinking and behavior belie a lack of understanding of the human heart and our motivations.

Any theory of human motivation must begin with a biblical understanding of who we are. What we do is driven by what is in our hearts. Emlet sums up the word *heart,* which he explains "captures the totality of the fundamentally moral nature of a human being as creature-before-Creator."[9] The Bible speaks with clarity on this issue as well: "As water reflects the face, so one's life reflects the heart" (Prov. 27:19).

The heart comes up frequently in Scripture. It is not an obscure concept, by any means. Throughout Scripture we see the full breadth of what the heart can do or be:[10]

Think	Hate	Love God
Remember	Lust	Faithful
Know	Love	Upright
Discern	Give	Deceive
Store things	Turn away/to	Set up idols
See	Pray	Become hard
Meditate	Rejoice	Seek God
Fear	Become proud	Repent
Grieve	Sing	Believe

This teaching may be familiar to many Christians, but I often find it is not *functionally* believed. We believe the heart is the source of our behavior, but when marital issues plague us, we quickly shift blame to our past, our spouse, or our body. Tim Keller writes,

---

9. Michael R. Emlet, "Understanding the Influences of the Human Heart," *Journal of Biblical Counseling* 20, no. 2 (2002): 48.

10. I'm indebted to Dr. Tedd Tripp, who spoke at a parenting conference for us at Parkside Church. This formulation of what the heart can do/be is from that conference.

Whatever captures the heart's trust and love also controls the feelings and behavior. What the heart most wants the mind finds reasonable, the emotions find valuable, and the will finds doable. It is all-important, then, that preaching move the heart to stop trusting and loving other things more than God. What makes people into what they are is the order of their loves—what they love most, more, less and least. That is more fundamental to who you are than even the beliefs to which you mentally subscribe. Your love shows what you actually believe in, not what you say you do. People, therefore, change not by merely changing their thinking but by changing what they love most. Such a shift requires nothing *less* than changing your thinking, but it entails much more.[11]

Let me clarify what I am *not* saying. I am *not* saying that our past history, family of origin, or current environment have zero effect on us. I *am* saying, however, they are not *determinative* of our behavior. Influential? Yes! Determinative? No.

Every counseling system can be critiqued—and should be. One of the critiques leveled at biblical counseling is that it seems behavioristic. A counselor identifies a sinful pattern of behavior and asks the counselee to change the behavior. While some have experienced this sort of counseling and been hurt by its simplistic approach, I believe true biblical counseling will go deeper than behavior. It will be incredibly attentive to the heart. And in being attentive to the heart, we will seek to understand the various influences on the heart. Mike Emlet writes, "Ignoring the influences on us results in a failure to engage with counselees, to incarnate the love of Christ, and to truly understand the context in which beliefs and motivations become expressed."[12]

As counselors, how can we have a more fully formed understanding of both husband and wife? Jeremy Pierre writes, "Caring for people requires understanding the delicate interplay between the internal responses of people's hearts and the external factors of their situation."[13] What are those external factors we must consider? Let me offer four principles for us to consider: [14]

1. We are physically embodied.
2. We are socially embedded.

11. Timothy Keller, *Preaching* (New York: Viking, 2015), 159.
12. Emlet, "Understanding the Influences of the Human Heart," 47.
13. Jeremy Pierre, *The Dynamic Heart in Daily Life* (Greensboro, NC: New Growth Press, 2016), 9.
14. I'm indebted to David Powlison for these categories (nested circles) of understanding who we are. They have proven immensely helpful in counseling ministry, and I believe accurately depict a holistic understanding of who we are.

3. We are spiritually embattled.
4. We live in God's world.

We are individuals who are physically embodied.

God created us both soul *and* body. At various times in church history, pendulums have swung and emphasized one of these over the other.[15] As counselors, we seek to strike a biblical balance between the two. The Bible does not denigrate or hold the body in low esteem. In fact, Scripture says the body is an integral part of our sanctification (1 Cor. 6:13–14). Believers will spend eternity in the new heaven and new earth worshipping God as fully-embodied beings (Is. 65:17–25; 1 Cor. 15:48–49; Rev. 7:9–10; 21:4–5). Far from being an afterthought, the body plays an important role in our growth in godliness.

In 1 Kings 19, we see the prophet Elijah afraid for his life and running from Jezebel. We are told in verses 5–9, "Then he lay down under the bush and fell asleep. All at once an angel touched him and said, 'Get up and eat.' He looked around, and there by his head was some bread baked over hot coals and a jar of water. He ate and drank and then lay down again. The angel of the LORD came back a second time and touched him and said, 'Get up and eat, for the journey is too much for you.' So he got up and ate and drank. Strengthened by that food, he traveled forty days and forty nights until he reached Horeb, the mountain of God. There he went into a cave and spent the night."

God cares for Elijah's physical needs first, before addressing other issues (1 Kings 19:9–18). We see that God cares about the body and its physical needs *along with* the spiritual components of our struggles and difficulties.

In counseling, we want to be attentive to the body and the way it influences and mediates the worship of the heart. What physical weaknesses or limitations are present that need to be factored in? What disabilities or hindrances does your counselee have? Recently, in counseling, I had a husband who struggled to complete homework I would assign. I thought it was a lack of engagement with the assignment until he confessed he had been diagnosed with dyslexia. Reading was incredibly difficult for him, and most of my assignments had been oriented to reading various passages and articles. To help with this, we were able to purchase

---

15. I believe part of the reason there has been an inattentiveness to the bodies is due to a reaction against the body-worship dynamic that is present in much of modern medicine and psychiatry. Biblical counselors want to be careful in locating personal agency and responsibility within the heart of the individual, and thus, we risk not rightly speaking and prioritizing the body. Can the body make an individual sin? No. But the body certainly plays a significant role in our lives. Emlet writes, "At most, the body can only *influence* our hearts to make that righteous or sinful choice" (Emlet, "Understanding the Influences of the Human Heart," 49).

an audio Bible for him, and he was able to listen to Scripture during his commute to work.

Understanding that the person in front of you is a physically embodied being will inform the way you counsel. Mike Emlet writes, "We want to call people to obedience and responsibility to the extent that it is appropriate, in view of bodily strength and/or weakness."[16] The body never absolves us of our personal responsibility to live a life that is pleasing to God, but it can certainly affect that process to varying degrees based on our physical strengths and weaknesses.[17] Tim Chester offers a helpful summary, "Only when we understand the role of our hearts can we truly understand the role of our circumstances in sin. Our struggles and temptations often trigger sin, but they never cause it. The root cause is always the heart and its sinful desires. We choose how we respond to circumstances, and what determines our choices are the thinking and desires of our hearts."[18]

We are individuals who are socially embedded.[19]

Ryan and Sarah could not have come from two more different family backgrounds. Ryan grew up in a Christian home with two parents who loved the Lord. Ryan and his siblings attended Christian school their whole lives, but when it came time to choose a college, Ryan decided he wanted to attend a state school. His parents were slightly concerned with his decision, but felt that his time at home had prepared him for this next stage of life.

At college Ryan experienced a level of freedom he had not been able to enjoy at home: no curfew, no rules on media consumption, no one monitoring how much time he spent on his phone. The newfound freedom coupled with a moderate ability to maintain his grades led to a first year of partying and late nights, which he was able to keep hidden from his parents.

Ryan was invited by one of his roommates to a Campus Crusade meeting where he met Sarah. The connection was instant, and before long they were dating. Sarah's background was the opposite of Ryan's. Sarah's mother had given her up

---

16. Ibid.

17. For further reading on this topic, I highly recommend Ed Welch's *Counselor's Guide to the Brain and Its Disorders*. Welch writes, "The unique contribution of the body to the whole person is that it is the mediator of action rather than the initiator. As mediator, it is not the source of sin . . . the body can influence the heart" (Edward T. Welch, *The Counselor's Guide to the Brain and Its Disorders: Knowing the Difference Between Disease and Sin* [Grand Rapids: Zondervan, 1991], 39).

18. Tim Chester, *You Can Change* (Wheaton: Crossway, 2010), 67.

19. The case study below uses "socially-embedded" on a micro scale, i.e., the counselee's immediate family background. No less important is the "socially-embedded" on a macro scale, i.e., the counselee's world or social setting. The world we live in (cf. Rom. 8:18–25) must be considered as well. From cultural practices and values to the media choices we consume, all play a factor in shaping who we are and what we love.

for adoption at a young age, and she had spent her childhood in and out of foster homes. The last foster home she was in before she headed to college was a Christian foster home, and it was there she went to church for the first time. After getting involved in a youth group, Sarah committed her life to Christ.

When Ryan and Sarah became engaged, the excitement of life took over, and they only gave their family backgrounds and history a cursory look. Here were two young people in love, wanting to be married. Against the judgment of his parents, Ryan and Sarah were married between his sophomore and junior years of college. Sarah dropped out of school to work and help pay for Ryan's schooling. Within the first six months, they began to experience trouble in their marriage. They reached out to their Cru leaders for help, but after a few meetings—with Ryan storming out and Sarah in tears—they came to me for help.

After a few sessions of meeting with Ryan and Sarah, it became clear that their family background and childhood experiences played a significant role in shaping their expectations in marriage. Ryan's childhood was, to some degree, idealized. Looking in from the outside, his family was the ideal home: two Christian parents who sent him to a Christian school. His parents rarely fought, and for the most part, things in the home assumed a routine, a cycle which felt very easy. The idea that marriage, and relationships in general, took effort and work was unfamiliar to Ryan. Furthermore, the idea that Christ and the power of the gospel were what make marriage work was even more foreign to him. When Ryan left home and the constraints of his routine wore off, he began living to please himself.

Contrast all of this with Sarah, whose history was instability and chaos. She had made a practice of not getting too close with people because she knew at any point she could be moved to another home. She wanted deep relationships, but she knew she could not let herself get too close to someone—until she met Ryan. Here was a "good guy" who came from a Christian home. This was what she had been looking for! Ryan's apathy about the marriage surprised her, and Sarah's neediness scared him. What were they to do? After spending time exploring their past and their family histories, it became clear what was happening in their marriage, and they were able to biblically reorient their expectations and responses.

If our counseling had bypassed these aspects of their history, it could have led to counsel which was *biblical* in content, but *harmful* in its application. I could have instructed Ryan to be a better husband, be more attentive to Sarah. Remember, however, that Ryan grew up in a home where being "good" and "Christian" was driven more by routine and culture than the gospel. Ryan could have cleaned up his act a bit and been a better husband, but apart from the gospel, it would not be lasting change. I could have counseled Sarah to lower her expectations as they related to Ryan. Give Ryan some time to adjust in marriage—be a submissive wife. But in doing so I would have missed the real desires churning below the surface: a desire to be loved and in relationship with Ryan.

The people you counsel are human beings who come to you with histories, stories, and values. They come from social environments that have shaped their lives. To ignore this devalues the way God created us. Is Ryan and Sarah's past *determinative* of who they are? No! But is it significant? Yes! Emlet explains: "The Scriptures also affirm the influence of others, *but* without suggesting that these influences (these people) must be *determinative* of who we turn out to be or how we act in a specific situation."[20] People's history and social situation are never determinative, but they often play a significant role in their present circumstances. Be mindful of this when you offer care and counsel.

We are individuals who are spiritually embattled.

We are people who are physically embodied, socially embedded, and we are also people who are spiritually embattled. As I mentioned earlier, the church can sometimes swing from one extreme to another. In some corners of the church, the spiritual battle we are immersed in is overemphasized, leading to a "demon-behind every bush" mentality. At the opposite end of the spectrum are those who live in functional denial of the spiritual realm. In Ephesians 6, the apostle Paul soberly offers us a glimpse behind the curtain of reality: "Be strong in the Lord and in his mighty power. Put on the full armor of God, so that you can take your stand against the devil's schemes. For our struggle is not against flesh and blood, but against the rulers, against the authorities, against the powers of this dark world and against the spiritual forces of evil in the heavenly realms. Therefore put on the full armor of God, so that when the day of evil comes, you may be able to stand your ground, and after you have done everything, to stand" (Eph. 6:10–13).

I'm always surprised when this portion of Ephesians is disconnected from the larger context of Paul's letter. Paul's teaching on spiritual warfare directly follows instruction and teaching on *relationships*:

- Within the church: 4:1–32
- Before the world: 5:1–20
- Husbands and wives: 5:21–33
- Children and parents: 6:1–4
- Slaves and slave masters: 6:5–9

---

20. Emlet, "Understanding the Influences of the Human Heart," 51.

The movement of the letter culminates with this section on spiritual warfare, and I believe Paul is indicating that the spiritual battle we are engaged in is not happening with lightsabers, pitchforks, and séances. It is happening in our relationships! Satan attacks our relationships within the church, marriage, parenting, and our work. What better way to disrupt God's plan than to attack God's people?

It is imperative to know and equip couples with this knowledge. Satan is against their marriage because he is against anything that testifies to the glory and majesty of God in Christ. He is the destroyer of godly relationships. I tell my counselees that Satan is not a kind little kitty nipping at your heels; he is a roaring lion seeking to absolutely devour you (1 Pet. 5:8).

How does this impact your counseling? Paul's instruction in Ephesians is incredibly helpful but often misunderstood. There is nothing *extra*ordinary about what he commands the Ephesians to do. In fact, what he tells them and what he tells us to do is quite ordinary: *be strong in the Lord*. Your union with Christ links you to the most powerful person in the universe. Your primary goal is to live out your union with Christ. Do you want to know how to offensively defeat the forces of darkness? Stand and be united with the Lord, arm yourself with God's Word, and pray in the Spirit. Live a faithful Christian life, immerse yourself in God's Word, and pray about everything.

We ultimately live in God's world.

Luke sums up the final layer of our existence in Acts 17:28, "For in him we live and move and have our being." We live in God's world. We are created beings with a majestic Creator. This is what distinguishes our anthropology and counseling from any other secular worldview or psychology. We did not come about by chance; we were created with purpose.

We live in a world governed and held together by a sovereign God, a God who is omnipresent, omnipotent, and omniscient. Ed Welch suggests that this helps counselors understand that the people you counsel are "at their very root people-who-live-*before*-God and people-who-are-to-live-*for*-God."[21] Welch connects the reality of living before God's face, sometimes called *coram Deo*, to the additional need to order our purpose and motivation around pleasing him. This full-orbed understanding of people keeps us from giving simplistic counsel, but it also helps us see the simplicity of the Bible's message: we are people created by God for his glory.

This is not Christianese to suggest that we simply offer a few well-timed verses; it means being attentive and addressing the whole person. When we commit to

---

21. MacDonald, Kellemen, and Viars, eds., *Christ-Centered Biblical Counseling*, 115.

addressing the heart, we commit to counseling husbands and wives in a way that is in keeping with how God created them to be. As always, God hasn't left us without resources for this endeavor. He gives us his Word and his Spirit: "The word of God is alive and active. Sharper than any double-edged sword, it penetrates even to dividing soul and spirit, joints and marrow; it judges the thoughts and attitudes of the heart. Nothing in all creation is hidden from God's sight. Everything is uncovered and laid bare before the eyes of him to whom we must give account" (Heb. 4:12–13).

 One Couple's Story

On our wedding day in 2004, neither one of us was a believer. Thirteen months later, we had both given our lives to Christ. As a newly married couple, we really didn't know what Christian living looked like, especially within the framework of marriage. There were long established sin patterns in our lives and we found they were deeply rooted. Despite gradual spiritual growth, we continued to struggle with these things, and we eventually turned to biblical counseling. Over the course of several years, we met on-and-off with Jonathan, and during our sessions there were some things we could count on:

- As we told our story and shared painful memories, it was clear that our words were being received with genuine Christlike concern and compassion.
- Almost all of our time together was spent in inward examination of the heart and the underlying motivation for "my" behavior, not focusing on what he or she did/said and the reasons why.
- The counsel we received was grounded in Scripture and we regularly were given hope that gospel-powered change was possible. When the outlook was bleak, we were reminded of the depths of God's grace.
- Jonathan put time and effort into these sessions, he held us accountable to do the same, and we were regularly given homework assignments that reinforced our discussion topics.

It's been a few years since we've met with Jonathan, and we don't always seem to be growing in grace as rapidly as we'd like, but there is evidence of God working in our marriage. Counseling taught us that the best way to improve our relationship as a husband and wife is by cultivating our relationship with God. We've learned that our efforts to "throw off everything that hinders and the sin that easily entangles" frees us to follow Christ and love each other unconditionally. As we press on, we now have the hope that God has equipped us to have a faithful, harmonious marriage that exalts Christ and brings glory to him.

Mike & Angie Kwietniewski

 ## Counselor Fieldnotes

Counseling individuals is tough. A counselor has to read the contours of another person's perspective—the beliefs and values they may not even be aware of that steer them as they traffic their little world. Counseling couples is even tougher. A counselor has two perspectives to explore—two different takes on the same marriage. These takes are usually inconsistent, sometimes unrelated, and often in direct conflict.

It would be much easier to skip the harrowing task of exploring two hearts and instead be satisfied with teaching general biblical principles of marriage. Counselors may find themselves attracted by the strategy of treating marriage counseling like a mini marriage retreat: give a vision of what marriage should be, and the couple will figure out how to get there.

If only. While giving a positive vision of marriage is necessary, it is not sufficient. Couples in trouble need help understanding *why* they are in trouble. It is not primarily because of poor communication strategies or even the external pressures of life. It is primarily because their hearts are in some way responding wrongly. They are seeing things incorrectly, being driven by values that fall short of God's, and committed to agendas that steer them into concrete walls.

In other words, their perspective of life needs to be directed toward God. When each spouse begins seeing not only their marriage but their entire life from God's perspective, they change. They change from the heart. They begin to love one another according to God's take on love. Marriage was designed to be a platform to display this for all the world to see.

Jeremy Pierre, PhD, Professor of Biblical Counseling,
Southern Baptist Theological Seminary

RESOURCES

Augustine, *Confessions*

Matthew Lee Anderson, *Earthen Vessels: Why Our Bodies Matter to Our Faith*

G. K. Beale, *We Become What We Worship: A Biblical Theology of Idolatry*

Michael R. Emlet, "Understanding the Influences on the Human Heart," *Journal of Biblical Counseling* 20, no. 2 (2002): 47–52

Elyse M. Fitzpatrick, *Idols of the Heart: Learning to Long for God Alone*

Robert W. Kellemen and Sam Williams, *Christ-Centered Biblical Counseling: How Christ Changes Lives* (ch. 7)

Heath Lambert, *A Theology of Biblical Counseling: The Doctrinal Foundations for Counseling Ministry* (ch. 7)

Jeremy Pierre, *The Dynamic Heart in Daily Life: Connecting Christ to Human Experience*

Robert L. Saucy, *Minding the Heart: The Way of Spiritual Transformation*

James K.A. Smith, *You Are What You Love: The Spiritual Power of Habit*

Edward T. Welch, *The Counselor's Guide to the Brain and Its Disorders: Knowing the Difference Between Disease and Sin* (more recently published as *Blame It on the Brain? Distinguishing Chemical Imbalances, Brain Disorders, and Disobedience*)

Chapter 3

STARTING, ENDING, AND REFERRING

In my beginning is my end.
T. S. ELIOT

Though the righteous fall seven times, they rise again.
PROVERBS 24:16

You are likely on the receiving end of many marriage counseling requests. At the church and counseling practice where I work, we receive inquiries for marriage counseling every week, and I've found pastors and ministry leaders typically respond to requests like these in one of two ways: they take on more than they can handle, or they refer out to someone else. Counselors often do more harm than good when we overcommit our time, energy, and resources and are forced to rely on our own wisdom rather than God's. Similarly, pastors can miss valuable opportunities to guide and shepherd their people in times of difficulty and hardship for fear of not being up to the task or not having enough time.

There are a number of preliminary considerations you should make *before* you commit to meeting with a couple. Proverbs 21:5 states, "The plans of the diligent lead to profit as surely as haste leads to poverty." Before you take on a marriage counseling case, it is wise to pause and consider the following concerns.

TAKING ON MARRIAGE COUNSELING CASES

Are there any conflicts of interest?

Sometimes there will be situations that might be best for you to refer or bring in another counselor. Below are some potential conflicts of interest that should be evaluated.[1]

Are you related?

You may be called on to offer formal counseling to a brother, sister, or other related family member. As a pastor and counselor, you must wisely evaluate whether or not your family relationship could adversely affect the counsel you offer. Are you able to speak truth in love to your family member and their spouse? Or would you be tempted to hold back due to your family relationship? In some cases, you might be tempted to confront too easily or speak too quickly *because* you have a previous relationship. Both aspects must be considered and evaluated. Because family members share a common history and background, there can be a tendency to lean on prior knowledge and family tradition than spending the adequate amount of time investigating and gathering relevant data.

Are you colleagues?

Your professional environment is another potential conflict of interest. Do you serve on a pastoral team with this husband? Do you serve on the same church staff as the wife? Is he a fellow elder on your church board? Again, this relationship does not preclude your ability to do formal counseling but could be a reason for you to refer them to another individual.

Are there other entanglements?

I recently had a pastor refer a member of his church to me because the two had entered into a financial contract. The husband had offered to do some construction work in the pastor's home. While working on the home project, the husband shared with the pastor that he was in need of marriage counseling. He asked the pastor to meet with him and his wife, but the project had not yet been completed. To avoid a *quid pro quo* relationship, the pastor asked if he could refer him to me, not by way of avoidance, but to keep their relationship above reproach.[2]

---

1. These areas or conflicts of interest are not disqualifying in a biblical sense, but I do believe wisdom invites us to consider them before entering a counseling relationship.

2. While I haven't personally encountered this in counseling, other pastors and counselors have shared with me how they have felt manipulated at times by people they are counseling because the counselee

Are you attracted to one of the spouses?

This should definitely inform your counseling decision. If there is a physical attraction to one of the spouses in counseling or an unhealthy emotional connection with one of the spouses, the counselor should not only disclose this immediately but seek to put in place proper structures of accountability. Sometimes a counselor might be at a vulnerable spot in their own marriage, and unhealthy emotional bonds can be formed when the counselor begins to identify too closely with one of the spouses.

Take stock of your time, energy, and resources.

As a pastor, there is no shortage of people seeking your time and attention. There are sermons to write, people to be visited, bulletins to proofread, and books to be read. Pastors frequently say to one another that there are not enough hours in the day to get everything done. This can be a good thing when it helps us understand our limitations as human beings. We are not God, and we cannot do everything. We are dependent beings (2 Cor. 2:16).

That being said, when couples in your church need help, you must evaluate whether or not you have time to meet with them. Too often pastors can over promise ("Sure, I'd love to meet with you and Sandy! I'm happy to do whatever I can do to help. Call me at any time.") and under deliver ("I'm sorry Rick. I just don't have the time to do another meeting. Why don't I send you a referral?"). A better dynamic is to under promise ("Rick, I would love to meet with you and Sandy. Why don't we schedule a time to get together and chat? From there we can make a better informed decision on how to move forward.") and over deliver ("Rick and Sandy, it was good to be with you today. There are a few more things I would like to cover with you, so why don't we schedule another meeting to get together and talk?"). At times, when I haven't set appropriate expectations and guidelines, counselees have been hurt by a perceived lack of attention or care.

Over promising sets up expectations that may not be met, while under promising sets expectations that can be met and even exceeded at times. You do not want to commit to something—even something good like counseling—if you are unable to fulfill your commitment (Matt. 5:37). Certainly, there are always unforeseen circumstances that might lead to a change in the counseling relationship, but as much as is possible, seek to establish reasonable and right expectations with your time.

---

has some sort of financial interest in the church or they are seeking counsel that would be favorable or predisposed toward them in counseling.

Know your gifting.

Jay Adams explains yet another reason why a counseling relationship might be terminated: "[It should] be terminated early when it becomes apparent that you, as a counselor, are not up to handling the problems in the case. It is right to let your counselee know this fact. Recommend and refer him to some other biblical counselor and pray for them both. There is no disgrace in not knowing something; disgrace ought to be heaped on the one who will not learn, however. When you refer the counselee, refer yourself as well. Perhaps you can learn from the new counselor."[3]

There will be times in marriage counseling when what is required is beyond your gifting. Whether it's the chronic nature of the problem or the seriousness of the issue (e.g., intimate partner violence, serial adultery) you may realize the issue is beyond your skill and competency. As Adams mentioned, this is not a sign of weakness but an honest awareness of your limitations and an opportunity to learn and grow.

WHEN TO END MARRIAGE COUNSELING CASES: POSITIVE REASONS

The conclusion of a counseling relationship is often referred to as *termination*. The term itself can sound dire and foreboding. Termination is an important part of marriage counseling, yet it is often ignored or haphazardly handled. Jay Adams writes, "Counseling, in most instances, should neither end abruptly nor simply peter out."[4] Adams identifies two dynamics which can happen in pastoral marriage counseling. In the first scenario, pastors can be meeting with a couple, offer counsel, but for whatever reason the counseling ends. In the second scenario, counseling appointments become infrequent and inconsistent. In either scenario, there exists a bit of ambiguity. Who contacts whom to schedule a follow-up appointment? Should the couple be working on something in the meantime? Will you be scheduling a checkup in six months?

Proactive and intentional termination plays an important part in establishing the end of a counseling relationship. Whether formal or informal, a clear statement about the state of the relationship is one way you can love the couple. Whether it's scheduling a six-month check-in or making a referral, pastors and counselors should be clear about the expectations surrounding the end of the process.[5]

---

3. Jay E. Adams, *Critical Stages of Biblical Counseling* (Stanley, NC: Timeless Texts, 2002), 203.
4. Ibid., 169.
5. If official, legal paperwork has been submitted, termination is an important part of counseling.

Jeremy Pierre and Deepak Reju write in *The Pastor and Counseling*, "The decision to bring the counseling process to a close is sometimes clear, but often not. You will probably be aware, with some uneasiness, that not every problem has been solved. You will sense the need for more growth or the person's desire that counseling continues regularly. But these are not adequate reasons to perpetuate counseling. When to end counseling is always a judgment call that requires wisdom. It's best to frame the decision with some clear criteria."[6] Two positive criteria I use to know when to end counseling are:

1. Is the couple experiencing true, biblical change, and/or
2. Is there someone else better equipped to care for the couple?

True, biblical change is taking place.

There are positive reasons for counseling to end. Namely, if the couple is experiencing true, biblical change in their marriage. Change is possible in marriage when couples seek to apply God's Word to their lives and live in a way that brings glory to God.

Jay Adams looks for progress in four areas of counseling—has the counselee: solved their significant *problems*, understood the biblical *passages*, replaced sinful patterns with biblical *practices*, and are they able to put into words the major *principles* they have learned in counseling?[7] Let us take time to examine each of these in greater detail.

Problems. Have the significant problems in the marriage been addressed? Remember the goal of progressive sanctification in life and in marriage is not the complete absence of sin and struggle. If you were to wait to end marriage counseling based on the absence of sin, you would never end marriage counseling. However, have the major problems and struggles been addressed? Are they seeing progress in how they handle their problems? Do they understand their struggles from a biblical perspective?

Passages. Are your counselees able to view their struggle through the lens of Scripture? Is Scripture informing their conversations and communication? When times are tough, and they are feeling misunderstood, do they run to God and his Word for comfort rather than their own unhealthy coping mechanisms?

It formally closes the relationship, thus leaving you less open to potential litigation. If your church uses any sort of legal intake paperwork or informed consent, be sure to explain the termination process. Visit www.parksidechurch.com/counseling or https://fieldstonecounseling.org/services for sample counseling forms.

6. Jeremy Pierre and Deepak Reju, *The Pastor and Counseling* (Wheaton, IL: Crossway, 2015), 89.

7. Adams, *Critical Stages of Biblical Counseling*, 209.

Practices. Change always happens in the details of life. Sanctification is not an abstract principle but a tangible reality. How is the couple experiencing change in their lives? If one were to use Romans 12:9–21 or Galatians 5:22–24 as a framework, how is the couple doing at embodying and living out these marks of a Spirit-filled life?

Principles. Near the end of marriage counseling, I like to ask the husband and wife to write down five to ten principles they have learned. This will give you good insight into their ability to summarize the truths you taught and passed. Do they have a biblical view of forgiveness? Do they have a biblical view of conflict?

Someone else emerges to offer biblical care for the couple.

Pastors must guard against the temptation to end counseling prematurely simply to pass or delegate the care of a couple to another because it's convenient or easy. We should not end counseling with a couple because we don't like them or find them to be an inconvenience. If this is the case, we must pause, confess, and repent from such notions. People are our ministry!

However, it may be that over the course of counseling, other individuals or resources rise to the forefront and prove to be more helpful than the counsel you are able to provide. Later in the book we will discuss how pastors can labor to make good referrals and develop relationships with biblical counselors or mental health professionals in the community. Most pastors are not built for long-term counseling, so it's not unreasonable to think someone else *will* be needed and necessary to provide more consistent care and counsel.

Another way pastors and counselors can help share the load of counseling is to develop the use of advocates. *Advocacy* is a term that describes members of the body of Christ coming alongside the couple in need and providing biblical friendship, support, and care during the time of counseling. Reju and Pierre explain, "If you are counseling in the context of the local church, you will be utilizing other couples or individuals to come alongside a counselee. Often, these other individuals become more effective than you in addressing the issues of this person's heart. This is not a threat to your position as pastor or counselor, but rather a mark of how the church should work. It should thrill you that others demonstrate a skill or have an insight that you didn't. If you recognize this as the case, it may be best to transition them to the care of others."[8]

Here is how our training materials describe the role of an advocate in the counseling ministry of Parkside Church:

---

8. https://www.biblicalcounselingcoalition.org/2015/07/27/when-do-you-stop-counseling.

If you have read this far, we believe that the Lord has called you to be a Proverb 17:17 kind of friend right now. It is an absolute privilege to be an advocate, standing in the gap for your friend or loved one in their time of need. You do not have to have extensive counseling training or schooling in dealing with "deep psychological issues." If you have had training in biblical counseling, that is great; but it is not necessary to be an advocate. Sometimes, in God's providence, he allows us to be trained in certain areas in order to help others. However, most of the time he allows us to help others in order to be trained ourselves.[9]

As couples develop a larger network of care—advocates, pastors, elders, professional biblical counselors, medical professionals—you might find your counseling needs to take a pause. In either of the above cases, clearly communicate that counseling has ended. Here are some items to consider going over in the final session:

Review basic principles that were covered. Are there any final passages of Scripture you want to leave them with? Any poignant principles of counseling that need to be reinforced? Spend the last session highlighting a few for their benefit. Or even better, ask them what was most helpful in the counseling process. Their answers may be surprising and helpful!

Remind them of the gospel. I like to think of this as a time to remember all God has done in and through them in counseling. Reminding couples of where they have been, where they are, and where they are headed has the potential to offer a good deal of hope.

Relinquish control to God. There will come a time in counseling when you will ask yourself, How long do I keep going? At some point, pastors and counselors need to relinquish couples to God's care. However, let them know you are there to help in the future, if need be. Some couples will feel a bit uneasy ending formal counseling. Reassure them that you and the other leaders of the church are eager to help if that becomes necessary. Let them know that if they need to reach out again, it is not indicative of weakness but rather strength and humility.

Recommend additional resources. Give couples resources—not just books to read, but things to listen to, conversations to engage in, and activities to enjoy together. Make them aware of any upcoming marriage conferences or workshops being offered in your area.

Rejoice with them. Help them to see that the termination of counseling is a good thing. Adams again has a helpful word, "All in all, termination should be

---

9. A full copy of our advocate manual is available at www.parksidechurch.com/counseling.

a happy time, a time when you both rejoice in what God has done and a time of anticipation of good things in the future. Be sure to make it so; don't simply stop counseling in some abrupt manner that fails to acknowledge God's goodness."[10]

Issue written communication that the formal counseling relationship has ended. Either through email or a letter, let them know the formal counseling relationship has come to an end. In this letter or email, I like to communicate my thankfulness for our time together as well as my hopefulness for their future as they pursue Christ together.

In C. S. Lewis's *Prince Caspian* there is a lovely scene where Lucy is finally reunited with Aslan after being away from Narnia. In the ensuing dialogue between Lucy and Aslan, Lucy comments on the fact that Aslan seems bigger to her:

> "Aslan, Aslan. Dear Aslan," sobbed Lucy. "At last." The great beast rolled over on his side so that Lucy fell, half sitting and half lying between his front paws. He bent forward and just touched her nose with his tongue. His warm breath came all round her. She gazed up into the large wise face.
> "Welcome, child," he said.
> "Aslan," said Lucy, "you're bigger."
> "That is because you are older, little one," answered he.
> "Not because you are?"
> "I am not. But every year you grow, you will find me bigger."[11]

Lewis writes about a dynamic I hope couples under my care experience: as they look at themselves and as they look at God, they will see God as righteous, powerful, mighty, gracious, forgiving, and so much bigger than they ever could have imagined. This is not because God has changed—he is immutable and unchangeable. The difference is that husbands and wives have grown in their knowledge and love for God and their spouse.

WHEN TO END MARRIAGE COUNSELING: NEGATIVE REASONS

Our counseling sessions ended on a tense note. It was clear there were marital dynamics going on that would not be resolved overnight. Joel had kept his cool throughout the session, but I could tell he was slowly simmering internally. Vanessa

---

10. Jay E. Adams, *Institute for Nouthetic Studies*, http://www.nouthetic.org/nouthetic-counseling/adams-answers/69-you-talk-about-nothing-else-but-sin.html.

11. C. S. Lewis, *Prince Caspian: The Chronicles of Narnia* (New York: Macmillan, 1951), 136.

had brought up several stories of Joel getting angry with her and the kids, and it was the first time Joel's facade of self-control began to crumble.

As they walked out of the office and into the parking lot, I could hear them arguing. I looked out my window and could tell something was wrong. Joel got into the car without Vanessa and peeled out of the parking lot. Vanessa came back to the office visibly shaken. When I asked what happened, Vanessa cried, "Joel told me that if I ever pulled something like that again in counseling, I would pay for it." Somewhat shocked, I inquired as to what he meant by "pulling something like that again." Vanessa said that Joel had told her not to bring up those stories of him losing his temper with the kids.

Later that week I reached out to Joel to discuss what had happened, and to see if we could schedule a follow-up appointment. Joel tersely replied that he was not interested in continuing counseling because, "Nothing is changing, and I'm not going to have the two of you gang up on me like that again." After putting forward a few options—meeting alone with him, offering another pastor on staff—Joel remained implacable. What does one do in situations like this?

These four factors or criteria are helpful in knowing when counseling should end:

1. One of the spouses ends counseling prematurely.
2. You discover that one of the spouses is engaged in abusive behavior.
3. The couple is not changing.
4. You are in personal danger or feel threatened.

Does the husband or wife end counseling prematurely?

In Joel and Vanessa's case, marriage counseling came to an end because Joel refused to come in for another session. Counselors, like all people, have limitations and cannot *force* spouses to come in for counseling. I've been on countless phone calls with desperate spouses asking me to reach out to their spouse to come in for marriage counseling. In most of these situations, I'm happy to make a phone call or send an email request for a session, but ultimately the decision lies with the spouse.

God must work in the counselee's heart to bring about a sense of need and conviction. It is in his power and the Spirit's timing that I must rest. There have been many times where counseling has ended abruptly because it was beginning to reveal and uncover areas in a counselee's heart and life that needed to be addressed.

If one spouse refuses to come in for marriage counseling, then our marriage counseling itself comes to an end. As a man, I personally find it best to engage the help of another woman in cases where the husband chooses not to continue but the wife wishes to remain in counseling.

Is abuse taking place?

There are also circumstances when marriage counseling comes to an end because of domestic abuse. Counselors must be aware of and attuned to the dynamics of abuse (cf. chapter eleven). When abuse of any kind is taking place, it is counterproductive to marriage counseling. Brad Hambrick writes, "Abuse is a matter of personal responsibility, not a shared relational culpability. When one person is willing to harm another in order to get his way, no amount of working on 'us' will remedy the problem. Marriage counseling becomes a distraction from what needs to change first and most."[12]

You cannot do effective marriage counseling when abuse is taking place. Counseling must come to a pause (and oftentimes an end) so that individual care and productive counsel for each spouse can begin.

Are the basic dynamics of the marriage changing?

I had been seeing Don and Tina for three months over the summer. When they first came in, the problems seemed overwhelming and insurmountable. It was the second marriage for Tina and the first marriage for Don, who had two children with a previous woman. The couple had dated for two months, were quickly engaged, and then married three months later. It was a whirlwind romance!

Problems arose the day after they married. As the plane landed at their honeymoon destination, Don got off the plane, retrieved his luggage, and waited for Tina to catch up. Tina was surprised by Don's impatience and hurriedly tried to gather her things to catch up with Don in the baggage area. When she finally collected her things, Don told her to hurry up as they were about to miss their ride to the resort. Tina asked him why he was so upset. Don confessed he had realized he had just made a huge mistake in marrying her. Taken aback, Tina asked why he would say something like that. Don didn't say anything. He stared straight ahead as the driver drove them to the resort.

By the time I met with them, the problems had increased exponentially. They were two months into the marriage and nothing was going well. Initially, I tried to gain an understanding of their story, their personal histories and backgrounds, their relationship, and what brought them into counseling. Tina shared the story from the airport, and how it had left her unsettled. Don did not offer much, other than the fact that the Tina of today was not the Tina he had dated and fallen in love with.

We spent the first three months making slow progress—dealing with their unbiblical patterns of communication, developing a structure to their devotional

12. Brad Hambrick, "The Situationally Explosive Self-Centered Spouse," October 23, 2012. http://bradhambrick.com/the-situationally-explosive-self-centered-spouse/.

life, and finding a small group at church they could attend. Things began to plateau soon after that, however. Don and Tina would consistently come to sessions late, often in the midst of an argument. Don refused to do any of the homework, while Tina would complain about Don's lack of efforts in marriage counseling. After repeated attempts to engage them and call them each to repentance, I finally told them we had reached the end of marriage counseling. As a pastor and counselor, I had done all I could.

As a general rule, you should not be doing *more* work than your counselees. Your role as a counselor is to listen, engage, and instruct. It is neither your role nor your right to live the life of faith *for* your counselee. In ending marriage counseling with Don and Tina, I gave them clear instructions so they could reengage the counseling process if they chose to get serious about their walk with Christ. Jeremy Pierre and Deepak Reju concur: "Regarding effort, as you meet with people over the course of time, be careful not to do most of the work in counseling. Consider what we call the $80/20$ rule. The person you're helping needs to be responsible for eighty percent of the work in any given counseling session, with you guiding him or her with good questions, a few Scripture texts, and appropriate advice."[13]

You feel threatened or personally endangered.

The dynamics of abuse and people refusing to change are common in marriage counseling. If you are personally threatened, this is another reason marriage counseling (or any counseling) should come to an end. Recently, I was involved in a counseling situation where my personal safety was threatened.

Adam called me one afternoon to let me know his wife was in the midst of a manic episode. As a church, we had tried to offer help and counsel at various times to Adam and his wife, but neither had been willing to come in to meet with someone. When they finally agreed to meet, Adam came in early for the appointment and proceeded to explain his wife's manic episodes. He relayed that she had made threats of physical harm against him and their children. I told Adam that given this recent information, I did not feel comfortable meeting with Allison, his wife. When she came in for the appointment, I told Allison we would not be meeting, given the nature of the recent events Adam had shared with me. I encouraged her and Adam to seek professional medical help.

Allison became enraged and made a threat of physical violence to me and my family. At that point, we called the local police, and she was taken away by local law enforcement. This may sound like an extreme situation, but some pastors and

---

13. Pierre and Reju, *The Pastor and Counseling*, 86.

counselors will encounter manic counselees or those who are experiencing psychotic breaks.[14] When this happens, pastoral counseling is not helpful; professional medical help is needed.

In each of these four scenarios, the issuing of written communication, either through email or letter, is necessary to end the formal counseling relationship; it helps to document the termination of the relationship in a way that protects your ministry from subsequent misunderstanding and misrepresentation.

WHEN AND HOW TO MAKE A REFERRAL IN MARRIAGE COUNSELING

A referral is not an abdication of responsibility. When making a referral to another counselor, you have a significant responsibility to help the counselee make a good transition to the next stage of care. In addition, a referral is not a technique to avoid counseling cases that prove to be difficult. As mentioned earlier, when your personal gifting and ability is exceeded by the nature of the problem, then referral can be a helpful step.

Labor to make good referrals. A referral should be a thoughtful and wise transition to someone better equipped to offer counsel and care. A common struggle many pastors have is a lack of strong connections or relationships to local counselors (professional or paraprofessional). Here are some practical ways you can build relationships with your community to help make better-informed referrals for your people:

- Identify mental health professionals in your congregation and community and spend time building relationships with them. Get to know their stories and their philosophy of care.[15]
- Talk to other pastors in your area and find out who they refer to. From whose help have they benefited?
- Are there other counseling resources in your area? Are there certified biblical counselors from well-known biblical counseling organizations?[16]

---

14. Additionally, you should make a referral when you suspect there are other medical issues at play, such as changes in mental acuity, marked personality changes, heavy substance abuse, disordered eating, severe anorexia, psychosis, hallucinations, etc. (Mike Emlet, https://www.ccef.org/shop/product/when-pastors-should-refer-micro-session).

15. Brad Hambrick has a helpful article on vetting potential counseling referrals: http://bradhambrick.com/vetcounselors/.

16. I'd recommend the Biblical Counseling Coalition's site: https://www.biblicalcounselingcoalition.org/find-a-biblical-counselor/.

Regarding referrals to other Christian counselors[17] or mental health professionals, Reju and Pierre offer a word of advice: "We would warn you more strongly against a professional Christian counselor who is weak in his biblical framework of human problems than against a psychologist who does not claim to be a Christian. The lines of distinction are at least clear in the latter case. In the former, they are blurry. If a professional Christian counselor offers advice that is largely based on unbiblical therapeutic models, then distinguishing between what stems from the Bible and what stems from an alternate model becomes difficult."[18]

David Powlison concurs, writing: "Psychotherapists whose personal faith is admirable typically counsel from a different perspective than what their faith professes."[19] What Reju, Pierre, and Powlison are suggesting is that as a pastor it will be easier to untangle a blatantly secular worldview from a semibiblical worldview. A couple who gets professional help from a secular therapist goes into the situation knowing the therapist is operating from a secular worldview. It's more difficult for a couple to discern the counsel offered by a professional *Christian* counselor when that counsel might deviate from what you have offered, thus pitting counselor against pastor. This is not to suggest you should avoid Christian mental health professionals! Just know that additional work may need to be done to help the couple process the counsel they are receiving through the lens of God's Word.

In the event you make a referral to another counselor, understand that this is not the end of your relationship with the couple. Stay connected to the case. Ask the couple for permission to stay apprised of their progress. Check in regularly. Ask the couple if you are able to sit in on sessions with them with the goal of (a) staying current with their counseling and (b) learning and developing your own personal skills as a counselor.

---

17. Tim Keller has an excellent summary of the various models of counseling in pastoral ministry. You can download it free here: https://gospelinlife.com/downloads/four-models-of-counseling-in-pastoral-ministry/. For those interested in a more detailed account, I would recommend Eric L. Johnson and Stanton L. Jones, eds., *Psychology and Christianity: 5 Views* (Downers Grove, IL: IVP Academic, 2010). David Powlison writes the chapter for biblical counseling (245–273).

18. Pierre and Reju, *The Pastor and Counseling*, 123.

19. David Powlison, *Speaking Truth in Love: Counsel in Community* (Winston-Salem, NC: Punch, 2005), 146. Powlison offers two reasons why this is so: (1) most Christian mental health professionals have a graduate level of counseling education but no formal training in the Bible, thus leading to a "Sunday school theology" and (2) Powlison notes the intense pressure for mental health professionals to deviate from Scripture. He writes, "Evangelicals doing psychotherapy almost invariably justify what they do as something qualitatively different from wise friendship and good pastoral counseling. Professional identity depends on possessing some unique area of knowledge and skill. How is this different from practical truth, genuine love, wide-ranging knowledge, and wisdom about all that pertains to being human (each in the biblical sense!)? The professional claim to unique expertise does not hold up under examination. A non-psychologist is often more insightful and helpful than a psychotherapist. The problems psychologists address are the same ones the Bible addresses" (Powlison, 147).

All of these steps—taking new marriage counseling cases, ending marriage counseling, or referring complicated marriage counseling—require wisdom and discernment. As a pastor you are entrusted with the serious responsibility of caring for people. Labor to be a good steward of their trust and of their lives. When you are unable to give them the level of care needed, seek a reputable counselor, but do not simply pass the couple off and leave. Stay as engaged as possible.

One Couple's Story

The process of counseling with Jonathan was truly a blessing for our marriage. It brought into focus the purpose that God had for our marriage and the role we each needed to play in order for that purpose to be fulfilled. He guided us through a process of teaching and time spent in the Word; he directed us to work specifically in areas where we were struggling; he prayed for us and with us, and through this helped to bring us to a place of healing we had needed for more than a decade.

We came to counseling when we felt we were at a dead end and it seemed there was no hope for our marriage. Our attempts to resolve conflict usually turned into arguments. A commitment to regular counseling sessions was key in whittling away at the obstacles that were causing a deep chasm in our relationship. We believe real change came through attending regular counseling, studying Scripture, and most certainly praying before, during, and after each session. Over time we each took steps to change, and we continue to enjoy the blessing of a more Christ-centered, cooperative marriage.

Biblical marriage counseling helped soften our hearts so we could experience the self-transformation (or correction) that then allowed us to work in partnership and draw together in marriage. Secular counseling had kept us focused on our own needs. Until Scripture opened our eyes to the truths about ourselves, we stayed self-focused and self-serving, so it was much more difficult to genuinely heal and stay together. Our belief that God is sovereign in all things, that he honors and blesses marriage, and that we can do all things through Christ who strengthens us is how we keep going.

Michael and Joanie Huff

Counselor Fieldnotes

I've had the privilege of walking with couples for over a decade. This experience has afforded me some specific lessons related to the starting and ending process.

One lesson is that most couples don't start marriage counseling until a relational crisis happens. This will likely be your experience as well. However, over the years I've had the opportunity of walking with a few couples who have sought out counseling simply to gain another person's perspective into their relationship.

Every marriage can develop blind spots, relational lethargy, or subtle unhealthy habits, and so every marriage can benefit from time in the counseling room. As a pastor, encourage those you shepherd to view marriage counseling as something anyone can benefit from. Challenge the assumption that requesting a counseling session first requires feelings of hopelessness and despair. Couples who start counseling in this manner will likely have fewer sessions, but their investment will result in focused relational progress.

Another lesson is remembering that you are ultimately not what your counselees need. Knowing when to refer or end a session may be just as important for your growth as it is for theirs. No matter how clearly you see the path, it is not your role to keep them on it. Every troubled marriage needs rescue, but it needs to be rescued by a Savior. Keep pointing them to Jesus. This will keep them from depending on you for marital improvement. This will keep you from the dangerous, though subtly tempting thought that the success of their marriage depends on your care.

Whether this is their very first or very last session, keep reminding them—and yourself—that their greatest need is not a counselor, therapist, workshop, or resource; it is Jesus.

Eliza Huie, MAC, LGPC; Executive Director,
Life Counseling Center Ministries; Council Board
Member, Biblical Counseling Coalition

RESOURCES

Jay E. Adams, *Critical Stages of Biblical Counseling: Finishing Well, Breaking Through, Getting Started*

Michael R. Emlet, "When Pastors Should Refer," 2015 CCEF National Conference, https://www.ccef.org/shop/product/when-pastors-should-refer-micro-session

Jeremy Pierre and Deepak Reju, *The Pastor and Counseling: The Basics of Shepherding Members in Need* (chs. 5, 6, and 8)

Winston Smith, "When NOT to DO Marriage Counseling," *Journal of Biblical Counseling* 27, no. 1 (2013): 72–76.

David Powlison, *Speaking Truth in Love: Counsel in Community* (ch. 15)

Chapter 4

TO FORGIVE OR
NOT TO FORGIVE

To forgive is to set a prisoner free and discover that the prisoner was you.

LEWIS B. SMEDES

Bear with each other and forgive one another if any of you has a grievance against someone. Forgive as the Lord forgave you.

COLOSSIANS 3:13

Kyle and Lydia were one of my first marriage counseling cases, and I'll never forget our first appointment. They came in, and immediately Lydia pulled her chair away from Kyle's and placed it next to mine. I quickly realized Lydia had different goals for this meeting than I had envisioned. She wanted a tag team offense against her husband.

I prayed, opened the session, and Lydia asked to speak first. I remember her exact words: "I know you're not supposed to keep a record of wrongs . . . BUT!" With that, she dug into her pocket and pulled out a small steno pad full of notes. Lydia proceeded to tell me she had been keeping a literal record of the many ways Kyle had sinned against her for the past five years.

I sat in stunned silence for the first few moments. I initially thought Lydia had been joking. But this was no joke, unfortunately. Lydia recited hurt after hurt, incident after incident. Kyle kept trying to interject, but Lydia would not let him get a word in edgewise. At the end of the reading, Kyle folded his arms defiantly and replied, "I've apologized for half that stuff already; I don't know what else she wants from me."

They both sat back in their chairs. Kyle was sullen; Lydia exhausted. This was obviously a frequent conversation and ongoing conflict in their relationship. What do you do with five years of wrongdoing, freely transacted by both parties? There are no quick fixes or date night suggestions that can bring healing to a relationship that has been repeatedly torn apart. What couples like Kyle and Lydia need is a wake-up call to the biblical command to forgive one another.

One of the foundational principles every pastoral counselor will need in marriage counseling is a biblical theology of forgiveness. I've never been in a marriage counseling situation where biblical forgiveness did not form a major centerpiece of the overall counseling.[1] It should not surprise us that forgiveness plays such a prominent role in marriage counseling given the fact that forgiveness is at the very heart of the gospel. For a couple to tell a story of redemption in their marriage (Eph. 5:31–32), they must be a couple who forgives one another. Paul Tripp writes, "I cannot think of a more essential ingredient in marriage than forgiveness."[2] On a larger scale, Keller says "forgiveness is at the very heart of what it means to be a Christian."[3]

Our culture buys the lie that humans are inherently good, but the church often promotes this message as well. While the church proclaims the message of the gospel, I still encounter many Christians who don't think they are sinful. Typically they are people who grew up in the church, possess moral virtue, and exhibit good behavioral tendencies. Of course they need to be saved, but to them salvation is more of a costume change than a heart transplant.

Why do I say this? Because it has profound implications for how we practice forgiveness. People who don't believe they need forgiveness of sins are people who find it difficult to forgive others who sin against them. Put another way, those who believe they have been forgiven little tend to forgive little. Yet the gospel is clear in its message—you are more sinful than you ever thought possible, but you are also more accepted and loved than you ever dared imagine.

Paul puts forth the reality of our sinfulness in clear and stark terms in the

---

1. The concept of forgiveness is present in secular marriage counseling too. However, what it means and how it is practiced varies widely depending on what you read. Winston Smith identifies why secular marriage counselors have such difficulty and lack precision when discussing forgiveness: "In a sense, psychologists have an impossible task. While forgiveness is something people do and can be observed, it's ultimately a supernatural act. God invented forgiveness, and his love is its foundation" (Winston T. Smith, *Marriage Matters: Extraordinary Change through Ordinary Moments* [Greensboro, NC: New Growth, 2010], 164).

2. Paul David Tripp, *What Did You Expect? Redeeming the Realities of Marriage* (Wheaton, IL: Crossway, 2010), 86.

3. Timothy Keller, "Serving Each Other Through Forgiveness and Reconciliation," (New York: Redeemer City to City, 2005), 1. https://gospelinlife.com/downloads/serving-each-other-through-forgiveness-and-reconciliation/.

book of Romans. A portion of Paul's audience in the church at Rome were Jewish Christians who thought they were doing pretty well when it came to moral behavior. Keepers of the law? Check! Circumcision? Check! Good deeds for the kingdom? Check! Paul does not mince words about their condition in chapter three when he quotes from the Old Testament and reminds them that

> There is no one righteous, not even one;
>> there is no one who understands;
>> there is no one who seeks God.
> All have turned away;
>> they have together become worthless;
> there is no one who does good,
>> not even one.
>>> *Romans 3:10–12*

One has to understand one's sinful state to see the beauty of the gospel message. In Romans 5, Paul goes on to describe us as powerless, ungodly, sinners, and enemies of God (Rom. 5:6, 8, 10). Make no mistake: you and I need forgiveness of sins if we are to have any hope of reconciliation with God the Father.

Too often in marriage counseling, we overlook this critical aspect of forgiveness. We jump to the horizontal aspect of forgiveness between spouses *before* we lay the foundation of understanding the forgiveness we need before God. Why is this so critical? Only people who realize the magnitude of forgiveness they have in Christ are likely to grasp and show a measure of that forgiveness in their personal relationships.

Imagine if Kyle and Lydia both fully understood and comprehended that they are weak, ungodly, sinners, and enemies of God. What if they truly saw that now, because of grace, they are justified through faith in Jesus Christ? Savoring and meditating on this truth necessarily propels a believer to be more forgiving in their posture and their actions. Paul reframes this in another letter, writing, "Be kind and compassionate to one another, forgiving each other, just as in Christ God forgave you." (Eph. 4:32).

Lay this foundation in your early sessions with a couple. Once you have done this, it is important to assess what the couple's current working model of forgiveness looks like in the home. In counseling, you will undoubtedly encounter bad theology about forgiveness. Instead of building on a bad foundation, take time in the session (or through homework) to dismantle their faulty theology to build a more biblical, healthy foundation.

8 COMMON MYTHS ABOUT FORGIVENESS

1. I don't need to forgive to have a good marriage.

Is forgiveness really that important? Recently a wife told me in counseling with her husband that she had figured out how to make things work with him. She excitedly told me that she had made a resolution to "let things slide off her back" and not be bothered by her husband's behavior. For her, forgiveness was one of several options for dealing with hurt and offense in her marriage. She had resolved, instead, to simply let things go; unfortunately, this only worked until the next time her husband said something she just couldn't let go.

If our marriages are to embody a story of redemption, then forgiveness— sincerely sought and genuinely granted—must be the central plotline, the thread that binds two sinners together in a transformative relationship.

2. Apologizing is the same thing as repenting and asking for forgiveness.

In my experience, this is one of the most common myths about forgiveness. The language of "I'm sorry" becomes the *lingua franca* of a relationship, and no care is given to biblical forgiveness. The problem with apologizing is that it is not a biblical concept! Often when you ask couples how they resolve conflict, they will say they simply apologize. Yet the problems continue to persist and no reconciliation takes place. A counselor must help couples see that the language of "I'm sorry" is not a substitute for the biblical pattern of repentance and forgiveness.

3. Forgiving means forgetting.

Forgiveness is frequently equated with forgetting. I've had scores of husbands and wives tell me they cannot forgive because they cannot forget the wrongs done to them by their spouse. In the economy of their relationship, forgiveness is withheld until the offense is forgotten. The problem with this myth, like many others, is that it is not grounded in Scripture. If our forgiveness is to embody and exemplify God's forgiveness of us in Christ, we will understand that Christ does not "forget" our sins in order to forgive them. Quite the opposite, in fact, is true—we are told he forgives and then *chooses* not to remember: "For I will forgive their wickedness and will remember their sins no more" (Jer. 31:34). This active disposition of forgiveness must be clarified and put into practice.[4]

---

4. An oft missed opportunity in the "forgive and forget" model of forgiveness is the fact that biblically-forgiven sins can actually be a point of hope and encouragement in marriage. Smith explains, "Being able to recall how God has delivered us through marital storms, empowering us to confess, forgive, and overcome,

4. I need to learn to forgive myself.[5]

Like myth number three, this is one of the most frequent myths surrounding forgiveness. This myth gets repeated so frequently in pop psychology that it has filtered down into Christian thinking and behavior. Simply put, forgiving oneself is not in the Bible.

Blogger Lara d'Entremont explains, "Self-forgiveness says that we have the authority to choose if our sins are forgivable or not. But that's not the case. Rather, Jesus paid the full price for your sins when He died on the cross and rose again. Jesus didn't pay a part of the price and then ask you to finish it off. He fully atoned for each of your sins and bore God's wrath that you deserved because of them."[6] Self-forgiveness might sound like a good technique to alleviate guilt, but the concept is not rooted in the gospel message.

Spouses might use this language to describe feelings of self-condemnation, self-loathing, guilt, shame, or unworthiness. Perhaps a spouse has difficulty letting go of past hardships, and it is hindering their ability to build healthy relationships here in the present. That individual may say, "I need to forgive myself so I can begin to trust my spouse." In a situation such as this, what typically underlies such a statement is a misunderstanding of the gospel. The spouse needs to be reminded to live out of the reality that God has truly forgiven them (cf. Ps. 32:1–2). When we are able to frame our feelings and experiences in light of God's forgiveness of us, it helps us better understand our identity and informs our behavior. Understanding and living out our status as forgiven sinners helps us apply this gospel truth in our relationships. Pastor H. B. Charles summarizes why self-forgiveness can be so deceiving: "To claim that I have been forgiven by God but I cannot forgive myself betrays that I do not understand, believe, or appreciate the gospel of Jesus Christ. It is a sinister attempt of the Enemy to get us to depend upon our own righteousness, rather than the grace of God."[7]

5. I don't need to forgive if they are not repentant.

We will address this more fully a bit later, but one common reason husbands and wives don't forgive is that forgiveness is only viewed and understood horizontally. In Luke 17:3–4, Jesus tells his disciples, "If your brother or sister sins against

---

can give us hope and an anchor in future storms. Stories of forgiveness and reconciliation can also become part of the way you seek to strengthen and encourage others in their marriages" (Winston T. Smith, *Marriage Matters: Extraordinary Change through Ordinary Moments* [Greensboro, NC: New Growth, 2010], 169).

5. For more on this topic, I'd recommend Robert Jones's booklet "I Just Can't Forgive Myself" (Phillipsburg, NJ: P&R, 2000).

6. Lara d'Entremont, "The Empty Pursuit of Forgiving Yourself," April 24, 2018. *Revive Our Hearts*. https://www.reviveourhearts.com/true-woman/blog/empty-pursuit-forgiving-yourself/.

7. H. B. Charles, "How Can I Forgive Myself?," https://www.hbcharlesjr.com/2017/07/17/how-can-i-forgive-myself/.

you, rebuke them; and if they repent, forgive them. Even if they sin against you seven times in a day and seven times come back to you saying 'I repent,' you must forgive them." Taking this verse out of context from other teaching on forgiveness seems to indicate that forgiveness is based on the offending person's repentance. But other verses such as Mark 11:25 clarify that we are supposed to forgive regardless of any action by the other person: "If you hold anything against anyone, forgive them, so that your Father in heaven may forgive you your sins."

Tripp helpfully explains the two aspects of forgiveness: "Forgiveness is a *vertical commitment* that is followed by a *horizontal transaction*."[8] This vertical commitment to forgive and entrust the other spouse to God is key in enabling you to extend forgiveness horizontally. It also prevents superficial forgiveness— forgiving in word but not in deed and heart.

6. Forgiveness is the same thing as reconciliation.

Forgiveness is not the same thing as reconciliation; forgiveness is an event that prepares the way for reconciliation. Tim Keller writes, "Forgiveness means a willingness to try to reestablish trust, but that reestablishment is always a process."[9] Helping couples see that forgiveness and reconciliation are two separate topics often brings hope. For too long spouses have conflated forgiveness and reconciliation. Because they cannot envision the fruits of reconciliation—renewed trust, renewed relationship, and positive emotions, they hold off on granting/seeking forgiveness.

7. Forgiveness erases consequences.

Spouses often withhold forgiveness because they fear it enables the other spouse to carry on without any consequences. The argument goes, "If I forgive them, then they have no consequences or repercussions for their behavior." Again, Scripture is clear that there are consequences for our actions. Paul writes in Galatians 6:7, "Do not be deceived: God cannot be mocked. A man reaps what he sows." Forgiveness of sin in a marital relationship does not remove consequences; however, it does give the couple a foundation of common acceptance and love to stand on as they deal with the consequences of sin.

I counseled a couple where the wife had secretly run up thousands of dollars of credit card debt unbeknownst to her husband. While dealing with the motive and reasoning that led to her actions, she humbly sought forgiveness from her husband. By offering forgiveness to his wife, he was able to come alongside to help deal with

---

8. Tripp, *What Did You Expect?*, 92.
9. Keller, "Serving Each Other Through Forgiveness," 4. In fact, the reestablishment of trust too quickly can often enable the other person to continue sinning against the spouse.

the immediate consequences of her sin (an enormous credit card bill) while not becoming embittered against her. Did forgiveness erase the bill? No, but it helped the couple grow in love and grace toward one another.

8. Forgiveness is a feeling or should be easy.[10]

"Why is this so hard?" One of the reasons people don't forgive is because forgiveness is more associated with feelings than obedience. When forgiveness is grounded more in one's personal feelings than obedience to God's Word, then forgiveness will most likely be difficult. Think about it for a moment: forgiveness almost always entails personal hurt or suffering, so why would we think negative feelings or emotions are unusual? Tim Keller explains, "Forgiveness, then, is granted before it is felt."[11]

Brad Hambrick explains the dilemma, "If we demand the benefits of forgiveness before we take the risk of forgiveness, we become trapped at the crucial point."[12] He goes on to explain that forgiveness is rarely easy because of the negative and raw emotions associated with the offending behavior. To wait for the absence of negative emotions runs counter to Scripture's emphasis on the timeliness of forgiveness.

HELPING THE COUPLE CULTIVATE A CULTURE OF FORGIVENESS

After spending time debunking the various myths that may be inhibiting the couple regarding forgiveness, the counselor then has the opportunity to build a stronger, more biblical foundation of what forgiveness is and is not.

God's forgiveness is both our motive and our model.

As I explained earlier, it is necessary for the husband and wife to understand their state and position before God. Apart from the saving grace of Jesus Christ, we all stand condemned for our sin. It is only through the atoning work of Jesus Christ that we can have forgiveness of sins (Matt. 26:28), and this forgiveness we receive as a free gift is both our model (we extend forgiveness to others freely) and our motive (we forgive because we are forgiven). Keller writes, "Both the power and the model for [forgiveness] is, of course, the gospel. Christ died for us while we

---

10. Adams notes in general that, "All day long, in order to be responsible to God and others, I must do many things against my feelings" (Adams, *Critical Stages of Biblical Counseling*, 23).

11. Keller, "Serving Each Other Through Forgiveness," 2.

12. Brad Hambrick, "Emotions and Forgiveness," February 22, 2013. http://bradhambrick.com/emotions-and-forgiveness/.

were his enemies. That action is not only the paradigm for us, but the thought of it becomes our power to follow through."[13] Every time a couple practices forgiveness they reenact the gospel story. Every story of forgiveness is a chance to retell and embody a story of redemption.

Understanding and meditating on our forgiveness in Christ is key in any situation where forgiveness is needed. The psalmist writes,

> Blessed is the one
>> whose transgressions are forgiven,
>> whose sins are covered.
> Blessed is the one
>> whose sin the LORD does not count against them
>> and in whose spirit is no deceit.
>> *Psalm 32:1–2*

A heart that understands the extent of one's sinfulness and the magnitude of God's grace is motivated to forgive. How can we not forgive in the face of such great and wonderful forgiveness shown to us?

Understand that forgiveness happens at two levels: vertical and horizontal.

Myth number five (I don't need to forgive if they are not repentant) briefly addressed this issue, but it bears repeating. Vertical forgiveness is releasing the offense against you to God (Mark 11:25). It is a necessary posture of the heart to enable you to forgive horizontally. Adams says of the vertical axis of forgiveness: "What he does is express *to* God his genuine concern to be reconciled to his brother (if possible) and his willingness to grant forgiveness to him. His prayer is to God."[14] Horizontal forgiveness is the extension of forgiveness to the other person based on their repentance (Luke 17:3).

Vertical Forgiveness	Horizontal Forgiveness
Unconditional	Conditional
Mark 11:25; Luke 23:34[15]; Acts 7:60	Luke 17:3–4
Between you and God	Between you and your spouse

---

13. Timothy Keller, *Romans: A Study Course in the Gospel* (New York: Redeemer City to City, 2003), 215.

14. Adams, *Critical Stages of Biblical Counseling*, 30.

15. Jesus's prayer in Luke 23 is instructive on a number of levels. Keller notes that Jesus does not "forgive

When there is a spirit of bitterness and lack of forgiveness in marriage, I will ask spouses if they have forgiven their spouse vertically. After hearing an explanation of the concept, they will confess they haven't. Once a spouse has forgiven vertically, releasing the offense and attending bitterness to God, many find the horizontal forgiveness that had previously been withheld is now much easier to extend.

What recourse has God given us to forgive those who are not repentant? Jesus tells us in Luke 17:3, "If your brother or sister sins against you, rebuke them; and if they repent, forgive them." When there is no repentance from an offending spouse, Jesus tells us there is a way forward: you are to *rebuke them*.[16] This language[17] can sound harsh, but we must remember that biblical love involves speaking the truth in love (Matt. 18:15–17; Eph. 4:15–16). This does not mean a rebuke needs to happen every time a person is offended. We are instructed that "love covers over a multitude of sins" (1 Pet. 4:8), and in cases where the offended spouse can overlook an offense and cover it in biblical love, we are instructed to do so. Yet in situations where the sin is serious and part of a larger pattern, a rebuke may lead to repentance.

If the offending spouse is not repentant, even after a rebuke (honestly speaking the truth in love), what is an offended spouse to do? Forgive vertically. This is not easy to do; in fact, in my experience, it is only possible through the power of the Holy Spirit working in the offended spouse. Keller writes, "To forgive the unrepentant takes far more self-control and discipline."[18]

Know that forgiveness is costly.

When I was a kid, my sister and I stole bubble gum from our local Walmart. Fortunately, our kleptomaniac tendencies were a brief phase of our childhood. My mother took us back to the store to ask for forgiveness from the store manager. I'm not sure the manager understood exactly what was happening (i.e., my mom wanted him to scare us from ever shoplifting again), but he kindly and graciously

---

them," but rather does two things: (1) acknowledges that they need forgiveness of sin and (2) acknowledges their weakness and neediness, thus the need for help and forgiveness from God (Keller, Romans: A Study Course in the Gospel, 222).

16. The other side of this dynamic is that when we realize there is sin in a relationship, we are told to essentially drop whatever we are doing and go seek reconciliation (Matt. 5:23–24). Adams correctly describes what *should* happen in a situation like this, "Ideally you ought to meet each other on the way" (Adams, *Critical Stages of Biblical Counseling*, 17).

17. Adams again is helpful, "There are two words in the NT for rebuking. One means 'to so prosecute a case against another that he is convicted of the crime of which he was accused.' Needless to say, that is not the word used here. The others, which Jesus uses in this connection, means to 'rebuke tentatively.' That is to say, when you go, you must do so with caution. You go with the facts as you see them. You present the facts. Then you wait for any possible forthcoming explanation that might clear up a misunderstanding or that might mitigate the situation. If there is none, the offense has been committed, and if your brother or sister repents, you are to forgive him or her" (Adams, *Critical Stages of Biblical Counseling*, 18).

18. Keller, *New Relationship*, 220.

forgave us. While the manager was able to forgive us, that forgiveness came with a price. Yes, he offered us forgiveness, but now his store would have to eat a loss of $1.99. My sister and I had received all the benefits of forgiveness, but that did not mitigate the cost the Walmart manager incurred.

If the cost of an offense were always so obvious and small, it would be simple to pay back the loss (make restitution), and forgiveness would be far more pleasurable and less costly. However, when the damages of an offense are internal, interpersonal, and emotional, the costs to the offended may exceed the offender's ability to fully comprehend or ever repay. In such cases, restitution by the offender is practically impossible. Forgiveness can only be offered freely—without restitution. This happens when the offended party, motivated by Christ's example, personally absorbs the cost of the offense willingly and without compensation. Forgiveness is a costly exchange, what Keller calls "voluntary suffering."[19] Spouses need to realize that forgiveness is not always accompanied by good feelings, and may lead to negative emotions and pain. Brad Hambrick relates, "Similarly, forgiveness is a God-sized action that when written into our life pushes at the edges of our humanity to such a degree that it is sometimes deathly painful."[20]

Role-play and assign meaningful homework.

At some point you will need to assess the relational capabilities of your couple to see if it is possible to introduce the concept of forgiveness into their marriage. One way I have sought to assess their readiness for this is to see if they are able to seek and grant forgiveness for an everyday conflict, preferably something that has happened recently.[21] I will ask the husband to pause and take a moment to think, pray, and consider what he can and should seek forgiveness from his wife for. We will take a few moments, and then I'll ask him to speak directly to his wife.

If there is blame-shifting,[22] rationalizing,[23] or justifying language, I gently interject and remind him of what we've learned about forgiveness. It shouldn't surprise you to find that the first time you run through this exercise in a session, most spouses find it difficult to say those three simple words, "Please forgive me." Eventually, most get around to doing it, but they may need time, patience, and guidance. During this time, I ask the other spouse to remain silent and to pray for God's strength to truly listen and be ready to forgive when asked.

---

19. Keller, "Serving Each Other Through Forgiveness," 1.

20. http://bradhambrick.com/lewisonforgiveness-2/.

21. Typically, there is no shortage of issues or conflicts from which to draw. Try not to choose something that would require significant time.

22. "I'm sorry if I hurt your feelings when I yelled at you."

23. "I know what I did was wrong, but when you yell at me, I have no choice but to respond . . ."

After the husband asks for forgiveness, I share with the wife that she now has three options: "Yes, I do forgive you," "No, I don't forgive you," or "I need some time to think about it." If the husband is genuine in his request,[24] more often than not, the wife will respond with forgiveness. For couples who have more entrenched patterns of conflict, the response might be a request for more time to process. If the reply is a strong *no*, I ask the spouse why they cannot forgive. In this case, additional instruction about forgiveness is often needed.[25]

When the answer from the spouse is affirmative, remind them about the promises that forgiveness embodies:[26]

1. *"I will not dwell on this incident."* Do not replay the person's offense against you mentally over and over again. This promise must be renewed daily, even hourly, in the immediate aftermath. It requires God's grace and the remembrance of your own forgiveness in Christ to accomplish this.

2. *"I will not bring up this incident again and use it against you."* Don't go into the garbage can of the past to find ammunition for your conversation today. It is one thing to use a past incident illustratively and lovingly. It is another thing to use an incident from the past to inflict shame or additional hurt.

3. *"I will not talk to others about this incident."* Do not slander or gossip about your spouse's sin to other people. In marriage counseling, I find this promise to be especially pertinent with in-laws, siblings, and close friends of the husband or wife. Retelling your spouse's sins to gain the sympathies of your mother or close friend is not compatible with biblical forgiveness.

4. *"I will not let this incident stand between us or hinder our personal relation-ship."* Love does not keep a record of wrongs (1 Cor. 13:5). Biblical forgiveness does not allow forgiven sins to keep a couple from growing together in the grace and knowledge of our Lord Jesus Christ.

The first promise of forgiveness undergirds the other three. Helping the wife *choose not to remember* her husband's sin because of the power of biblical forgiveness will give her greater ability to fulfill the other three promises. Paul Tripp explains, "You simply can't continually rehearse in your heart all someone's perceived wrongs

---

24. If you sense that the spouse is not being genuine in their request (e.g. joking, cynical, or sarcastic), I recommend pausing and reevaluating. You do not want to allow the counselee to take the exercise and turn it into a joke. This will only further deepen the couple's problems with trust and future opportunities to forgive.

25. It is difficult to remain unmoved in the face of a true seeking of forgiveness.

26. Ken Sande, founder of Peacemaker Ministries and Relational Wisdom 360, has excellent resources and tools for issues related to conflict resolution and forgiveness. Four Promises of Forgiveness, https://rw360.org/four-promises-of-forgiveness/.

against you and grow in affection toward him or her. You can't argue with yourself daily that the person you live with is the chief cause of the wrongs that you do, and want to move close to them."[27]

There are several reasons to role-play and practice forgiveness in session when possible:

1. If a couple cannot forgive in the small things (the humdrum of life), then they probably will not be able to forgive in the larger things (the more entrenched patterns of sinful practice and communication).
2. If you can help a couple practice forgiveness in a small area in the session, it can provide them with a glimmer of hope for their future. Many couples come into marriage counseling with little to no hope. A small movement in the right direction is one of many graces God can use to revive a struggling relationship.
3. If there are issues in the session where forgiveness needs to be sought and granted, what better way to show them the practicality and immediacy of forgiveness than to do it right then.

Remember the gospel and act on the gospel.

In marriage counseling, you teach and instruct by way of reminder (Jude 5, 17). Couples need to choose not to remember the other person's faults and sins, while they simultaneously choose to remember God's grace to them in forgiveness. It is this simultaneous and conscious choice to forget faults and remember grace that makes forgiveness so beautiful. Tripp helpfully reminds us, "When you remember, when you carry with you a deep appreciation for the grace that you have been given, you'll have a heart that is ready to forgive. That doesn't mean that the process will be comfortable or easy, but it will mean that you can approach your needy spouse remembering that you are just as in need of what you're about to give to him or her."[28]

When we fail to follow up cycles of sinful behavior and corrosive conflict with biblical forgiveness, we lose an opportunity to display the life-changing power of the gospel. No sin is too great to be forgiven, and yet in our sinful thinking, we obscure the power of biblical forgiveness and find ourselves mired in marital discord. Couples must believe, live, and embody biblical forgiveness. Only then will they be able to give testimony and witness to the far greater forgiveness shown to them in Jesus Christ.

---

27. Tripp, *What Did You Expect?*, 71.
28. Ibid., 97.

I'll conclude this chapter with a word from J. C. Ryle on forgiveness:

Do we know what it is to be of a forgiving spirit? Can we look over the injuries that we receive from time to time in this evil world? Can we pass over a transgression and pardon an offence? If not, where is our Christianity? If not, why should we wonder that our souls do not prosper? Let us resolve to amend our ways in this matter. Let us determine by God's grace to forgive, even as we hope to be forgiven. This is the nearest approach we can make to the mind of Christ Jesus. This is the character which is most suitable to a poor sinful child of Adam. God's free forgiveness of sins is our highest privilege in this world. God's free forgiveness will be our only title to eternal life in the world to come. Then let us be forgiving during the few years that we are here upon earth.[29]

 One Couple's Story

By the time we arrived in front of Jonathan for biblical counseling, we were at a crossroads in our marriage. Unsure whether we were going to be able to stay together, we decided to try counseling as our last hope. Many years of turning to other things besides God had left us with a damaged marriage that crumbled to pieces one weekend.

The first moment we sat with Jonathan, a glimmer of hope began to emerge. He immediately began to lay the foundation for leading us back to Christ and into a community of believers through a strong understanding and application of biblical principles. We never felt condemned but were always encouraged to reflect on our own behaviors in light of the Bible and to more fully understand the gospel and its message of grace, hope, love, and forgiveness.

We were continually nudged forward in our thinking and in our actions, which forced each of us to look deeply into ourselves and examine how fragile our relationships with God had become. We were always given hope and encouragement, and although we often left our sessions feeling drained, it was worthwhile soul-building work that has completely transformed our marriage and our walk with God.

---

29. J. C. Ryle, *Mark: Expository Thoughts on the Gospel* (Carlisle, PA: Banner of Truth, 2012), 189.

We are now five years beyond that pivotal weekend. God has blessed us with a strengthening in our marriage we would have never imagined before. He is growing and transforming each of us in his own time and in his own way because of the path Jonathan led us down—a path of reconciliation to God first, then to one another. We are finally able to begin putting the pieces in place spiritually that impact every aspect of our lives and are able to reach out with hope and encouragement to other hurting couples.

Don and Kim Davis

Counselor Fieldnotes

Forgiveness is oxygen in the lungs of marriage. You breathe in mercy from the Lord for your iniquities. You exhale forgiveness for your spouse. Both of you urgently need it. But the reality is that couples often hold their breath in two ways: by refusing to express humble and earnest sorrow for their sin and by withholding heartfelt and regular forgiveness. It's no wonder many marriages are slowly suffocating and dying. Forgiveness in marriage must be as regular as breathing. Facilitating forgiveness is part and parcel of marriage counseling. It's the counselor's responsibility to gauge their ability to forgive and help them make forgiveness and reconciliation as vital and common to their relationship as breakfast is in their day.

But here's where the metaphor breaks down. Forgiveness, unlike breathing, does not come easily or naturally. Depending on the transgression(s), it can often be quite complex and requires an understanding of the impact of the sin, how it may have redefined the marriage, and how it has devastated the couple. Infidelity, betrayal, abandonment, and a violation of trust and intimacy deeply change the course of a couple's marriage. Sometimes a couple comes to counseling in crisis. The failure and offense are visibly on the table. But in other situations, it lies unseen, only spoken of indirectly. These couples don't seem to respond to counseling. Their level of conflict may decrease, but trust, intimacy, and unity don't flourish. Here, there is often a marital wound that led to one person's silent decision never to trust, depend on, or place oneself in the other's hands. Forgiveness, in these more complex situations, requires patience and skillfulness.

It will not be a single "transaction," but a process of helping the "sinned against" spouse to describe and explore the painful experience. Maybe for the first time, the person articulates the impact and significance of what happened. With gentle persistence, the outrage and anger come into the light along with fear, helplessness, hurt, and shame.

Almost always, the one who sinned will need support and encouragement to hear and understand the significance of their actions or negligence. Together, the couple grieves and expresses their sorrow and loss. Humbly, the "offending" spouse is moved from defensiveness and denial (or ignorance) to taking responsibility and feeling remorse for what happened. For the first time, compassion and care are expressed in a way that fosters the rebuilding of trust and intimacy. Forgiveness finally becomes a reality—a part of their story and something that becomes a regular part of their marriage. What a privilege it is to serve a couple and see the Lord redeem their marriage from very difficult circumstances!

Aaron Sironi, CCEF faculty member, LCPC

RESOURCES

Jay E. Adams, *From Forgiven to Forgiving: Learning to Forgive One Another God's Way*
Ruth Ann Batstone, *Moving On: Beyond Forgive and Forget*
Steve Cornell, "How to Move from Forgiveness to Reconciliation," https://www.the gospelcoalition.org/article/how-to-move-from-forgiveness-to-reconciliation
Nancy Leigh DeMoss, *Choosing Forgiveness: Your Journey to Freedom*
Dave Harvey, *When Sinners Say "I Do": Discovering the Power of the Gospel for Marriage* (ch. 6)
Ken Sande, *Peacemaking for Families: A Biblical Guide to Managing Conflict In Your Home*
Robert D. Jones, *Pursuing Peace: A Christian Guide to Handling Our Conflict* (chs. 8–9)
Timothy Keller, *Serving Each Other Through Forgiveness and Reconciliation*
Timothy S. Lane, *Forgiving Others: Joining Wisdom and Love*
Winston T. Smith, *Marriage Matters: Extraordinary Change through Ordinary Moments* (chs. 12–13)
Aaron Sironi, "From Your Heart . . . Forgive," *Journal of Biblical Counseling* 26, no. 3 (2012): 46–61.
Ryan Troglin, "Must We Forgive Those Who Sin Against Us If They Don't Repent?" https://www.thegospelcoalition.org/article/must-we-forgive-those-who-sin-against -us-if-they-dont-repent
Walter Wangerin Jr., *As for Me & My House: Crafting Your Marriage to Last* (chs. 4–8)

Chapter 5

ALL YOU NEED IS LOVE

Christian: Love is a many splendored thing,
  Love lifts us up where we belong, all you need is love.
Satine: Please, don't start that again.
  MOULIN ROUGE

This is love: not that we loved God, but that he loved us and sent
his Son as an atoning sacrifice for our sins.
  1 JOHN 4:10

People come to counseling for a variety of issues, but over time you begin to see certain patterns emerge from their situations and problems. Whether husbands and wives voice it in counseling or not, one of the core, existential questions they are asking is: Who *can* love me? Out of this question flows a second question: Who *will* love me?[1] Time and time again, I've seen husbands and wives struggle in their marriages because they don't have a biblical answer to these two questions.

We use the word *love* in a variety of ways. I love reading books. I love a good movie. I love finding an empty parking space near the front of a store. My wife loves getting a good deal. She loves the Cleveland Cavaliers. She loves hosting people in our home. In each of these scenarios, the word *love* conveys feelings and desires, but they aren't all the same. The way we love our children should look different than the way we love eating at Chipotle. With such range to a simple word, it should not surprise us that love in marriage needs greater definition—a biblical definition. If couples don't understand what biblical love is, it will be difficult to practice it in their relationship.

---

1. The first is a question of ability. The second is a question of desire.

If you were going to explain God's love to a husband and wife, where would you begin? To what Scripture would you bring them? John 3:16? 1 Corinthians 13? How about Romans 1? Would you begin a discussion of the love of God with the wrath of God? Surprisingly, that's exactly how Paul begins his magisterial letter to the Romans.

As he unpacks the glorious riches of the gospel, Paul writes in Romans 1:18, "The wrath of God is being revealed from heaven against all the godlessness and wickedness of people, who suppress the truth by their wickedness." We don't like to speak about God's wrath, but that may be because we misunderstand it. J. I. Packer writes, "God's wrath in the Bible is never the capricious, self-indulgent, irritable, morally ignoble thing that human anger so often is. It is, instead, a right and necessary reaction to objective moral evil."[2] In other words, God's wrath is not the same as human anger. God's wrath is his righteous action against sin and evil.

Paul methodically lays out the case that every single human being bears the wrath of God: "They have become filled with every kind of wickedness, evil, greed and depravity. They are full of envy, murder, strife, deceit and malice. They are gossips, slanderers, God-haters, insolent, arrogant and boastful; they invent ways of doing evil; they disobey their parents; they have no understanding, no fidelity, no love, no mercy. Although they know God's righteous decree that those who do such things deserve death, they not only continue to do these very things but also approve of those who practice them" (Rom. 1:29–32).

A few chapters later, Paul states clearly: "All have sinned and fall short of the glory of God" (Rom. 3:23). Who can stand in the gap for us and satisfy the wrath of God and pay the debt for our sin? From Abraham to Moses to David, human history has been looking for that one person who can reconcile sinful humanity to a righteous God. Our answer and hope is revealed in Romans 5 where Paul wrote some of the most important words in the entire Bible: "While we were still sinners, Christ died for us" (Rom. 5:8).

Peace with God? After what Paul has just written about God's wrath being revealed against all of us? How does this happen? We certainly did nothing to earn this reprieve from God's just punishment of our sin. Paul writes that this happened at a time when we were powerless and ungodly. When we were completely *unlovable*, Jesus Christ died for us. He bore the punishment for our sins. He stood in our place condemned. Tim Keller writes of the magnitude of God's love for us shown in Christ on the cross, "We must say to ourselves something like this: 'Well, when Jesus looked down from the cross, he didn't think 'I am giving myself to you because you

---

2. J. I. Packer, *Knowing God* (Downers Grove, IL: InterVarsity Press, 1993), 151.

are so attractive to me.' No, he was in agony, and he looked down at us—denying him, abandoning him, and betraying him—and in the greatest act of love in history, he STAYED. He said, 'Father, forgive them, they don't know what they are doing.' He loved us, not because we were lovely to him, but to make us lovely."[3]

When we were at our worst and most unlovely, Jesus died to make us holy and reconciled to God. Only when we understand that the wrath of God necessitated and required the death of God's only Son, Jesus Christ, can we begin to understand the immensity and depth of God's love for us. John Piper writes, "The love of God provides escape from the wrath of God by sacrificing the Son of God to vindicate the glory of God in forgiving sinners. That's the gospel."[4] Charles Wesley wrote about it in his hymn:

And Can It Be?

And can it be that I should gain
An int'rest in the Savior's blood?
Died He for me, who caused His pain—
For me, who Him to death pursued?
Amazing love! How can it be,
That Thou, my God, shouldst die for me?

Whenever we are tempted to doubt the depth and security of God's love for us, we need look nowhere else but the cross of Christ. It is on the cross that the wrath and love of God perfectly meet and intersect for his glory and our redemption. D. A. Carson writes, "God in His perfections must be wrathful against His rebel image-bearers, for they have offended Him; God in His perfections must be loving toward His rebel image-bearers, for He is that kind of God."[5]

Paul concludes his first section in Romans by not only telling us of God's love in Christ but also assuring us of God's *forever* love in Christ: "For I am convinced that neither death nor life, neither angels nor demons, neither the present nor the future, nor any powers, neither height nor depth, nor anything else in all creation, will be able to separate us from the love of God that is in Christ Jesus our Lord" (Rom. 8:38–39).

Pause for a moment and consider how this truth practically impacts the couples you are caring for right now. How might the dynamics of their marriage

---

3. Timothy Keller and Kathy Keller, *The Meaning of Marriage* (New York: Dutton, 2011), 109.
4. Sam Storms, "Is the God of Love Also a God of Wrath?", January 13, 2015. http://www.samstorms.com/enjoying-god-blog/post/is-the-god-of-love-also-a-god-of-wrath.
5. D. A. Carson, "God's Love and God's Wrath," *Bibliotheca Sacra* 156 (1999): 388–90.

change if a husband and wife knew they were fully loved by God and they were secure in that love? Think with me through a few scenarios.

Ryan and Meredith have been married for ten years, and they have two children. Ryan has your typical nine-to-five job, and Meredith stays at home to care for the kids. Over the past few months, the distance between Ryan and Meredith has been growing. Meredith has tried to ask Ryan what is going on but is met with short explanations and a silence that says, "Leave me alone."

After being "shut out" by Ryan, Meredith might be tempted to pursue several tactics in response. She could retaliate against Ryan, shutting him out in return. She could get angry and bitter. She could become whiny and needy. She could move on and act as if nothing is wrong. Or, out of her understanding of God's love for her, Meredith could choose to move toward Ryan. Just as God moved toward us when we would have nothing to do with him, Meredith could move toward Ryan in sincere love (cf. Rom. 12:9) without expectation of getting something in return.

Tim Keller writes,

> In any relationship, there will be frightening spells in which your feelings of love dry up. And when that happens you must remember that the essence of marriage is that it is a covenant, a commitment, a promise of future love. So what do you do? You do the acts of love, despite your lack of feeling. You may not feel tender, sympathetic, and eager to please, but in your actions you must BE tender, understanding, forgiving and helpful. And, if you do that, as time goes on you will not only get through the dry spells, but they will become less frequent and deep, and you will become more constant in your feelings. This is what can happen if you decide to love.[6]

Jeff and Laura are a newly married couple of six months. Jeff is an avid tennis player but during the chaos of their engagement, he took a break to help Laura plan their wedding. After the wedding Jeff resumed his old schedule of playing tennis, but it takes him out of the house two nights a week. At first Laura did not seem to mind, but she felt more and more neglected, so she asked Jeff to cut back his tennis to one evening a week. Jeff's response? "Why do I have to give up a night of tennis to prove I love you?"

How could Jeff have responded if he had a better understanding of God's love for him? What if Jeff understood that self-sacrifice was more than *an* expression of love for Laura, but *the* very embodiment and demonstration of true, biblical love? As the apostle John states in 1 John 4:10: "This is love: not that we loved God,

---

6. Keller and Keller, *The Meaning of Marriage*, 104.

but that he loved us and sent his Son as an atoning sacrifice for our sins." What if Jeff were to understand and live out of an understanding of the self-sacrificial love of Jesus? Would the sacrifice of an evening of tennis still be hard for him? Probably, yes. But in light of the love of Christ, such a sacrifice is both encouraged and empowered.[7]

Nick and Crystal have been married for five years, and for the most part, they enjoy a happy marriage. One recurring struggle is when Crystal makes a harmless comment that Nick interprets as a not-so-subtle dig at him. Last week she made a comment about how he mowed the lawn, and this week it was about his aggressive driving. At first, Nick let the comments slide off his back, but he finds it increasingly more difficult to shake them off. The final straw broke last night when Crystal made a joke about the steaks Nick had "burned" on the grill. Nick lost it. "I can't do anything right that makes you happy," he yelled, slamming down his plate and leaving the dining room.

What is really going on in Nick's heart? Is this anger? Is it a lack of self-esteem? Or is it something deeper? What if what Nick needs is a deeper understanding and assurance of God's love for him? What if Nick truly believed that he was known, loved, and accepted by God? If Nick is satisfied and secure in God's love for him, then it gives him a different framework in which to hear and receive Crystal's comments. Instead of letting them fester internally or being mentally undone by them, Nick can choose to speak to Crystal about how her words hurt him. Instead of fearing how Crystal might react to his vulnerability, self-sacrificial love can move Nick toward his wife, not away from her.

In all of these situations, a more durable, robust, and biblical understanding of love is needed. As husbands and wives understand God's love for them, you, as a counselor, can begin to call them to love each other biblically.

Let's start by defining exactly what we mean by love, in light of Paul's teaching: *Biblical love in marriage flows out of our relationship with Christ into a covenantal commitment to self-sacrifice in small and large ways for the spiritual, emotional, and physical well-being of my spouse.*

This definition embodies the heartbeat of what biblical love in marriage is all about. Biblical love requires not only *understanding* the love of God but *functioning* and *living* out the reality that you are loved by God. It's not enough to *know* you need to love your spouse; you must *do the actions* of love.

Some spouses (wives in particular) often push back on this definition because sacrificial love gets filtered through certain social and political lenses. I've had husbands and wives both tell me that sacrificial love—in their understanding—means

---

7. I'm not communicating that Jesus's sacrifice for us makes our sacrifices unimportant but that Jesus's sacrifice informs and motivates our self-sacrifice.

letting their spouse do whatever they want, becoming a doormat to their spouse's desires. They believe that loving another sacrificially means putting yourself in a position where you are easily taken advantage of by the other person. Others see it as a life of self-denial and self-negation. Professor Elizabeth Krumrei-Mancuso counters, "So, what is the solution, then? For me, the starting point is the idea that if Christianity is true, it has to be possible to take a positive view of self-sacrifice without promoting oppression. If Christ gave his life as a sacrifice for others, then it has to be possible to live a life of sacrifice in a way that does not, ultimately, harm my relationships or myself."[8]

Mancuso goes on to note that even secular research supports the view that, "more positive views of sacrificing early in marriage predicted positive relationship outcomes."[9] If research supports the view that a self-sacrificial love ethic promotes health in relationships, then how much more positive could marriage relationships be when that love is rooted in Christ?

When husbands and wives are confident in God's love for them, it frees them to offer and to seek love, expecting nothing in return. This is more than just romanticism. This is more than mere sentimentality or feeling. This is the love of God incarnated in marriage. Imagine with me for a moment the dynamic change in marriages when husbands and wives grasp the height, breadth, and depth of God's love for them. This kind of love has the power to change marriages because it's the same kind of love that changed you and brought you from the kingdom of darkness to the kingdom of light.

> Therefore if you have any encouragement from being united with Christ, if any comfort from his love, if any common sharing in the Spirit, if any tenderness and compassion, then make my joy complete by being like-minded, having the same love, being one in spirit and of one mind.
>
> PHILIPPIANS 2:1–2

HUSBANDS AND WIVES AS LOVERS

With a foundational understanding of love in place, we can begin to consider how self-sacrificial love works itself out in marriage. What does this look like practically? How can you equip couples to love one another self-sacrificially? Here are

---

8. Elizabeth Krumrei-Mancuso and Bradley J. Mancuso, "Love & Marriage: He Said, She Said," February 13, 2017. *Biola Center for Christian Thought*: https://cct.biola.edu/love-and-marriage/.
9. Ibid.

four principles to walk through that will help couples move from a "me-oriented" marriage to an "others-oriented" marriage. Self-sacrificial love:

- repents of innate selfishness
- acts before it feels
- happens in the details of marriage
- pursues spiritual health and oneness

Self-sacrificial love repents of selfishness.

The starting point for husbands and wives is a fundamental understanding that the bent of their heart is toward themselves. We are, as Martin Luther famously said, curved in on ourselves by nature.[10] Keller writes, "The main barrier to the development of a servant heart in marriage is . . . the radical self-centeredness of the sinful human heart."[11] Encourage husbands and wives to examine their hearts (cf. Ps. 139:23–24) and ask the Lord to reveal blind spots of selfishness to them. Take a husband or a wife to Philippians 2:3–5 and ask them if they have the same mindset as Christ Jesus.

More likely than not, if couples are honest with themselves and each other, you will get some acknowledgment that selfishness is part of their problem. If you can get a husband and wife to pause in their marriage and recognize their self-oriented bent, there is an opportunity here for them to repent and change. Instead of playing the blame game, spouses can take a small step toward looking inward and taking personal responsibility. When they confess and repent to God, they find that he is a God who is faithful and just to forgive them and restore them (1 John 1:9).

Self-sacrificial love acts before it feels.

One of the biggest issues you will face in marriage counseling is getting couples to live out their theology. They may read passages that tell them to *love one another* (John 13:34), but because they don't *feel* love for their spouse, they fail to fulfill God's command. Tim Keller reminds us, "Our culture says that feelings of love are the basis for actions of love. And of course, that can be true. But it is truer to say that actions of love can lead consistently to feelings of love."[12]

---

10. Martin Luther, *Lectures on Romans* in vol. 25 of *Luther's Works: The American Edition* (St. Louis: Concordia, 1972), 345.

11. Ibid., 56.

12. Ibid., 103.

How, then, can pastors and counselors teach, model, and equip couples to love each other?

C. S. Lewis writes,

But though natural likings should normally be encouraged, it would be quite wrong to think that the way to become charitable is to sit trying to manufacture affectionate feelings. Some people are "cold" by temperament; that may be a misfortune for them, but it is no more a sin than having bad digestion is a sin; and it does not cut them out from the chance, or excuse them from the duty, of learning charity. The rule for all of us is perfectly simple. Do not waste time bothering whether you "love" your neighbor; *act as if you did*. As soon as we do this we find one of the great secrets. When you are behaving as if you loved someone, you will presently come to love him. If you injure someone you dislike, you will find yourself disliking him more. If you do him a good turn, you will find yourself disliking him less. There is, indeed, one exception. If you do him a good turn, not to please God and obey the law of charity, but to show him what a fine forgiving chap you are, and to put him in your debt, and then sit down to wait for his "gratitude" you will probably be disappointed. . . . But whenever we do good to another self, just because it is a self, made (like us) by God, and desiring its own happiness as we desire ours, we shall have learned to love it a little more, or, at least, to dislike it less.[13] (emphasis added)

Lewis hits the proverbial nail on the head. More often than not, when we take actions of love, feelings will follow. I find that couples waste precious time in their marriage waiting on their spouse to love them or waiting for feelings of love for their spouse to return before they, in turn, will act in love toward their spouse. The result is a vicious cycle of rejection and selfishness. A wife withholds love for her husband, waiting for him to affirm her, encourage her, and attend to her. When he doesn't, her feelings for him grow cold and brittle. "I don't deserve to be treated this way," she concludes and then resolves, "I'm not going to take his rejection forever." Ironically, on the other side of the marriage, the husband is thinking to himself, "Loving my wife is like curling up to a porcupine." Each is waiting for the other to take action.

Often in counseling sessions, couples will talk about their love languages: giving and receiving gifts, acts of service, physical touch, words of affirmation,

---

13. C. S. Lewis, *Mere Christianity* (New York: HarperCollins, 2001), 130–31.

and quality time. These lenses can be wonderful when they are used as a guideline for selflessly loving a spouse outside one's own comfort zone and according to the spouse's unique needs. However, I've also seen some couples weaponize the love languages, misusing them to legitimize selfish snobbiness about the kind of love they want to receive. They drill down on one particular "language" and say that the only way their spouse's love is good enough is if it is expressed in exactly the way they want to be loved, according to their self-perceived needs and standards. This is not biblical love. God's Word does not tell us to accept or reject our spouse's love according to their masterful sensitivity to our personal preferences or love languages. What he does call us to do is love our spouse self-sacrificially and selflessly. This must be lived out in how we selflessly *give* sincere love to our spouse according to *their* bent, but also in how we selflessly *accept* sincere love from our spouse according to *their* bent. Awareness of one another's love languages does not excuse us from the mandate to elevate the other's needs above our own.

Self-sacrificial love happens in the details of marriage.

The concept of self-sacrificial love sounds a lot easier and better than actually *living* a life of sacrificial love in marriage. How does a husband's "I love you" translate into the everyday details of marriage? How does a wife's "I love you" manifest itself in the everyday actions of marriage? God desires more than our professions and confessions of love, he desires actions which correspond to our beliefs!

Paul reminds us in Romans 12:1–2 that God desires all of us: body and soul. He is not content for husbands and wives to have only a cognitive awareness of salvation; he wants faith that leads to action (James 2:14–26)! In Romans 12:9–21, he lays out a vision for what this presentation of both body and soul might look like. While his thinking goes beyond the marital relationship, what he says helps us see how our "I love yous" become embodied practices in our marriage.

One exercise I've found helpful with couples is to ask them to think through Paul's statements in Romans 12 from a different vantage point. Try helping them pray through Romans 12:9–21 with their own selfishness in mind. Here are a few sample verses:

Love must be sincere. Hate what is evil; cling to what is good.

Lord, I confess my love is often hypocritical, especially when it comes to my spouse. My love can be manipulative and self-serving. I don't always hate what is evil, but have sometimes actively pursued things I know are bad for our marriage.

Be devoted to one another in love. Honor one another above yourselves.

Lord, I want to be devoted to my spouse, but I often pursue my own desires and expectations. In fact, I often find others to be annoying, frustrating, and an all-around source of hardship. I don't enjoy showing honor to others, but seek to do the bare minimum requirement, which for me is not saying much.

Live in harmony with one another. Do not be proud, but be willing to associate with people of low position. Do not be conceited.

Lord, I confess I'm conceited and think highly of myself—my opinions, my way of doing life in the home. My pride often gets in the way of confession and repentance. I try to build myself up by putting my spouse lower, instead of embracing a humble attitude and letting you lift us both up in your time.

Do not repay anyone evil for evil. Be careful to do what is right in the eyes of everyone.

Lord, I confess my propensity to repay evil for evil. I need to be honest about how I treat my husband. I'm a master scorekeeper and avenger when you call me to be a masterful forgiver and peacemaker.

Do not be overcome by evil, but overcome evil with good.

God, I confess that this sounds difficult and almost impossible. Help me to give grace and goodness in the face of hardship and rejection. God, forgive me for the times I've allowed myself to become overwhelmed with despair without seeking and seeing your goodness in the small, everyday moments of our marriage.

Paul reminds us that sacrificial love is love in action. Christ's love for his people is not theoretical or abstract. It is real and tangible. He entered into our world. He emptied himself and made himself nothing. He loved us in the details of life. Husbands and wives must embrace and embody Jesus's mission of love, and by loving each other in the details of life, they will present themselves to God as a living, holy, and pleasing sacrifice.

Self-sacrificial love pursues spiritual health and oneness.

I'm convinced that every kind of authentic intimacy—physical and emotional—flows from a robust spiritual intimacy. You cannot give what you do not have. Without fail, every couple I counsel with marital problems is simultaneously lacking intimacy with God. Pursuit of God in marriage helps build deeper spiritual intimacy. As husband and wife draw closer to God, they will draw closer to one another.

As a husband and wife pursue God, the distance between the two of them narrows. Intimacy with God has at least two positive dynamics in marriage:

1. It focuses responsibility on the individual spouse. The focus is on you and your relationship with God. It's about cultivating and tending to weeds of sin which easily crowd out your love for God. It's about pruning and shaping your desires for Christ and others. It's not about you changing your spouse.

2. It entrusts responsibility for change to God, and not to your own abilities
    to manipulate or motivate that change. When husbands and wives keep
    their eyes on Christ, I'm amazed to find that they have less time to critique,
    blame, and badger their spouse. Instead, they realize that those techniques
    they have tried time and time again are of little use. Spouses must be
    entrusted to God, who alone can change the hearts of men and women.

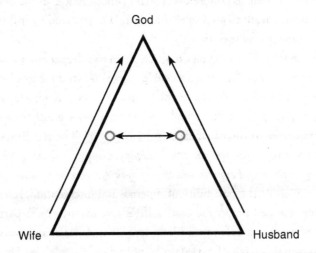

At some point in the counseling session, I try to get a full picture of what each
spouse's devotional life looks like. I've found most people give generic answers, e.g.,
"I read my Bible here and there, not as consistently as I would like to," or "I listen
to a lot of sermon podcasts when I drive in to work." Generic devotional lives lead
to generic spiritual lives. Spiritually robust devotional lives lead to spiritually robust
intimacy with God.

Here are some helpful questions I ask spouses to get a sense of their spiritual life:

- Describe your daily routine with God, including time in the Word and
  in prayer.
- Do you and your spouse spend time praying with one another?
- Describe a recent time you felt especially close to God. Where were
  you, and what were you doing?
- What is your favorite verse? Why?
- What is a line or a stanza from a recent hymn or song which has
  impacted you? Why?
- Describe a recent time you felt the conviction of the Holy Spirit.
- When was the last time you sought your spouse's forgiveness?

- How often do you attend church?
- Where do you serve or how do you exercise your spiritual gifts?
- When was the last time you saw something in nature that truly provoked a sense of awe and wonder for God?

These questions are not only good for counseling couples, they are good for us to consider as well, as counselors. You don't need to ask all the questions at one time. These are meant to go deeper than just, "Do you read your Bible and pray?" Help the couple to get specific.

Based on their answers, you can guide them to a deeper and more robust spiritual intimacy. One of the most accessible ways you can do this is by encouraging couples to pray together.[14] Recently, the *Washington Post* put out a fascinating article detailing empirical proof that couples who pray for one another experience more positive outcomes in their marriage. Why is this so? Thomas Burnett concludes the article, writing, "Yet how exactly does prayer improve relationships in so many ways? *None of these studies presumed that the prayers were being answered by a divine being.* Setting aside the possibility of supernatural intervention, research suggests that partner-focused prayer increases selfless love towards one's partner. It could also help reorient a couple toward long-term shared goals, and away from short-term, adversarial behavior focused on 'winning' conflicts."[15] (emphasis added)

What I find fascinating is that the prayers in these various studies are not presumed to be heard or answered by any sort of god. What a difference there is between this understanding of prayer and biblical prayer! Christian couples who engage in prayer are not simply completing an exercise in mysticism, they are communicating with the Creator of the universe. "I call on you, my God, for you will answer me; turn your ear to me and hear my prayer" (Ps. 17:6).

Husbands and wives can have confidence when they pray to God that he will answer them. What joy to know that God, our Abba Father, delights to hear the cries of his children!

On the subject of prayer and marriage, the apostle Peter writes, "Husbands, in the same way be considerate as you live with your wives, and treat them with

---

14. In situations where there is chronic conflict, abuse, or anger, prayer together as a couple will be something they need to work toward. Couples who cannot even talk together will find it hard and difficult to pray together. Progress on either end (prayer or conversation) will inevitably aid the frequency and goodness of the other. Be mindful of simply prescribing a spouse to sit down and pray with their husband/wife when there is not a good foundation in their relationship.

15. Thomas Burnett, "Frustrated with your spouse? These scientists suggest a specific kind of prayer," August 7, 2017. *The Washington Post*: https://www.washingtonpost.com/news/acts-of-faith/wp/2017/08/07/frustrated-with-your-spouse-these-scientists-suggest-a-specific-kind-of-prayer/?utm_term=.26484e3c115c.

respect as the weaker partner and as heirs with you of the gracious gift of life, so that nothing will hinder *your* prayers" (1 Pet. 3:7, emphasis added). The *your* in the final half of the sentence is plural in the Greek. If Peter were from the South, he might have written, "so that nothing will hinder *y'alls* prayers." John Piper offers three ways this verse can be interpreted:

1. First possibility: Our prayers are hindered because sin obstructs our relationship to God. (cf. 1 Pet. 3:12)
2. Second possibility: Our prayers are hindered because sin obstructs the unity of the husband and wife in prayer, making it less likely God will respond favorably. (cf. Matt. 18:19)
3. Third possibility: Our prayers are hindered because a broken relationship makes it hard to kneel in prayer together.[16]

Commentators agree that all three of these are legitimate interpretations of the passage, but regardless, the common thread binding them is this: prayer is important in the marriage relationship, and sin hinders your ability to pray.

The couples you counsel must reclaim a biblical vision for love in marriage for that marriage to fully display the glory of God. Left to themselves, husbands and wives will act out of self-interest and selfishness rather than responding in love to the needs of their spouse. Only the power of the gospel can draw husbands and wives out of this self-oriented dynamic. It is only when husbands and wives know they are fully loved and fully known in Christ that they will have any hope of moving toward their spouse in self-sacrificial love.

When spouses know and are convinced of God's love for them, it frees them up to love their spouse *expecting nothing in return*. Love in marriage is not sentimental or superfluous; it is the living incarnation of the gospel. Every time a husband or wife self-sacrificially loves the other they embody Jesus's sacrifice for them. What an opportunity for our marriages! Imagine if husbands and wives felt the gravity of the apostle John's command and teaching: "No one has ever seen God; but if we love one another, God lives in us and his love is made complete in us" (1 John 4:12).

As God's children, husbands and wives are active storytellers in God's larger story. Through their actions and feelings, they make the love of God for humanity concrete and real. They remind us we are loved and known by God, and that, in turn, propels our hearts to worship and yearn for the day when we will see God and experience his loving, majestic presence for all eternity.

16. John Piper, "Your Prayers Hang on Your Marriage," March 29, 2016. *Desiring God*: https://www.desiringgod.org/labs/your-prayers-hang-on-your-marriage.

One Couple's Story

There have been a couple times during our marriage that we sought biblical counsel. Neither time were we thinking drastically; we weren't tempted to end our marriage. Rather, we wanted to strengthen it, but had simply reached a point where we needed help understanding each other and guidance in applying Scripture to our lives and marriage. We are always quite open about the fact that we sought counsel because we know the Lord used it to bolster our relationship and believe marriage counseling can be such a helpful tool for the health of any marriage.

We urge others to seek help without shame. Relationships can simply be difficult at times, and it is responsible to tend to a marriage with care. We both went into counseling recognizing sin was present in each of us. Jonathan helped us communicate, but, more importantly, helped us through the process of repentance. Identifying and putting off our sinful habits and expectations was one step; the next was to build better habits that were God-honoring because they were rooted in his love and mercy.

God created marriage; he also designed us to be relational and live in community. To seek help from our community for our marriage relationship seemed very natural. We are very thankful for the help we received and the peace it provided. It has impacted our marriage and benefitted us personally, but also helps us to share Christ through our marriage with a watching world. We wouldn't hesitate to seek biblical counseling again.

Joe and Katti Simkanin

 Counselor Fieldnotes

It is surprising when a married person does not want to follow God's plan to help their spouse grow in Christlikeness. A wife will excuse her neglect of addressing sin in her husband's life and wrongly label the neglect as submissiveness. A husband will abdicate his role of leading his wife spiritually and explain he is just trying to keep the peace. Husbands and wives have the greatest vested interest in the spiritual growth of their own spouse. No one else is going to benefit more from a husband's spiritual growth than his wife. Conversely, no one is going to suffer more if he fails to grow.

Marriage brings intimate contact and many opportunities to influence one another to grow into the image of Christ. Matthew 18:15 commands, "If your brother or sister sins, go and point out their fault, just between the two of you." Believing husbands and wives must remember that first and foremost they are brothers and sisters in Christ. They can help one another in many practical ways, but sanctification is of primary import. No spouse is responsible to change the other. No human being can play the role of the Holy Spirit. Rather, marriage is a call to be an instrument in God's hand to lovingly serve one's spouse and encourage spiritual growth—not through nagging or oppressive domination but through speaking the truth in love to one another.

Curtis W. Solomon, Executive Director, Biblical Counseling Coalition

RESOURCES

Alexander Strauch, *Leading with Love*
Paul David Tripp, *What Did You Expect? Redeeming the Realities of Marriage* (chs. 11–12)
Timothy and Kathy Keller, *The Meaning of Marriage: Facing the Complexities of Commitment with the Wisdom of God*
Tim Savage, *No Ordinary Marriage: Together for God's Glory* (ch. 3)
Joel R. Beeke, *Friends and Lovers: Cultivating Companionship and Intimacy in Marriage*

Chapter 6

STRUCTURING YOUR INITIAL SESSIONS

> The question I put to myself is not "How many people have I spoken to about Christ this week?" but "How many people have I listened to in Christ this week?"
>
> EUGENE PETERSON

> Plans fail for lack of counsel,
> but with many advisors they succeed.
>
> PROVERBS 15:22

To this point, we have covered the pastor's call to counseling, our need to understand the struggles of the human heart, and a few significant themes that come up in marriage counseling. In this chapter I want to get practical and outline for you a way to envision and structure your initial counseling sessions with a married couple.

The father of modern biblical counseling, Jay Adams, poignantly reminds counselors that the first session they have might possibly be the *only* session they have. Adams lists several reasons why there is not a second session: the problem is solved in the initial session, the counselee will not come back for another session, or you refuse to continue counseling.[1] Most often, I've found that couples don't return for a second session because the expectations for the counseling relationship are not properly communicated in the first meeting. Some pastors approach the

---

1. Jay Adams, *Critical Stages of Biblical Counseling* (Stanley, NC: Timeless Texts, 2002), 9.

first session with a couple in crisis haphazardly. They lack an overarching agenda, and this can lead to sessions that are unproductive at best. While there are those rare cases where the issues can be addressed in only one session, I find that with most marital counseling cases, you will need more than that.[2]

Pastors must also guard against the tendency to view a counseling session as another opportunity to preach to the couple. Counseling, unlike preaching, represents opportunities for interaction: the give-and-take, observation and interpretation, prayers, confession, and repentance. In counseling, we say and do things that matter in the moment. Keep in mind that you won't be able to say everything you want to say. David Powlison describes it this way: "The task in any ministry moment is to choose, emphasize, and 'unbalance' truth for the sake of relevant application to particular persons and situations. You can't say everything all at once—and you shouldn't try. The Bible's authors minister in this way. They say one relevant thing at a time."[3]

In light of this, how should you structure your initial sessions to say something that truly matters to a couple in need of help and hope? While the amount of time[4] you have in the first session may vary, here are five objectives for your initial session:

1. Communicate care
2. Communicate the gospel
3. Communicate the big picture
4. Communicate hope
5. Communicate what will happen next

COMMUNICATE CARE

For a counselor, communicating care is an important step in the initial session. If the couple with whom you are meeting does not sense you truly care about them, the chances are small that they will return to you for counsel. As a counselor, you communicate care in three ways: you listen, pray, and ask.

---

2. Adams is helpful in his work, providing wise guardrails for meeting with couples for an extended period of time and ending counseling with couples prematurely.

3. David Powlison, *How Does Sanctification Work?* (Wheaton, IL: Crossway, 2017), 34.

4. The amount of time you spend with a couple in counseling varies from pastor to pastor. As a rule of thumb, I like to divide a ninety-minute session into thirds: 1/3 catching up and reviewing the past week/month, 1/3 going over homework, 1/3 dedicated to instruction and teaching. When sessions go longer than this, attention spans tend to wane, focus is dissipated, and you tend to begin circling back to previous things already said/done.

Listening

In those initial moments when a couple comes in and pours their hearts out to you, the first thing you want to do is express care and gratitude. Look them in the eyes and thank them for coming in to see you.

- Thank you for coming in to see me today and entrusting me with difficult things.
- Thank you for coming in today and airing out your dirty laundry before your pastor.
- Thank you for coming in and being brave enough to say we can't keep going through this cycle.
- Thank you for coming in and giving counseling a try.
- Thank you for letting me in to see some of the messier parts of your marriage and offer God's life-giving words and perspectives.

Couples who come in for counseling are hoping that the first words they hear from you are not words of condemnation and critique, but words that offer life and hope. It shouldn't surprise us, but showing true humility and gratitude go a long way in developing rapport and relationships with the hurting and hopeless. Couples in crisis can be disarmed and engaged through a simple thank you and a desire to listen. Consider how the psalmist exults over God's "listening ministry" in Psalm 116:1–2:

> I love the LORD, for he heard my voice;
>> he heard my cry for mercy.
> Because he turned his ear to me,
>> I will call on him as long as I live.

What an amazing truth! The Creator of the universe is eager to hear our cries for help. Indeed, when people come to us, our prayer as counselors is that people find we display this type of inclination and disposition, one that leans *toward* people and their story, not away from them in disgust, horror, or surprise.

Professor and author David Augsburger writes, "Being heard is so close to being loved that for the average person, they are almost indistinguishable."[5] Actor Kelsey Grammer played the famous psychiatrist, Dr. Frasier Crane, on the hit show *Frasier*. People would call into his radio show with various problems, and Frasier's

---

5. https://www.huffingtonpost.com/janice-taylor/the-9-do-nots-of-active-l_b_5852646.html.

invariable tagline would be infamously offered—"You're on with Frasier Crane, and I'm listening." The irony of the interaction was that half the time, Frasier was doing anything but listening. Pastor, don't model your counsel or listening skills after Frasier. Model your counsel after the Wonderful Counselor. Listening to the cares and concerns of your brothers and sisters in Christ is an act that not only displays love but also incarnates the priorities of our God.

When we listen to couples, we want to model for them a God who bends his ear near to us so he can hear our struggles and our cries for help. This is not a God who is distant and indifferent, but a God who is vitally interested in your life and, by extension, your marriage. When people come in for counseling, this is the flavor I want to bring to that first session (and Lord willing, subsequent ones as well). When couples come into your home or office, they need to be assured that you are *for* them!

Communicating care happens through our posture. How we lean in toward them and position ourselves toward them can speak volumes to a couple. Do you sit behind an imposing desk, or do you come out toward them, near to them? In my college days, I remember visiting with one of my professors. Whether it was an advising appointment or an opportunity to talk about his course, he would sit behind a fortress of books, papers, and other sundry items. I always had a sense he had something better to do, another paper to grade, or a book to read. I'm sure I was reading too much into his posture, but regardless, our connection was not as vital and personal as it could have been.

In marriage counseling, there will be many variables outside your control, things that can influence the dynamics of your session. But there are also things you *can* control, and though they are small, they can make a big difference. Sometimes it may be a small gesture of hospitality ("Can I get you both a cup of coffee or something to drink?"), a kind invitation ("Let's go take a walk and talk"), or simply repositioning yourself ("Let me pull my chair around here so we can be face-to-face")—all of these are actions that can create small dynamic changes to the session.

Praying

We are human beings, made to be dependent on our Creator for everything. Being a counselor is not about being the best therapist the world has ever seen or fixing the unfixable. We do this work humbly, and as service to God. In order to do this work, we must be people who pray. Our prayers work in two directions: first, we pray to be counselors who are Spirit-filled and Spirit-dependent; secondly, we pray for our counselees. Praying silently in the midst of the session is one of the ways you show care for the couple. Whether your couple knows it or not, you are caring for them in the session when you reach out to the Holy Spirit in silent prayer for wisdom, guidance, and direction. You acknowledge in each and every minute of that session that you don't have anything to offer them, unless you have Christ. At the end of the day, all the world's best advice and counsel is powerless to change hearts; there's only one thing that carries that guarantee, and that is the good news of Jesus Christ.

Consider for a moment the impact of prayer, offered both silently and out loud. You are going before God himself, seeking grace and mercy to help you in your time of need. This is something a secular therapist cannot offer. In a relationship governed by professionalism and clinical detachment, praying with counselees would be considered a breach of the professional and ethical code of counseling. But as a pastoral counselor, I realize that the most ethical, beneficial action I can do for a couple is to pray and lift their burdens to the Lord. I offer the kind of prayer Peter writes about in 1 Peter 5:7, "Cast all your anxiety on him because he cares for you," a prayer that happens best in community—and in pastoral counseling situations! Ed Welch writes, "Knowing others well enough to pray for them—that's help at its most basic and its best."[6] May we be counselors who seek to know *and* pray for our counselees!

Asking

We'll delve into this a bit more in coming chapters, but in the first session, the counselor should be asking a fair amount of questions. These are not random questions to fill time and space but thoughtful and intentional questions aimed at helping you maximize the time you have with the couple. The author of Proverbs writes, "The purposes in a person's heart are deep waters, but one who has insight draws them out" (Prov. 20:5).

Like listening, asking questions is more than a Freudian expedition into the past; it represents a thoughtful, inquisitive methodology lived out by God himself. Our God is a God who asks questions, seeks answers, and desires to hear what people say. Note how often he uses questions to draw us out and to show us our need for him:

- To Adam: "Where are you?" (Gen. 3:9)
- To Cain: "Why are you angry? Why is your face downcast?" (Gen. 4:6)

6. Edward T. Welch, *Side by Side: Walking with Others in Wisdom and Love* (Wheaton, IL: Crossway, 2015), 84.

- To Hagar: "Where have you come from, and where are you going?" (Gen. 16:8)
- To Job: "Where were you when I laid the earth's foundation?" (Job 38:4)
- To Jonah: "Is it right for you to be angry?" (Jonah 4:4)
- To Nicodemus: "You are Israel's teacher," said Jesus, "and do you not understand these things?" (John 3:10)

Once a month, I gather with our lay counselors and we watch video from some of my counseling sessions. I take it as a compliment when my counselors tell me after viewing a session, "It's not that hard! I can do that!" Often they're getting at the straightforward process of asking questions, the skill of probing thoughtfully but purposely, and the various strands of narrative that aim to help the counselee see the inner workings of their heart.

Here's how this portion of the conversation might begin:

"Jeff and Jennifer, do you mind if I ask you a few questions to help me get a better sense of who you are and what you are going through? You each might have different answers, but let's seek to have each person give their answer in an uninterrupted fashion."

Here is a sample of some initial questions you might try to cover in that first session:[7]

- Tell me about yourself. Give me the ten-minute autobiography of your life.
- How did you come to faith in Christ?
- How long have you been experiencing trouble in your marriage?
- On a scale of one to ten (ten being "we're filing for divorce"), where would you put yourselves?
- What have you done already to help solve the various issues you're facing?
- Who else knows there is trouble in the marriage?
- Am I the last person you've reached out to or the first? Why?
- What do you hope to gain from our time together?
- If you could write out a best-case scenario for this counseling, how would it read?
- Is there anything else I need to know to help me better understand the two of you?
- Was there anything I said that didn't make sense or was unhelpful to you?

---

7. These questions represent a framework. It is important to tailor the questions to be in your unique voice.

Communicating care is an important aspect of all marriage counseling. But it is less of a "step" and more of a mindset you should have. Throughout the time together, you are seeking to communicate love and care. This isn't just a priority in the first session; it must be a consistent and persistent component of your entire time together.

REDEFINE THE PURPOSE OF MARRIAGE

Additionally, in that first session, it must be communicated that our only hope is in Jesus Christ and the good news of the gospel.

A large majority of the couples we have counseled at Parkside Church and Fieldstone Counseling have at one point or another sought out secular professional counseling. They have been through and experienced what the world has to offer by way of techniques and systems of change. To one degree or another, they've either found those systems ineffective or the results haven't been long-lasting. They may be coming to you as a last-ditch attempt to get a word from someone "religious" or receive a "pastoral" opinion. This is why the initial appointment is so critical. If you give them something they've already had by way of a trite platitude or self-help scheme, you're likely to lead them further down the road of despair and disillusionment. Give them something different, something personal and powerful, and you're likely to surprise them in the best of ways.

As a Christian counselor, I recognize that my primary role is to be an ambassador for Christ who calls spouses to be reconciled to God and one another (2 Cor. 5:20). This influences how you and I counsel in significant ways. Our primary role and goal as counselors is not to make couples have happy and successful marriages, but to glorify God in the way we counsel.[8] Author Gary Thomas sums it up succinctly, "What if God designed marriage to make us holy more than to make us happy?"[9] This statement can be revolutionary if understood and embraced. Most couples are surprised when I tell them my number one concern for them at the outset is not that they would have a good marriage. While it's often arresting and surprising to hear this, it allows you, the counselor, to clearly communicate to them your primary goal for your time together.

---

8. Obviously, these two outcomes are not mutually exclusive. Indeed, we would hope that they're complementary to one another; however, the counselor must keep in mind that pleasing God is their primary role. Couples can experience temporary happiness and peace in their marriage, but not apart from authentic, biblical change.

9. Gary Thomas, *Sacred Marriage* (Grand Rapids: Zondervan, 2000), 13.

The statement that marriage is not primarily about our happiness but our holiness is something the majority of couples don't fully grasp. "You mean to tell me that my current marital struggles could actually be a part of God's plan for my life?" This concept is radically reorienting for most of them. And for those that have heard this idea before, I find that most don't understand the premise and what it means. The fact that God could be using their marital struggles to sanctify them and bring them closer to him should actually serve to encourage us, not discourage us.

I love how pastor and author Tim Savage puts it:

Marriages . . . need a galvanizing agent, something external to what the partners themselves bring to the relationship . . . only one thing qualifies: the glory of God. Here is something so powerful that it transcends the most difficult challenges of life. Here is a provision so dependable that it can lift marriages to awe-inspiring heights. Here is a beacon so intense that it can show the way out of the darkest crisis. Here is a vision so permanent that it can outlast every temporary obstacle. Here is something supernatural, something beyond what mere human beings bring to a partnership. Here is the cement of marriage. Here is the rope that binds. When husbands and wives unite for the glory of God, they unite indeed.[10]

Do we believe this is true in a practical sense? Does it flesh itself out in how we counsel? If the glory of God is really the most important aspect of any marriage, then it should not surprise us that the gospel takes front and center in our marriage counseling.

I've seen couples visibly relieved to know that the marriage counseling process is not about them getting back to a particular state of "happiness" or "calm." There are many couples who are happy but not holy. There are many peaceful, conflict-free homes, but they're not homes where the gospel and glory of God is on full display. The glory of God in marriage must be the primary goal in our marriage counseling, because without it, we go from conflict to conflict, dust-up to dust-up, without ever addressing the core issues of the heart. Without a focus on the glory of God, we're potentially leading the two people to a modicum of human success apart from the enabling power of the Holy Spirit.

---

10. Tim Savage, *No Ordinary Marriage* (Wheaton, IL: Crossway, 2012), 24–25.

COMMUNICATE THE BIG PICTURE

We often get bogged down in the details of life. As Paul Tripp aptly puts it, we shrink the world down to the size of our world.[11] And we all do this. Think about your own life. You've had a difficult day at work. Your computer is working slower than traffic on the interstate during rush hour. Your lunch appointment was thirty minutes late. You finally get home, and you walk into your house and are immediately bombarded by a thousand requests for mediation from your three children. This life we live can crush us and lead us to believe our lives are nothing more than one chaotic encounter after another. Life is hard!

Couples who come to you probably feel these difficulties even more acutely. That's why they're meeting with you! Their marriage feels lifeless and dull. It's filled with difficulty, heartache, and sadness. Interactions are full of anger and vitriol. They feel things are never going to get better. That's why they need to be reoriented to the God of the Bible. Marriages need a fresh, hopeful, biblical perspective. One of the blessings you bring to couples in crisis is a ministry of perspective. You can help couples see several things:

- God created the world and ordained marriage as a way to bring him glory (Gen. 1–2).
- Life is hard; this world is broken (Gen. 3).
- You married a sinner, but they aren't the biggest problem. You are. (Rom. 3:23).
- God's promises of redemption, reconciliation, and justification are for people like you: the hurting, the broken, the disappointed, the depressed, the angry, the bitter.
- Repent, trust, and believe the good news of the gospel, and your marriage can begin to change.

When couples have a vision of the big picture of the Bible and how their marriage intersects with that story, you can pull husbands and wives out of the vortex of their small, hermetically-sealed world into a glorious journey of worship and mission for God. James K. A. Smith writes of the benefit of such reoriented worship, "Worship that *restores* us is worship that *re-stories* us."[12] Pastors and counselors, you can help re-story marriages for God's glory!

---

11. Paul David Tripp, "4 Ways to Experience the Fullness of Life," June 28, 2017. https://www.paultripp.com/wednesdays-word/posts/4-ways-to-experience-the-fullness-of-life.

12. James K. A. Smith, *You Are What You Love* (Grand Rapids: Brazos, 2016), 95.

COMMUNICATE HOPE

Throughout the session, the couple must be offered true, biblical hope. In biblical counseling courses, there is much discussion about giving hope to couples and people in crisis. I remember sitting in my classes thinking to myself, "Yeah, yeah . . . let's get on to the important stuff!" But I've realized that one of the most crucial things you can do as a counselor in that first session is to offer them hope. The people coming to you are possibly at their rope's end after decades of marital discord. They're reaching out because their spouse has threatened to walk away from eighteen years of marriage. They're broken, they're weak . . . they're hopeless. They need to be reminded of the hope Peter calls us to: "In his great mercy he has given new birth into a living hope through the resurrection of Jesus Christ from the dead, and into an inheritance that can never perish, spoil or fade" (1 Pet. 1:3–4).

Remember, they've most likely tried several times to fix the situation either on their own or with the help of a professional counselor. Don't give them more of the same—give them real, personal hope. The hope of Christ.

Read the words of Hebrews 4:14–16: "Since we have a great high priest who has ascended into heaven, Jesus the Son of God, let us hold firmly to the faith we profess. For we do not have a high priest who is unable to empathize with our weaknesses, but we have one who has been tempted in every way, just as we are— yet he did not sin. Let us then approach God's throne with confidence, so that we may receive mercy and find grace to help us in our time of need."

COMMUNICATE WHAT WILL HAPPEN NEXT

One of the ways we can love the people we minister to is through the thoughtful communication of what to expect and how the counseling process will unfold. Here are some basic items to communicate with the couple before they leave:

- Is there paperwork that needs to be completed?[13]
- When and where the next session will be held, and how that meeting gets set up.
- How should they follow up with you if anything comes up between now and their next session, e.g., phone, text, email?

---

13. If the counseling taking place is formal counseling and your church has a process and protocol for such things, be sure to have the paperwork on hand. If your counseling is more informal and conversational, then paperwork might not be a factor.

- Are there homework assignments? Give them clear instructions and hard copies if necessary.
- Ask them what their preference is if you run into them at church or somewhere else. Some couples prefer their counseling be anonymous, and some type of public gesture or embrace might raise questions. This is an issue to which you should be sensitive.

By communicating care, the gospel, the big picture, hope, and what will happen next, you are helping set the stage for a healthy, biblical, Christ-centered counseling relationship. These steps are more than action points; they are guideposts for how you interact and love people in crisis. As a pastor, small group leader, or Bible study facilitator, these are things I am confident you are equipped and able to do. As Paul told the church in Rome, "I myself am satisfied about you, my brothers and sisters, that you yourselves are full of goodness, filled with knowledge and competent to instruct one another" (Rom. 15:14).

Counselor Fieldnotes

One thing I've found helpful in the initial sessions with a couple is to share three phases that marriage counseling will go through: stabilizing, reconciling, and rebuilding. This helps the couple know you have a plan, gives direction, and promotes a sense of security. While each of these phases has its own character, the phases are flexible and a couple may float between them. Here are some examples for each stage:

Stabilizing: bringing order and peace out of chaos and conflict so the couple can begin to heal.

- Teach a communication strategy to avoid arguments between counseling sessions.
- Enlist prayer and practical support for each spouse.
- Teach spouses to pause and pray when tempted to indulge in angry or suspicious thoughts or words.

"Have mercy on me, my God . . . I will take refuge in the shadow of your wings until the disaster has passed" (Ps. 57:1).

Reconciling: leading spouses to confess sin and receive forgiveness from God and one another.

- Explore heart causes and gospel cure for marital conflict.
- Teach principles of confession and forgiveness. Provide guidance so each spouse experiences reconciliation with God and each other in a safe environment.

"As God's chosen people, holy and dearly loved, clothe yourselves with compassion, kindness, humility, gentleness and patience. Bear with one another if any of you has a grievance against someone. Forgive as the Lord forgave you" (Col. 3:12–13).

Rebuilding: helping couples rebuild their marriage on a Christ-centered foundation.

- Help couple understand how the gospel impacts marital vision, communication, conflict resolution, intimacy, roles, and mutual service.

"Be filled with the Spirit. . . . Submit to one another out of reverence for Christ" (Eph. 5:18, 21).

Pat Quinn, Director of Counseling, University Reformed Church

RESOURCES

Jay E. Adams, *Competent to Counsel: Introduction to Nouthetic Counseling*
Richard Baxter, *The Reformed Pastor*
Heath Lambert, *A Theology of Biblical Counseling: The Doctrinal Foundations of Counseling Ministry*
Jeremy Pierre and Deepak Reju, *The Pastor and Counseling: The Basics of Shepherding Members in Need*
Jeremy Lelek, *Biblical Counseling Basics: Roots, Beliefs, and Future*
David Powlison, "The Pastor as Counselor," *Journal of Biblical Counseling* 26, no. 1 (2012): 23–39
———, *Speaking Truth in Love: Counsel in Community*
———, *Seeing with New Eyes: Counseling and the Human Condition Through the Lens of Scripture*
Paul David Tripp, *Instruments in the Redeemer's Hands: People in Need of Change Helping People in Need of Change*
Robert W. Kellemen, *Gospel-Centered Counseling: How Christ Changes Lives*
———, *Gospel Conversations: How to Care Like Christ*

Bob Kellemen and Kevin Carson, ed., *Biblical Counseling and the Church: God's Care through God's People*

Edward T. Welch, *Side by Side: Walking with Others in Wisdom and Love*

———, *Caring for One Another: 8 Ways to Cultivate Meaningful Relationships*

Lauren Whitman, "What Does a Good First Session Look Like?," *Journal of Biblical Counseling* 28, no. 1 (2014): 53–63

PART 2

SPECIFIC ISSUES YOU WILL FACE IN MARRIAGE COUNSELING

Chapter 7

MY SPOUSE CHEATED ON ME!

Monogamy is impossible, but anything else is worse.
FRANCOIS TRUFFAUT

You adulterous wife! You prefer strangers to your own husband!
EZEKIEL 16:32

You are disgusting," he screamed with contempt, "How could you? I can't even look at you right now."

"I know, I know, I'm so sorry. I was so hurt by what you had done to me that I was looking for someone to love me."

"Are you joking? Are you saying you cheated on me because of something I did to you? Are you serious? You're trying to blame this on me?"

"No, I know what I did was wrong, and I'm so sorry. What I'm trying to tell you is that I did this because I was so unhappy in our marriage, and I thought he could make me feel better about myself."

"I don't know what you want me to say," he replied, shaking his head, "I don't even know what to do. But I know this, you can't be in the house tonight. Either you go and stay with your mom, or I'm out of here. I can't do this right now."

Adultery. Sooner or later every pastor or counselor will encounter stories of marital infidelity. Remember how one of my first counseling cases was marital infidelity? To this day, I remember how unprepared I was to walk that long road with the couple.

As I write this chapter, the country is reeling from three consecutive hurricanes—Harvey, Irma, and Maria—which have wreaked untold havoc on the southern United States and Puerto Rico. Hundreds of thousands of people have been displaced from their homes; millions have been without power and electricity. The financial price tags for Harvey and Irma alone are currently estimated at $180 billion and $100 billion respectively.[1]

The factors (ingredients) it takes to make a hurricane are fascinating. Bob Larson of Accuweather explains:

> These ingredients . . . are the right amount of wind and warm water. A steady and quiet wind is important in sustaining a hurricane. If you were to try to light birthday candles in front of a fan, it would blow out the candles. Similarly, if there is a lot of wind high in the atmosphere, it will not let the hurricane form. . . . Enough wind speed or a sudden change in direction could change the rotation of the top or even knock it over. Warm water is the second ingredient a hurricane needs. . . . Imagine that warm water is fuel to the hurricane in the same way that gasoline powers a lawn mower or a car.[2]

Infidelity in a marriage can feel like a hurricane. The factors of a hurricane look fairly harmless—water temperature, wind strength—but in the right timing they become a force for destruction. Similarly, if some seemingly harmless factors are present in a marriage, it can be a recipe for disaster. Gary Shriver, coauthor of *Unfaithful: Hope and Healing After Adultery*, explains his own descent into adultery, "I never really thought I was a prime candidate for adultery. I was committed to our marriage, and I didn't think I was what you would call 'high risk.' So how did I get here? The best description I ever heard was 'baby steps.' I let myself get into an intimate friendship with another female."[3]

FACTORS AND INGREDIENTS FOR INFIDELITY

Disappointment

Every couple I've counseled through infidelity began at the gateway of disappointment. It starts with a singular disappointment—he doesn't love like I deserve, she doesn't respect me the way I deserve. Then the disappointments pile up. Why doesn't he affirm me more often? Why is she always on my case about when I come

---

1. Umair Irfan, "The stunning price tags for Hurricanes Harvey and Irma, explained," September 18, 2017. *Vox:* https://www.vox.com/explainers/2017/9/18/16314440/disasters-are-getting-more-expensive -harvey-irma-insurance-climate.

2. Alexa Lewis, "Explain hurricanes to kids," https://www.accuweather.com/en/weather-news/ how-to-explain-hurricanes-to-kids-how-hurricanes-form-damage-from-storms/47422516.

3. Gary and Mona Shriver, *Unfaithful* (Colorado Springs: Cook, 2009), 45.

home from work? When is he going to start helping me discipline the kids? Why does her mother always have to get involved in our personal business?

When a spouse does not have a biblical framework to handle the inevitable disappointments that enter any marriage, they often internalize them rather than constructively discussing them and working them out. Disappointments come from unmet expectations, and unmet expectations stem from unspoken expectations.

Dabble

Laughter. That's what did it for Michael. As he walked over to Christy's cubicle at lunch to chat and engage in small talk, it was her carefree laughter that engaged him. Not only did it engage him, it also kept him coming back for more. She laughed at his jokes and sense of humor. She seemed genuinely interested in what he had to say.

Most people don't go into relationships thinking to themselves, "I want to commit adultery with _____." In fact, only 6 percent of men plan to have an affair and "fall into bed together."[4] Yet time and time again men and women fall into the trap of adultery. Why? It is because they dabble with the boundaries of their marriage in order to satisfy the disappointment they feel.

The author of Proverbs writes, "Can a man scoop fire into his lap without his clothes being burned?" (Prov. 6:27). This image accurately describes what I often see in marital infidelity. Men and women slowly dance around the fire, longing for it, looking at it, being entranced by it, thinking they will not get burned by it or that they can control it, only to find themselves engulfed in its flames and left with nothing but ashes.

Delight

The laughter moved slowly to an invitation for lunch from Michael. It seemed harmless enough, nothing more than grabbing lunch at the local deli down the road. After a few months of casual lunches, Michael confided to Christy that his marriage was not well. From there things escalated quickly and within the week Michael and Christy were in the throes of an adulterous affair.

What are some of the warning signs that these three initial stages of infidelity are happening?

- You really look forward to seeing this person.
- You are willing to go out of your way to make sure that you have regular interactions with them.

---

4. Josh Squires, "Take Action Against Adultery," February 2, 2016. *Desiring God*: https://www.desiringgod.org/articles/take-action-against-adultery.

- You rearrange your calendar to find ways to sneak more time in with that person (like early morning meetings, long lunches, late evenings, and more).
- You are growing increasingly critical of your spouse, especially as compared to that other special someone.
- You are looking for reasons to be away from your spouse.
- Your recreational life becomes more and more exclusive of your spouse.
- Your desire to be intimate, physically or emotionally, with your spouse is dwindling.[5]

When these first three factors are present—disappointment, dabbling, and delighting—some sort of attraction, either emotional or physical, begins to develop. Sinfully, spouses tell themselves to keep this sort of thing to themselves—which is exactly what you should *not* do. Paul writes in Ephesians 5:11, 13–14 (emphasis added), "Have nothing to do with the fruitless deeds of darkness, *but rather expose them.*" If a spouse finds themselves delighting in the company of another individual, it is imperative to disclose it.[6] Honesty in marriage is a disinfectant for the hidden disease of delight in someone other than your spouse. Honesty provides opportunities for repentance and accountability.

Denial

After his first encounter with Christy, Michael swore he would never cross that line again. Internally he berated himself but vacillated between overwhelming guilt and shame to excitement and anticipation at seeing Christy again. After each liaison, Michael told himself that he needed to end things with Christy before one of them got hurt. Michael even had conversations with Christy telling her that things needed to end. Christy would plead with Michael not to cut things off. "I'm fine with this until you're ready to leave her," she would entreat him. Michael kept telling himself he was going to come clean with his wife and let her know what was going on.

Discovery

Unfortunately, the opportunity for Michael to come clean never came. As Denise, his wife, was going through their phone bill, she noticed they had gone over their allotted data usage. Finding it odd, she combed through the phone bill and

---

5. Ibid.

6. Gary and Mona Shriver quote noted adultery specialist, Shirley Glass, "When we share our hidden feelings about another person with our spouse, the intensity and fascination of that secret are greatly diminished. We let reality into fantasy" (Shriver, *Unfaithful*, 201).

found multiple calls to the same number—Christy's number. Denise confronted Michael when he came home from work that day. She slammed the bill down on the table and demanded Michael explain who he was calling and texting so much.

Michael fumbled over his words and offered several explanations—all lies. Realizing he was caught, he offered a half-hearted confession. Yes, he and Christy had been calling and hanging out at work. He got carried away, and things "went too far" between them. Denise demanded to know exactly what "too far" meant.

Despair

Denise was devastated and angry. A rollercoaster of emotions swept over her; she had to get out of the house and talk to someone. She called her best friend, Sally, and they met at a park. Denise sobbed through all that had transpired at the house just a few short hours ago. "I don't know how he could do this to me and to the kids. He's a monster!" Sally tried to console her and offered a few words of encouragement.

"You should go and talk to someone at church. The least they can do is let you know what your options are," Sally replied.

While these ingredients—disappointment, dabbling, delight, denial, discovery, despair—might be present over a short amount of time or a longer amount of time, they are all present in most cases of infidelity. As a pastor and counselor, the spouse or couple will most often come to you at the end of this process broken, hopeless, and in need of help.

INITIAL STEPS IN COUNSELING

The affair must end.

There can be no progress made in marriage counseling if the spouse who is engaged in the affair[7] does not end it immediately. Ending the affairs entails:

- No meeting up of any kind.[8]
- No electronic communication of any kind, including texting, calling, emailing, or social media.[9]

---

7. There are numerous sorts of affairs. Tim Lane describes several different kinds you will encounter: http://timlane.org/blog/are-all-affairs-alike.

8. In cases where there are work entanglements, finding a new place to work might be the best option. When Jesus speaks of radically dealing with your sin in Matthew 5:29–30, I believe this is one of the practical ways this verse can be put into action. If the spouse works closely with the person they were having an affair with, it will continue to put them in the path of temptation on a daily basis. Part of the repentance process entails doing whatever is necessary to live in a way that pleases God (cf. 2 Cor. 7:10–11).

9. Brian Meismer says, "Although I am a fledgling therapist, it has been remarkable to me that every case of married infidelity I have seen has involved some form of indiscretion committed

- No third-party communication. Occasionally, some individuals will continue to work around accountability measures put in place by communicating through a coworker or a friend.
- Disclose any contact to your spouse immediately, e.g., you randomly see or run into the person at a restaurant, a store, or a local place of business. When this happens, it is best to be up-front with your spouse and let them know, regardless of whether or not there was communication or recognition on the part of the other person.
- Getting rid of any gifts, cards, clothing, jewelry, or mementos that the other person gave to you.

There are several helpful resources that can help you navigate this initial step.[10]

Make a full disclosure and confession.

When a couple comes in for an initial session following the discovery of adultery, a confession from the offending spouse may or may not have taken place. I ask the couple if there has been a full disclosure of what happened. Depending on the level of disclosure, I find it helpful for couples to have a definitive conversation where—away from the heat of the moment—a full confession can be made by the offending partner. For offending spouses, I recommend writing this down. This disclosure should not veer into shifting blame to the other spouse for the affair and should be as full and complete as possible. If significant details come out later in the counseling journey, it has the potential to destroy any rebuilt trust that has been acquired through forgiveness and repentance. A great deal of prayer should go into this step of the journey (cf. Psalm 139:23–24). In this case, progressive revelation is not a good thing.

What should be discussed in this full disclosure of the affair? Listed below are some helpful categories to organize the content and information:

---

on a phone. I have even spent whole (paid!) sessions helping couples learn how to manage their phones. Called 'remote infidelity,' this new kind of cheating is wildly popular and, according to some polls, is on the rise. (https://www.washingtonpost.com/news/the-intersect/wp/2014/10/03/back-up-husbands-emotional-affairs-and-the-rise-of-digital-infidelity/?utm_term=.3749aca79f13) The list of offenses I have seen runs the gamut from straight-up pornography usage to phone sex or text message flirting. The discovery of such sins by the offended party is often traumatic and shrouded in deceit and confusion. Although much remote infidelity never actually leads to physical infidelity, the damage that it tends to do is comparable." Brian Meismer, "Is Your Smartphone Endangering Your Relationships?" July 25, 2017. *Midlands Directory*: https://www.midlandscbd.com/articles/is-your-smartphone-endangering-your-relationships-4926.

10. Tim Lane, http://timlane.org/blog/immediate-actions-to-end-an-affair; Brad Hambrick, http://bradhambrick.com/how-to-end-an-extra-marital-relationship-2/.

- Take responsibility for what happened.
- a basic timeline of the affair (when did it start, duration, when did it end)
- who was involved[11]
- what methods were involved to keep the affair hidden
- were gifts exchanged
- a summary of what happened[12]

A common issue that comes up is the concern that too much information might create mental images or memories that will be difficult for the offended spouse to handle. This rationale overlooks the fact that any aspects of the affair that are not disclosed create room for the offended spouse's imagination to run wild, and this can cause a significant deal of harm. Gary and Mona Shriver explain, "Spouses often report being inundated with graphic images prior to hearing any details. We believe knowing what happened actually can decrease those thoughts and images . . . better to err on the side of too much disclosure than too little."[13]

As a counselor, help the offending spouse understand that this disclosure and confession is a tangible part of the repentance process and is ultimately done for God (cf. 1 John 1:9).

Do not make any big decisions in the aftermath.

Tim Lane writes, "Rebuilding a relationship after infidelity is not easy, but neither is dissolving one, particularly if there are children involved. Regardless of the choice to leave or stay, it is wise to discourage a quick decision when emotions are running high."[14] Proverbs 19:2 says, "Desire without knowledge is not good—how much more will hasty feet miss the way." Because there is always a rollercoaster of emotions present after an affair, it is not wise to make a final decision about the marriage at this time.

In particular, decisions about divorce should be postponed in the immediate aftermath of an affair. I've seen couples run the gamut of commitments and ultimatums post-affair, from threatening divorce to promising total reconciliation.

---

11. Most of the time affairs are kept secret, but on some occasions, others are aware and perhaps even facilitating the infidelity. This needs to be disclosed during the time of confession. A general principle I find helpful in marriage counseling is that someone outside the marriage should not have more information about the affair than the offended spouse.

12. Alasdair Groves, https://www.ccef.org/shop/product/what-should-i-tell-my-spouse-about-my-sexual-sin; David Powlison & Cecelia Bernhardt, https://www.ccef.org/resources/podcast/how-specific-should-i-be-confessing-sin.

13. Shriver, *Unfaithful*, 150.

14. Tim Lane, "Adultery: Divorce or Rebuild?," October 29, 2013. http://timlane.org/blog/adultery-divorce-or-rebuild.

Spouses who threaten divorce often make a decision based on their emotions at the time. Spouses who promise total reconciliation[15] often make a decision based on their faith, without understanding the full weight of how this will affect them.

During this initial period, do not be surprised if each counseling session you find yourself dealing with what seems to be a completely different couple. During session one, the offended spouse wants to end things. In session two, they believe the marriage can be restored. In session three, they're back to wanting to end things. As a counselor, you incarnate the steadying hand of God. Encourage them to take things slowly. In Psalm 46:10, God calls on his people to remain calm amid trial and upheaval, "Be still, and know that I am God."

Each spouse needs to get checked for sexually transmitted diseases.

A couple I met with post-infidelity was working toward reconciliation. The wife began to experience some significant health challenges. When she went to the doctor, she discovered that she had Hepatitis B and it had adversely affected her liver. When the doctor began to ask questions, she realized she had been infected by her husband. The Hepatitis B could have been treated earlier and more efficiently had it been detected through a routine STD screening.

This step of the process often involves a significant amount of shame and embarrassment for the spouse who has been sinned against. Ask questions to see if there is a way you can help mitigate that shame. See if they would like a friend to go to the appointment with them. Remind them that this is not their fault but is a precaution they must take.

Be prepared for a rollercoaster of emotions.

Anger. You need to be prepared for it in all its forms and varieties. The Shrivers give good advice to angry spouses: "There are a couple of principles that can help you deal with unresolved anger. Don't allow your anger to control you. If we are out of control verbally or physically, we are in sin. And the truth is that no real work gets done in that atmosphere."[16]

Grief. One of the emotions and processes pastoral counselors can miss is that of grieving. We normally think of grieving with death, but infidelity is a sort of death for the offended spouse, a death of a certain way of life. It is important that you walk through this grieving process with the spouse in a patient and

---

15. I'm not saying you do not want spouses to commit to reconciliation in marriage, only that actually *doing* reconciliation is much more difficult than *saying* you want to reconcile.
16. Shriver, *Unfaithful*, 152.

understanding way. Cindy Beall writes, "Encourage them to grieve. They have experienced a death. The death of a dream, a commitment, a trusting marriage. They are in immense pain and, honestly, the last thing they want to do is feel the pain. But they must. In order to heal through the paralyzing agony they are living in, they must grieve. They must ache, weep, and lament. Tell them this is part of the journey. If they try to go around the pain and ignore it altogether, it will be waiting for them on the other side. This is not fun but absolutely necessary."[17]

LONG-TERM CARE

Dealing with forgiveness.

The seeking and granting of forgiveness for marital infidelity is something that will need to be addressed. However, before forgiveness can be offered or granted, it is best to spend a portion of time addressing what biblical forgiveness is (see chapter four for a full explanation). Pastor and counselor Dave Dunham writes, "The first great danger in counseling those who've been betrayed by their spouse is to push for forgiveness too quickly."[18] To help prevent this, a number of issues must be addressed:

1. Has the offending spouse demonstrated biblical repentance for their sin?
   There will be an initial impulse to offer apologies and plead for forgiveness.[19] They feel the weight of their sin and the magnitude of the rupture in their marriage, and their initial response is to do whatever it takes to restore the relationship. Acknowledge that their desire is good, but caution them to take time and meditate on what the Bible has to say about godly sorrow versus worldly sorrow (cf. 2 Cor. 7:10–13).[20]
2. Does the offending spouse know what they are seeking forgiveness for?
   In the aftermath of an affair, the offending spouse knows in principle what they are seeking forgiveness for: committing adultery. A thoughtful and robust seeking of forgiveness, though, must be more thorough in its

17. Cindy Beall, "How to help the spouse who stays in marriage after an affair," May 11, 2016. *Care Leader*: https://www.careleader.org/help-spouse-stays-marriage-affair/.

18. Dave Dunham, "Counseling after Adultery," February 22, 2017. *Biblical Counseling Coalition*: https://www.biblicalcounselingcoalition.org/2017/02/22/counseling-after-adultery/.

19. This scenario entails a situation where adultery has taken place and the offending spouse desires to end the affair and be reconciled in the marriage relationship. There are marriage counseling cases where the offending spouse *does not* want to end their affair or does not want to work on the marriage, in which case these steps would not be appropriate.

20. On the topic of repentance, I haven't found a better book than Richard Owen Roberts, *Repentance: The First Word of the Gospel*.

scope. Why did they commit adultery? What led them to it? Listen below for how a sample dialogue might go:

Mark, I need to ask you to forgive me for what I did; how I sinned against you. I confess I went outside our marriage covenant to find happiness, excitement, security, and love. I fell short in my role as your wife to love and respect you, and in doing so I found my worth and significance in another person. Throughout the time of our affair, there were many times where I was deceitful, where I lied to you, where I kept the whole truth from you. Please forgive me. I know that in seeking your forgiveness, we are not promising to forget everything and brush it under the rug, but that we are committing to one another to piece this marriage back together with Christ as the foundation and the focal point of our marriage.

For spouses seeking forgiveness, I encourage them to spend time in prayer and God's Word, asking for his wisdom in knowing what to confess. I encourage spouses to write down their thoughts in advance to allow them time to organize their thinking so they can clearly communicate and seek their spouse's forgiveness. Be sure to encourage them to be specific and concrete.

3. Does the spouse who has been sinned against understand what is required in extending forgiveness?

Not only do you want to prepare and help the spouse who is confessing and seeking forgiveness, you also need to prepare and equip the offended spouse to know how to respond biblically. This is not a step in the rebuilding process you want to rush, but neither is it a step you want to drag out unnecessarily. As a counselor, you can simultaneously urge thoughtful contemplation and also lead them toward biblical reconciliation.

   a. Commit yourself to prayer before, during, and after your spouse's confession.

   b. Listen actively and seek to not interrupt.

   c. If there are areas of disagreement about the content of your spouse's confession, do not interject, but wait until they are done speaking.

   d. Remind yourself that forgiveness does not mean forgetting; forgiveness is not the same thing as rebuilding trust.

   e. Know that reconciliation cannot happen until forgiveness is sought and given.

   f. If you are not ready or able to offer forgiveness in the moment, communicate to your spouse that you need additional time to consider their request.

    g. Rehearse and remind yourself of the four promises made implicitly in forgiveness:

        i. I will not dwell on this incident.

        ii. I will not bring up this incident again and use it against you.

        iii. I will not talk to others about this incident.

        iv. I will not let this incident stand between us or hinder our personal relationship.[21]

4. Is the couple ready to commit themselves daily to prayer in order to develop and maintain the culture of forgiveness in their marriage?

I currently have a couple in counseling that is recovering from marital infidelity, and they have hit a few bumps in their rebuilding process. While both of them have sought forgiveness from each other and granted it, they came in last week expressing how difficult it was to make progress. I asked them if they were committing every day to forgive each other and remind themselves of the forgiveness they had granted. Their reply was, "No, we thought we only needed to do that one time." I gently reminded them that forgiveness was a daily lifestyle they needed to commit themselves to. Every day they would need to spend time with God asking for supernatural, Spirit-empowered strength to not only forgive but also seek each other's forgiveness when necessary. The four promises of forgiveness they made to each other need to be rehearsed, remembered, and lived out each day.

Rebuild trust.[22]

When adultery happens, trust is lost in a moment but can take years to rebuild. The process of rebuilding trust after infidelity is a long and arduous road. Proverbs 18:19 says, "A brother wronged is more unyielding than a fortified city." This is an apt metaphor for a couple post-affair. The offended spouse is like a fortified, walled-off city and they are not about to open the gates for their spouse to walk back in and hurt them. The offending spouse may feel shut out of their spouse's life. They can feel punished, cut off, and emotionally isolated. Gary Shriver described trust as "something I'd never appreciated having until I lost it completely."[23]

What does rebuilding trust look like in a post-affair marriage? Rebuilding

---

21. Ken Sande, "Four Promises of Forgiveness," https://rw360.org/four-promises-of-forgiveness/.

22. For a further, in-depth look at the topic of rebuilding trust: http://bradhambrick.com/10-step-progression-for-restoring-broken-trust/.

23. Shriver, *Unfaithful*, 181.

trust will entail each spouse growing first and foremost in their relationship with God and in turn moving in trust toward their spouse. Steve Cornell writes, "Differing from forgiveness, reconciliation is often conditioned *on* the attitude and actions of the offender. While its aim is restoration of a broken relationship, those who commit significant and repeated offenses must be willing to recognize that reconciliation is a process. If they're genuinely repentant, they will recognize and accept that the harm they've caused takes time to heal."[24]

Help them write a new story.

Another aspect of counseling couples after adultery is helping them live out a new story and a new identity. Adulterer is not their primary identity. I worked with a woman who had committed adultery, and she would frequently come in and speak of how she could not get rid of the enormous weight of guilt of what she had done. She would describe herself as "worthless" and "gross." We spent time reading through Hebrews 10, and I reminded her of Jesus Christ's once-for-all sacrifice for her sins. I asked her, "Did you confess your sin to Christ? Did you turn away and repent of what you did?" Christ offered a once-for-all sacrifice for her sin, and he chooses to remember it no more! This is the good news of the gospel. There's no other message that can offer this hope.

The world has no category for dealing with the pain of the past. The past is either everything (Freudian determinism) or the past is nothing (complete denial). The Bible, however, says that your past is something—your past is redeemable and able to be restored because of Jesus's sacrifice. One of my favorite lines from Lewis's *The Lion, the Witch, and the Wardrobe* is after Aslan has had a private conversation with Edmund regarding his treachery and betrayal of his brother and sisters. Aslan brings Edmund out of their meeting and presents him to his siblings. He says to them: "Here is your brother and there is no need to talk to him about what is past."[25] Only the gospel can bring about this type of forgiveness for the past and also hope for the future.

Plan for ongoing temptation and battles.

I often tell couples that Satan is not a cute kitten nibbling at the heels of their marriage. Peter writes, "Be alert and of sober mind. Your enemy the devil prowls around like a roaring lion looking for someone to devour" (1 Pet. 5:8). It would be foolish to think the Evil One is content to sit on the sidelines and watch

---

24. Steve Cornell, "How to Move from Forgiveness to Reconciliation," March 29, 2012. *The Gospel Coalition*: https://www.thegospelcoalition.org/article/how-to-move-from-forgiveness-to-reconciliation/.
25. C. S. Lewis, *The Lion, the Witch, and the Wardrobe* (New York: Macmillan, 1951), 136.

as marriages wrecked by adultery are restored and reconciled (cf. Eph. 6:10–17). Andreas Köstenberger brings a sobering perspective, "Marriage and family are not exempt from the cosmic conflict that is raging between God and his angels on the one hand and Satan and his demons on the other. Because marriage and the family are not merely human conventions or cultural customs but divine institutions, it should be expected that Satan, who seeks to rob God of his glory would attack them."[26]

Post-adultery, couples must be constantly on guard, acknowledging their vulnerability. Gary and Mona write, "You have to admit your vulnerability before you can recognize the need for protective measures."[27]

With the help of a counselor, some of these protective measures can be discussed and put in place. Protective measures could include but are not limited to:

- Is there a plan in place for rebuilding trust?
- Does each spouse have an accountability partner?
- What are the parameters for interaction with members of the opposite sex?
- How do you deal with current conflicts?
- What does healthy sexual intimacy look like?

FINAL THOUGHTS

Counseling couples through adultery requires endurance, patience, and wisdom from above. It's not easy; it can be discouraging at times—even lonely. Let me encourage you to stick with this; stick with *them*.

Despite all the hardship and the long hours, you do have something to offer couples in crisis: true and authentic hope. This is not a hope that erases the hurt and pain of adultery, but a hope that is honest about the suffering. A hope that the adulterer can be forgiven (cf. David and Psalm 51) and that this sin does not change the person's identity in Christ. A hope that says broken marriages have the potential to tell the gospel story in a way that is deep and profound. A hope that says God is in the business of taking broken, hopeless situations and bringing something good out of them.

---

26. Andreas J. Köstenberger, *God, Marriage, and Family: Rebuilding the Biblical Foundation*, 2nd ed. (Wheaton, IL: Crossway, 2010), 156. Köstenberger goes on to note that to his knowledge there is not a current volume, resource, or book that addresses the topic of marriage in the context of spiritual warfare. As a result, he offers the most robust treatment of the topic I have found, on pages 156–65.

27. Shriver, *Unfaithful*, 201.

One Couple's Story

To anyone on the outside, our marriage likely appeared hopeless. Indeed, had God not intervened, there is little doubt in my mind it would have been over. My husband and I had spent ten years in a vicious cycle of hurting one another with words and actions, then making up and "trying again." There was emotional and physical abuse, broken trust with both physical and emotional affairs, as well as alcohol abuse. It was an ugly mess, with two little boys caught in the wreckage. Hopeless. But God . . .

Through God's grace, we both came to the end of ourselves and asked for forgiveness from God and one another. We started a journey of healing that included weekly marriage counseling. Counseling showed us that for too long we were focused solely on one another and how the other person should fill our every need. We looked to each other for identity, purpose, and fulfillment. It was a completely unrealistic expectation. Even a good spouse cannot fill those needs, let alone a "difficult" one! Once we began to look to the Lord for our worth and identity, the pressure to be someone else's "everything" was lifted.

Counseling also showed us the true meaning of forgiveness. We had many hurts to overcome. If we had not learned to look at Christ's example of forgiveness—unearned and undeserved favor—we could not have forgiven one another. Just as Christ forgave us, by faith, we, too, had to forgive. This did not happen instantaneously, but was a process that he was faithful to bring about. Learning to trust one another again was also a process and a true gift that Christ brought back to us, over time, through the guidance of wise counsel and his amazing grace!

Brian and Marsha Raymond

Counselor Fieldnotes

One of the hardest things for an offending spouse to realize is that confession does not make everything better. After confessing the affair and asking for forgiveness, it is tempting for the offending spouse to believe that everything will go back to the way it was. Often, however, the betrayed spouse will need time to process all the pain and damage. They will experience a rollercoaster of emotions. One day they are gracious and forgiving, the next they are angry and can't stand to look at their spouse. The offending spouse can quickly become frustrated and discouraged in this process.

Effective counselors want to help the offending spouse understand that it takes time to heal a relationship. Repentance doesn't stop after confession; it is only the first step. There will be many lengthy and upsetting conversations moving forward. It will require continued humility. They must be willing to hear the same questions, same frustrations, and same disappointments again and again as their spouse tries to process all that has happened. They will need to give the same answers again and again, clarifying details, owning sin, and acknowledging the hurt they have caused. They will not, of course, want to have these same conversations, but their spouse will likely need to have them. They must consider the needs of their spouse as more significant than their own (Phil. 2:3).

Humble and repentant people recognize the need to endure the consequences of their sin and do not demand a more rapid processing than is natural to the individual and the nature of the offense. Good counselors will want to help the offending spouse understand this and remain persistent in the relationship.

Dave Dunham, Pastor of Counseling and Discipleship,
Cornerstone Baptist Church

RESOURCES

*Dave Carder, *Torn Asunder: Recovering from an Extramarital Affair*
*———, *Close Calls: What Adulterers Want You to Know About Protecting Your Marriage*
Julie Ganschow, *Living Beyond the Heart of Betrayal: Biblically Addressing the Pain of Sexual Sin*
Brad Hambrick, "True Betrayal," http://bradhambrick.com/truebetrayal/
Robert Jones, *Restoring Your Broken Marriage: Healing After Adultery*
*Stephen M. Judah, *Staying Together: When an Affair Pulls You Apart*
Jim Newheiser, *Marriage, Divorce, and Remarriage: Critical Questions and Answers*
Mike Summers, *Help! My Spouse Has Been Unfaithful*
Russell Moore, "Does He Need to Confess Adultery to His Wife?" https://www.the gospelcoalition.org/article/does-he-need-to-confess-adultery-to-his-wife

*Frank Pittman, *Private Lies: Infidelity and the Betrayal of Intimacy*

Cheryl and Jeff Scruggs, *I Do Again: How We Found A Second Chance at Our Marriage—and You Can Too!*

Gary and Mona Shriver, *Unfaithful: Hope and Healing After Infidelity*

Winston T. Smith, *Help! My Spouse Has Committed Adultery: First Steps for Dealing with Betrayal*

Leslie Vernick, "After the Affair" https://christiancounseling.com/blog/uncategorized/after-the-affair-ten-steps-of-healing/

*These resources are not written from a biblical counseling perspective.

Chapter 8

I CAUGHT MY HUSBAND LOOKING AT PORN[1]

Pain is an appointment with God for him to do his deepest work in you, your husband, and in your marriage relationship for the glory of God.

DR. HARRY SCHAUMBURG

Everything exposed by the light becomes visible—and everything that is illuminated becomes a light.

EPHESIANS 5:13

There are a myriad of issues in marriage counseling that present the counselor with difficulty. Yet when issues of sexual immorality and impropriety come to light, the upheaval they create in a marriage is like no other. Sometimes it comes like an earthquake, quick and sudden. The revelation of an affair is jarring and disorienting. It calls into question so many different things, not the least of which are the very foundations of their marriage. Sometimes the upheaval is subtle, but no less disruptive and discouraging. Some sins are like a stone thrown in a pond,

---

1. In no way do I want to present a view where the husband is always the one who looks at pornography. I've counseled several marriages where the woman was engaged with pornographic materials too. That being said, for the balance of the chapter I'll refer to the offender as the husband, the wife as the offended.

and we watch the ripples cascade out imperceptibly. The chasm grows slowly, methodically, and the pain can last for years.

When the use of pornography is exposed in a marriage, you will find both of these dynamics playing out—the sudden destruction of the earthquake and the long-term effects of a stone thrown in a pond. However the sin is revealed, confessed, or discovered, the immediate reaction is cataclysmic but will have ripple effects for years into the future. Jennifer Ferguson, in a book coauthored with her husband, writes about her initial discovery of her husband's pornography addiction:

> It took me two years to find it, but find it I did. I happened to look at the history on the computer, searching for something I needed for my teaching job, and all these URLs with explicit names appeared on the screen . . . "I knew it!" But the validation of being right was quickly canceled out by the fact that I was right about something of which I wanted to be very, very wrong. . . . I remember wondering if I could ever trust him again. . . . There was no grace in my cutting words. I vented. I cursed at him.[2]

Discovery leads to feeling betrayed, betrayal leads to anger, anger leads to sadness and hopelessness. Emotions run the gamut from utter hopelessness and surprise to icy-hot anger and rage. This cycle will become a familiar one, and you should become acquainted with it.

INITIAL GOALS

Let's pick up where the quote we just read leaves off. Jennifer emails you the next day and the subject line reads: "We need to talk to you ASAP!" You scan the email, reading the words—accountability, pornography, counseling—and immediately you begin to scramble. Not again! Another pornography case? You don't have time for this! Where's John, the new youth pastor . . . can't he take this one on?

As a pastor, taking on a case like this can feel overwhelming. We've all been there. You put the various accountability measures in place, he messes up again and calls you in tears, asking for help to put things back together. You offer a sympathetic ear and the cycle continues. The wife meanwhile becomes more embittered as the months pass as she sees little change in her husband's behavior or patterns. Soon you're doubting whether you're up to the task of helping either

2. Jen Ferguson and Craig Ferguson, *Pure Eyes, Clean Heart: A Couple's Journey to Freedom from Pornography* (Grand Rapids: Discovery, 2014), 18.

Jen or her husband. What should you do? How can you best prepare to help Jen and her husband?

Some of the initial goals must begin with your own heart. Ask God to help you in the following areas:

- Acknowledge that the change in Jim and Jen's relationship is not dependent on you but God, and because of this you realize the important role prayer will play in your counseling.
- Be patient and listen to the details of their life rather than rushing to get to a solution or a quick fix.
- Be willing to engage others as necessary.
- Truth and time go hand in hand. Sometimes in marriage counseling, there can be a rush to prescriptive action before the hard work of uncovering motives is accomplished.
- Understand that repentance of this sin will not be established in one session or even two. Biblical repentance is a process with tangible characteristics—volitional, cognitive, emotional, and relational characteristics.[3] Repentance cannot be rushed.
- Work with trajectories, not preset timelines—particularly with the sin of pornography. A lot of counseling in this area mistakenly focuses on how many days/weeks have gone by since an individual last viewed pornography, rather than marking progress in the overall trajectory of the person's heart and affections.

QUESTIONS TO ASK

Below are some categories with a wide variety of questions to help aid you in drawing your counselee out (cf. Prov. 20:5).

Initial (triage)
- Tell me about the extent of your usage and interaction with pornography. How long has this been going on?
- What exactly are you involved in?[4]

---

3. There are several helpful resources on repentance, but two have proven indispensable to me: Richard Owen Roberts, *Repentance: The First Word of the Gospel*; and Thomas Watson, *The Doctrine of Repentance*.

4. One might hesitate to be this specific and explicit, but in my experience with both men and women, "pornography" as a category is much too broad of a term to use in counseling. Consider how viewing pornography online differs from soliciting random hook-ups on Craigslist. I've had people confess

- online chatrooms
- 1–900/800 phone sex operators
- solicitation of people on Craigslist
- usage of dating/hook-up apps like Tinder, Grindr, Hinge, Plenty of Fish, etc.
- strip clubs
- burlesque clubs
- massage parlors
- erotic fiction
- explicit text messages (sexting)
- solicitation of a prostitute
- voyeurism/web-cam based interactions
- TV/cable-based pornography
- print media (pornographic magazines)
- other: Is there anything I haven't mentioned which might fall into this category?

- Is the pornography heterosexual or homosexual in nature?
- At any point, did you view pornography that depicted a minor?[5]
- Were you discovered or did you confess? Tell me about how this unfolded.
- Is this the first time? Describe your history with pornography.
- Were you involved physically with another person? If so, have you been checked for STDs? Have you been intimate with your spouse since then? If so, has she been checked and evaluated?
- Have you spoken to your spouse about this? (If they're not coming in together.)

Survey

- Tell me about yourself. Give me a five-to-ten-minute biography.
- Tell me about how you came to faith in Christ.
- Give me an idea of what/how the spiritual disciplines play out in your life.

---

to additional instances listed above, with the caveat of, "Oh, I thought you meant just online porn." Also, the counselor needs to think carefully about the setting in which these questions are asked. Is the wife present? If so, how much detail should be shared?

    5. Child pornography is a federal offense. "Federal law prohibits the production, distribution, reception, and possession of an image of child pornography using or affecting any means or facility of interstate or foreign commerce (See 18 U.S.C. § 2251; 18 U.S.C. § 2252; 18 U.S.C. § 2252A)." If your counselee is involved with the possession or reception of child pornography, notify local police authorities (https://www.justice.gov/criminal-ceos/citizens-guide-us-federal-law-child-pornography).

- How would you describe the biblical process of change?
- Struggles with pornography rarely live in isolation from other besetting sins. Where else in your life do you struggle?
- Describe what biblical repentance in this particular area of your life would look like.
- Give me a sense of why you think you are here. What has led up to this point in your life?

Focused

- Give me your best explanation for what happened.
- Would you describe your issues with pornography as enslaving? Addicting? Hit or miss? Why?
- When was the first time you were exposed to pornography?
- Take me through a situation where you're tempted and give in to looking at pornography? What happens? What patterns exist?
- Is there a cycle or pattern you tend to follow?
- What kind of emotions and feelings do you experience post-interaction?
- Do you go through any "atonement-style" exercises?
- What role do guilt and shame play in your struggle?
- Who else knows about this struggle, and what role do they play in your life?
- Have you tried to overcome this sin in the past? How?
- What works, and what doesn't work?
- What advice or counsel have you received in the past regarding this struggle?

ISSUES TO CONSIDER

How much should you confess to your spouse?

This issue needs thoughtful and careful consideration. A large number of men will want to go through the motions (authentic or not) of expressing contrition and remorse about their behavior. In many cases, this comes before confession and forgiveness have happened before God (vertical relationship). Encourage confession and repentance before God, which helps prepare the offending spouse to confess and seek forgiveness from their spouse. A question to the wife from the counselor might be posed this way: "What degree of information and specificity would be helpful and appropriate for you to hear from your husband?" Reactions from wives typically fall into two categories:

1. Some wives want and desire a full confession. They believe at the time that they need details, context, setting, etc. in order to forgive, move forward, and rebuild trust.

2. Some wives don't need this level of specificity but want the basic broad brushstrokes of what has happened.[6]

Helping the Wife (or Husband)[7]

In a situation where sexual sin has occurred, the offender can often take up a large bulk of the time and attention. Helping, comforting, and walking alongside the offended should be a priority in counseling as well. Whether this is in joint sessions or separately, a plan for counseling and care should be thoughtfully laid out.

Spouses who have been sinned against often receive bad or faulty counsel. Any type of counsel which puts the blame on the wife for her husband's pornography or sexual sin must be avoided at all costs. I've heard some well-meaning pastors and counselors infer that if a wife were to be more sexually available to her husband then surely he would not be as tempted to go and pursue pornography. I once had a husband tell me that he wasn't getting "fed in the bed" as if that were a rationale for his sexual sin. Statements like this must be refuted gently, but if they persist, aggressively so.

Such counsel is patently unbiblical, and it places the offender's culpability in the wrong spot. Great damage can be done in marriage counseling if the pastor or counselor seeks to make accommodations for the husband's sexual sin by blaming the wife. Another dynamic to consider is the tendency—which many wives will naturally default to—to become a private investigator into their husband's behavior. After pornography is discovered, a wife's natural inclination lends itself toward seeking to monitor her husband's behavior more closely. Wives may become fastidious checkers of smartphones; discrepancies in schedules will be analyzed and combed through; unaccounted cash or money will be cause for speculation. Remember, this kind of behavior is natural.

Here are some helpful and guiding principles to offer offended spouses as they consider accountability and the role they should play:

---

6. Regarding confession of adultery to a spouse: Russell Moore, http://www.russellmoore .com/2016/04/26/if-youve-cheated-should-you-tell-your-spouse/. Regarding confession of lust to a spouse: David Powlison, https://www.youtube.com/watch?v=IRFdn6wSoKs.

7. Separate counseling for the spouse is something I like to offer in cases where sexual sin has occurred. Often the issues being discussed with the offending spouse are graphic and sensitive in nature. Additionally, if the spouse who has been offended is the wife, a same-gender counselor can be a wise and helpful choice in cases such as this.

- Understand what is within your control, and what is not. Entrusting the unknown to God is a step of faith and trust. Fulfill your calling first before trying to fulfill your spouse's calling.
- Check your own motivations. Are you hoping to discover something to prove a point, or is the investigation based on a genuine desire to help your spouse?
- Be honest with a counselor or friend if the investigating and checking in on your husband is distracting you from your primary duties and responsibilities.
- Rely on and meditate on the promises of a God who sees everything (Prov. 15:3), knows everything (Ps. 139:1–2), and will bring all things to light in his timing (1 Cor. 4:5).
- Realize that no amount of external accountability will ultimately change a person's heart. True change always comes from within and is motivated and empowered by the work of the Holy Spirit as the individual makes every effort to become more like Christ.
- It is not wrong for you to ask questions of your spouse. If you have concerns about his behavior or actions, move toward him and ask.

Here is how a sample conversation with the offended spouse might play out:

Jennifer, my heart is broken over what has been revealed today. I want you to know that what has taken place is in no way your fault. Jim is responsible for what he did, and we will take the necessary steps to come alongside him. In the meantime, what can we as a church do to help you? What are ways we can pray for you and your family? Is there any practical help you need during this time?

Ongoing Accountability

The wife's primary responsibility in the marriage is not to be her husband's accountability partner. For many wives this is relieving, for others, this can be difficult for them to entrust the responsibility to someone else. Please don't hear me wrongly on this point. I'm not saying that a wife shouldn't be involved and concerned about her husband's sanctification. However, the wife should not feel the weight and burden of asking her husband, "Have you looked at porn this week?" or "Were you surfing Craigslist again?"

The pastor and counselor's role in marriage counseling is to help the husband develop biblical, Christ-centered friendships where accountability can be cultivated. I'm not advocating for relationships where accountability is the catalyst and impetus. Those relationships tend to gradually fade away and can become perfunctory. The husband needs godly, same-gendered friendships, where accountability can grow alongside the varied joys of friendship and life together.

UNCOVERING HEART MOTIVATIONS

Something I have found helpful in counseling both men and women through this issue is helping the counselee identify what motivates him or her to seek out pornography.[8] In some ways, we might say the actual viewing of pornography is symptomatic of a deeper worship disorder happening in the heart. What motivates and precedes the viewing of pornography? Once that is identified, more specific biblical counsel can be offered.

Anger

Men who find their wives sexually cold or indifferent to them may turn to pornography as a way to satisfy their disappointment and dissatisfaction.[9] Disappointment is the pathway to anger.[10] Some men approach sexual intimacy not from a vantage point of service and love but from a position of entitlement and need. When those needs are not met, pornography becomes an outlet for sexual frustration and anger.

Boredom

This might sound benign, but many men find themselves viewing pornography out of pure boredom. They have nothing to do on a given evening, and they begin surfing the web, watching YouTube videos, and before they know what they are doing, they are accessing pornography. What started out as simple boredom and a lack of vigilance soon gives way to viewing pornography.

Reward and entitlement

One man I spoke with recently described his battle with pornography as a struggle of entitlement. After a long day of work, he felt his own self-gratification was something he deserved. It was a reward for him, a way he could make himself feel better. Pornography became a vehicle for him to feel good and experience pleasure.

---

8. This material is adapted from a post I wrote on the Biblical Counseling Coalition website: http://biblicalcounselingcoalition.org/blogs/2013/12/04/why-does-he-look-at-pornography/.

9. Teaching on the frequency of sexual intimacy in marriage has its appropriate place in marriage counseling. The wisdom of when and how to do so should be approached with wisdom and grace. Care must be taken to tactfully handle any discussions of sexual intimacy in their proper context without providing a rationale or excuse for the other person's sexual immorality. (See chapter fifteen, *Frozen Intimacy,* for further help.)

10. Simple equations I've found helpful in counseling are: disappointment + time = anger; and anger + time = bitterness.

Escapism and fantasy

Many men are very dissatisfied with their work life, home life, sex life, situational circumstances, and spousal relationships. This brooding dissatisfaction and discontentment leads them to seek satisfaction and contentment in a virtual world. In this virtual, on-demand world, the counselee can escape and create their own reality. Pornography becomes a haven from the "real world" they inhabit.

Fear of rejection

Some men have significant insecurities related to their sex life. They may sound something like this: "I fear rejection from my wife when I pursue sexual intimacy, so I pursue pornography where I am always accepted." Issues of self-image and performance soon preoccupy the mind and lead to paralyzing self-focus. The fearful man, afraid of rejection, can believe the lie that the people he views online always want him, love him, or need him. These insecurities surrounding sexual performance are only heightened and exacerbated by the ongoing use of pornography.

Easy

This motivation may also seem obvious, but many men pursue pornography because it is easy and accessible. It is easier to type in a web address than it is to pursue intimacy with my wife. It is easier to view pornography for a few fleeting moments than to build a deep and abiding relationship with my wife. It is easier to selfishly fulfill my desires with no expectation of self-giving, self-sacrificing love for my spouse.

Revenge

I have met and listened to individuals who have viewed pornography out of a heart of vengeance. Their reasoning goes something like this, "Because my spouse viewed pornography and hurt me, I'm going to do the same thing to show them what it feels like." Needless to say, the reasoning is specious and the result is always guilt, shame, and emptiness.

This summary of particular motivations is in no way meant to be exhaustive, but these are categories you may want to use to explore with your counselee. Many of these motivations are intertwined with each other, and some are perhaps more evident than others. A wise biblical counselor should seek to understand what is going on in the counselee's heart with the illuminating help of the Word.

Once a motivation has been more clearly uncovered, the promises and warnings of God's Word can be even more effective in counseling. Rather than dealing with pornography in a reductionistic and truncated manner, robust biblical counsel can be offered like valuable and restorative medicine.

SCRIPTURE IS SUFFICIENT, RELEVANT, AND NECESSARY

As pastors and counselors, we seek to counsel *biblically*. Scripture speaks with clarity and precision (Heb. 4:12). When we open its pages, we find a wealth of treasure out of which to counsel, care, and confront. As you consider your counseling relationship and intersecting the truth of Scripture, here is one place to begin with the offending spouse: James 1:13–15 and the progression of sin from desire.

James gives an incisive and illuminating inner pathology for what happens in the heart of the sinner. Before pornography has ever been viewed, an inner struggle in the heart has already taken place. A counselor must be aware of this, and James aids us through a series of four key categories:

1. tempted: v. 13–14
2. enticed: v. 14b
3. lured away: v. 14b
4. gives birth to sin: v. 15

James uses common fishing terminology, something familiar to his readers, to describe the inward process of temptation. Being enticed and lured away describes an inward heart dynamic where the heart is attracted, entertained, seduced, and ensnared. Like a fish angling toward the bait, the individual clamps down on the temptation only to realize he is now trapped and ensnared.

Most who have struggled with sexual sin will describe this process as something that happens in a very short window of time. The counselor can help the struggler identify the constituent elements of these dynamics in his own heart in an effort to help him mortify and kill his sin before it's ever externalized.

Here's how a sample dialogue might go:

Counselor: James is trying to help us understand the inner workings of our hearts so we can be more knowledgeable in our fight against sin. Where do these first three parts—tempted, enticed, lured away—happen?

Jim: Umm, inside of me?

Counselor: That's exactly right. Before you ever type something into a website or view that video on your smartphone, a battle is already being waged inside your heart. A process of attraction is leading to sin. What's the initial temptation you struggle with before you look at pornography?

Jim: I don't know exactly. I guess I'm just kind of bored and lonely.

Counselor: What do you mean? Bored from being married to Kim? Are you feeling lonely or isolated from your wife?

Jim: Sort of. We just aren't on the same page anymore. She's off doing her own thing with her friends, and I'm stuck at home with nothing to do. So I just stay up on my iPad at night and roam around.

Counselor: Good, now take it a step further. What are the next steps James mentions?

Jim: Being enticed and lured away.

Counselor: Exactly. James says after a person has been tempted, there's another step in the process. They begin to take a second glance . . . they pause, their attention has been captured. Their mind starts thinking about what they might be able to have.

Jim: That's what happens to me. Before you know it, I see an article online that one of my friends posted that has a questionable photo on it, and I think to myself, "I wonder what I'll see if I click that link." I know I'm going to find something inappropriate, but I'm just so curious. Plus, I'm bored, and I know Kim's not going to catch me because she's out.

Counselor: So, after this initial temptation—you're bored and lonely. You start surfing the web on your iPad. You see something, you read something, and it captures your attention. All the warning signs and things you know to be true go out the window, and you click on the link. Next thing you know, you're watching a pornographic video online.

Jim: Yes, pretty much.

Counselor: Do you see how this process all began? The use of pornography grew out of a heart-context where you were bored, lonely, and dissatisfied. Instead of pivoting and turning to Christ in your disappointment and loneliness, you're turning to something on a screen to satisfy you. Does that make sense to you?

From here, you might take Jim to Jeremiah 2:13:

> My people have committed two sins:
> They have forsaken me,
>   the sprint of living water,
> and have dug their own cisterns,
>   broken cisterns that cannot hold water.

Once Jim connects his use of pornography with filling an empty cistern in his life, you can help him see how futile and fruitless this is, according to Scripture. Jim doesn't have a porn problem as much as he has a worship problem, and making this connection can have helpful implications for his marriage. As Jim works on running to God as the true satisfaction for his soul, it will enable him to be a husband who treats his wife not as an object to receive satisfaction from but as a wife to love self-sacrificially.

From here, you can venture into other areas that need to be addressed (e.g., seeking the spouse's forgiveness, chapter four). A biblical counselor will need God's grace and wisdom to navigate through the complexities and messiness of pornography. The good news is that God can take sexual brokenness and redeem it for his glory and our good. There is no sin too great that the grace of God cannot reach.

Counselor Fieldnotes

If you have learned that your husband is involved with pornography, you may be questioning what is wrong with *you*. You most likely are wondering why you don't meet his sexual needs. You may suddenly feel insecure about your body, inadequate, and ashamed. You may be furious and scared. Above all, your heart is broken.

If we were sitting together right now, I would tell you that his pornography habit is not *your* problem. You haven't said or done anything that would "make" your husband watch pornography. I understand that you want him to change, but demanding that he "stop it" is rarely effective. You cannot badger him to stop lusting for pornography, and all the threats and manipulations in the world will not change him. You must give up the idea that you can control him because you cannot. Your husband's thoughts, beliefs, and desires are fixed on fulfilling the lust of the flesh. He has a serious spiritual problem, a lust problem that primarily demands a change of heart.

I have been involved in helping many women walk through these dark and murky waters. Let me encourage you by letting you know that there is tremendous hope for change, no matter how deeply your husband has fallen into sin. God is the heart changer, and he is deeply invested in the lives of his saints. He wants your husband to stop sinning with pornography even more than you do, and he has provided the means (salvation and the Holy Spirit) and the method (repentance and heart change) for that to happen.

Your prayers and patience as God does his work in your lives will be invaluable. Trust that God is at work, and that he intends to bring good out of this time of sorrow (Rom. 8:28–29).

Julie Ganschow, Executive Director,
Reigning Grace Counseling Center

RESOURCES

Andrew A. Boa, *Redeeming Sexuality: 12 Sessions for Healing and Transformation in Community*

Ellen Dykas, ed., *Sexual Sanity for Women: Healing from Sexual and Relational Brokenness*

Jen and Craig Ferguson, *Pure Eyes, Clean Heart: A Couple's Journey to Freedom from Pornography*

Julie Ganschow, *Living Beyond the Heart of Betrayal: Biblically Addressing the Pain of Sexual Sin*

J. Alasdair Groves, "Exposing the Lies of Pornography and Counseling the Men Who Believe Them" *Journal of Biblical Counseling* 27, no. 1 (2013): 7–25

Brad Hambrick, http://www.bradhambrick.com/falselove/

———, http://www.bradhambrick.com/truebetrayal/

Heath Lambert, *Finally Free: Fighting Purity with the Power of Grace*

David Powlison, *Making All Things New: Restoring Joy to the Sexually Broken*

———, *Coming Clean: Breaking Pornography's Hold on You*

Harry Schaumburg, *Undefiled: Redemption from Sexual Sin, Restoration for Broken Relationships*

———, *False Intimacy: Understanding the Struggle of Sexual Addiction*

Winston T. Smith, "When NOT to Do Marriage Counseling" *Journal of Biblical Counseling* 27, no. 1 (2013): 72–76

Vicki Tiede, *When Your Husband is Addicted to Pornography: Healing Your Wounded Heart*

Paul David Tripp, *Sex in a Broken World: How Christ Redeems What Sin Distorts*

David White, *Sexual Sanity for Men: Re-Creating Your Mind in a Crazy Culture*

Covenant Eyes has a number of helpful articles and resources: www.covenanteyes.com

Residential Treatment Facilities and Programs:

https://stonegateresources.org/
http://www.purelifeministries.org/
https://www.faithlafayette.org/restoration

Chapter 9

MY SPOUSE IS NOT A BELIEVER

No matter how much you want to, you cannot force your spouse to become a Christian. Yet it's equally important to emphasize that if you find yourself in a spiritually mismatched marriage, there *is* hope. Don't despair!

LEE & LESLIE STROBEL

Wait for the LORD;
> be strong and take heart
> and wait for the LORD.

PSALM 27:14

It's Tuesday evening, and you receive a text from Suzanne:

Hi Pastor. It's Suzanne. Can I come talk to you? Randall and I had another fight last night about how involved I am in the church. I don't know how much more I can take. I want to give up, but I know that's the wrong answer.

You put the phone down and pick it up to type a response, only to delete it. Suzanne attends your church, is a member in good standing, serves faithfully in women's ministry, and volunteers her time in the homeless ministry. Her husband Randall is not a believer and vacillates between antagonizing Suzanne and being utterly indifferent to her "way of life," as he calls it.

What do you say? What is the next step? In situations like these I find myself resonating with Paul's words to the Corinthians, "Who is equal to such a task?" (2 Cor. 2:16) Situations like this demand pastoral wisdom and care. A response to

Suzanne that bypasses the cultivation of good relational standing between pastor and counselee or that offers only a quick fix or abstract theological imperative might suffice for a moment. Yet such superficial responses will not adequately address the situation for the long term.

ENTER SUZANNE'S WORLD

It's common to underestimate the difficulty and suffering of the believing spouse of an unbeliever. Earlier, I wrote about several ways to build a relationship and rapport with your counselee, but a reminder here is appropriate. When someone like Suzanne reaches out for help, it's tempting to offer pragmatic advice: *Suzanne, it sounds as if you need to establish some boundaries with Randall on how he interacts with you.* Or you might punt the issue to another person: *Suzanne, it sounds as if it might be helpful for you speak with another woman about this issue.* In a worst-case scenario you might prematurely apply Scripture to her without understanding her situation: *Suzanne, it says in 1 Peter 3 that husbands may be won without a word by the behavior of their wives. Why don't you try practicing that, and see what happens?* One woman came to me relating how her pastor counseled her against confronting her unsaved husband on matters related to her faith because it might "make him angry."

I mention all of these by way of illustration because they represent the sort of counsel I have heard well-meaning pastors and counselors offer to people like Suzanne. Much of it sounds well-intentioned, but to the person standing before the counselor and laboring in the trenches of the marriage, these can represent the antithesis of loving care.

An appropriate response to Suzanne might be: *Suzanne, thank you for reaching out during this difficult time. Is it possible to stop by my office tomorrow to talk about this in person?*

Immediately you're seeking to move toward her. You are expressing gratitude, acknowledging her courage for reaching out, and seeking to understand. Resist the impulse to interrupt or to interpret her reply as seeking pity or playing the victim. Bias at the beginning of a conversation like this can prevent you from listening well and thus, offering a timely-spoken word (Prov. 15:23).

As you listen to Suzanne's story you'll undoubtedly hear difficulties and struggles. Jennifer McGehee offers some insight on common challenges for those in unequally yoked marriages, summarized below:[1]

---

1. Jennifer McGehee lists distinct reasons why being married to an unbeliever is so difficult. http://biblicalcounselingcoalition.org/2016/06/03/going-it-alone-part-1/.

- The inability to share with your spouse on a spiritual level because of their spiritual-blindness (1 Cor. 2:14).
- The irony of being called to share in the gospel mission with your spouse (Eph. 5:32) only to find your spouse *is* the mission field.
- The realization that many of the solutions the church advocates to find unity with our spouse—reading the Bible, prayer, input from biblical community, spiritual friendship, attending church—are not possible in an unequally-yoked marriage.
- Recognition that the consistency of your marriage is marked by its very inconsistency: at the very core you are different from your spouse— differing values, differing beliefs—and of utmost concern, differing eternal trajectories.

To operate from two fundamentally different worldviews on everything from parenting to finances can be exhausting. To go to church each Sunday while your husband remains at home may be spiritually and emotionally discouraging. To defend Christ and the church to your husband every time there's a disagreement can be demoralizing. Now imagine living those realities daily, 24/7.

Each of us can think of men and women in our congregation who are in this type of situation. What would they share with you about their experience? How does knowing their story help build empathy for their plight? As we listen to these stories, we need to understand that living with someone who is not a believer means living in an environment of loneliness, isolation—even suffering and persecution at times—that many of us cannot imagine, both for the believer and the unbeliever. When home is a "place of ministry" and marriage a "relationship of influence" then home is not a "place of rest" and marriage is not a "relationship of mutual encouragement."[2] Carol Cornish explains, "We need to understand that persecution is not always obvious or extreme in its manifestation. Subtle persecution can occur regularly in a marriage between a Christian spouse and an unbeliever. We just haven't thought about it in these terms. Failure to identify and *accurately* label the problem diminishes our ability to apply a biblical solution to it. Lack of insight into the true nature of the problem results in a vague sense of confusion and unrest."[3]

Remember that trust is earned in relationships; it's rarely given haphazardly. If you desire to be in a position where you can offer counsel and hope to Suzanne and

---

2. I'm indebted to Brad Hambrick for this helpful insight.
3. Elyse Fitzpatrick and Carol Cornish eds., *Women Helping Women: A Biblical Guide to the Major Issues Women Face* (Eugene, OR: Harvest House, 1997), 212.

others like her, be sure to understand their world. Don't bypass people's experiences by focusing solely on "getting to the point." This treats people as problems to be fixed rather than people to be loved.[4]

OFFER MEANINGFUL AND PRACTICAL HELP

People like Suzanne need a pastor who understands them, one who can ultimately point them to Christ. What are some potential paths you could take in ministering to those in unequally yoked marriages? After diligently pursuing them and understanding their world, how can you offer hope and help?

Offer to meet with the couple together.

If Suzanne is open to inviting Randall to counseling, either together or apart, then bringing him in could be an opportunity to get better insight into their world. Marriage counseling tends to work best when both spouses are present.[5] We should not presume that because Randall is not a believer that he is unwilling to come in and talk with a counselor. Some unbelieving spouses can be particularly hostile to their partner's faith, but that is not always the case. Unbelieving spouses can run the spectrum from being openly hostile to their spouse's faith to being openly supportive of their spouse's faith—as long as they're not forced to be involved.

You might wonder, "Can unbelievers be helped through biblical counseling?" Yes! Engaging the unbelieving spouse in marriage counseling can allow for greater communication between the two spouses. Often, the counselor can help the couple better understand each other's perspective.

Help the believing spouse see the big picture of God's plan.

Paul tells the church in Rome, "I am so eager to preach the gospel also to you who are in Rome" (Rom. 1:15). Why does he need to do that? Why preach the gospel to an established church? Apparently, Paul knows we need to hear this good news on a daily basis. When life is overwhelming, when fatigue sets in, and when a spouse's indifference to Christ seems like personal rejection, the believing spouse needs encouragement and strengthening.

It is easy for us to shrink our world to the size of our own personal context and experience.

---

4. Pastors can be guilty of being judgmental in times like this. Internally we think to ourselves, "Well, you're the one who chose to marry this person. What did you expect?"

5. For situations when marriage counseling should end, read chapter three: "Starting, Ending, and Referring."

Bobby never wants to talk about spiritual things.

I wish Josh was more like _____.

Lon is not interested in my life at church or anything, for that matter.

I bet Marsha never has to beg her husband to go to events at church.

Linda blames everything on God when things go wrong.

My marriage is always going to be like this.

He can make time to watch the football game, but he can't come to the church picnic?

It's not worth it to always be fighting.

I have heard phrases like these time and time again from brokenhearted men and women. Giving half-hearted hope to hurting people is like putting a Band-Aid on a gaping wound (cf. Jer. 8:11). Encourage the believing spouse with the fact that God hasn't forgotten them. In fact, God knows what it is like to be in a marriage where the spouse does not hold to the same beliefs and practices (cf. Jer. 3:8). Encourage the spouse to lift their gaze to God in these difficult times.

Begin with a line of questioning that helps them get an overall sense of who God is and how he works.

"Suzanne, let me ask you a question. What is your best guess at what God might be up to in this situation?"

"Well, I guess he wants me to love him and pray for him? Maybe this is just a trial I need to ride out."

You reach for your Bible and ask Suzanne to turn to Deuteronomy 8. "Remember how the LORD your God led you all the way in the wilderness these forty years, to humble and test you in order to know what was in your heart, whether or not you would keep his commands. He humbled you, causing you to hunger and then feeding you with manna, which neither you nor your ancestors had known, to teach you that man does not live on bread alone but on every word that comes from the mouth of the LORD" (Deut. 8:2–3).

You explain to Suzanne the context of the Deuteronomy passage. The children of Israel had been rescued out of four hundred years of slavery, and in the space of a few months were begging to go back to Egypt (Ex. 16; Num. 11, 14). How did this happen? They had forgotten what God had done for them. Beset by their own difficult circumstances, they complained and became angry.

Through Moses, God reminded the children of Israel that the big picture of their story was not merely to strand them in the wilderness on a *Survivor*-esque reality show, eating a diet of stale manna, but rather to "teach [them] that man does not live on bread alone." You remind Suzanne that God uses all of our life—the good, the bad, and the hard—for our growth in godliness. Yes, he'll even use an unbelieving spouse who makes fun of your faith. For the children of Israel, the time in the wilderness was not just a time for God to reveal their hearts but ultimately to draw them near to himself. Unfortunately, most of them failed to see what God was doing.

For women like Suzanne, being married to an unbelieving spouse may feel a bit like living in the wilderness. They often feel abandoned and left to fend for themselves. Pastor, help them see that nothing is outside of God's plan. Is God sovereign over their marriages? We can answer with a resounding yes. He's also a God who loves and knows the struggles of his children.

Leslie Strobel knew this reality well. She came to faith before her husband Lee. She writes, "If we abide in Christ, he can use our experiences as an unequally-yoked Christian to develop and mold our character in ways that never would have been possible without the struggles and difficulties we have faced."[6] This is the hope and perspective people like Suzanne need to hear. Don't airbrush past their current difficulties, but offer them a wise and redemptive perspective to motivate them to *make every effort* to press into the difficulty and find a God who is faithful in every way.

Help the spouse entrust the unbelieving partner to God.

One of the most difficult areas in counseling spouses married to unbelievers lies in their ability to entrust their spouse—and themselves—to God. Carol Cornish helpfully reminds us, "The wife of an unbelieving husband should seek to understand the limits of her responsibility before God."[7] Proverbs 3:5–6 puts it this way:

> Trust in the LORD with all your heart,
>   and lean not on your own understanding;
> in all your ways submit to him,
>   and he will make your paths straight.

Notice the totality of trust: *all* our heart, *all* our ways. He wants 100 percent of our trust, not 90 percent, not 95 percent—he wants it all. Entrusting the unbelieving spouse to God can be one of the most important things you can counsel them toward.

One of the reasons it is so hard for them to entrust their spouse to God is

---

6. Lee and Leslie Strobel, *Surviving a Spiritual Mismatch in Marriage* (Grand Rapids: Zondervan, 2002), 64.

7. Fitzpatrick and Cornish, *Women Helping Women*, 228.

that we like to be in control. This desire for control permeates and affects us all. I remember a conversation with a woman named Sandy. She said to me, "I just wish Jim would be more supportive of my faith. I wish he would just say 'thank you' every once in a while." I understood where she was coming from, but the gentle reminder for Sandy was that Jim's responses (or lack thereof) were ultimately outside her control. Now, entrusting someone to the Lord does not remove our ability to influence them for good. Quite the opposite. When we are relieved of the burden of controlling others, it is easier to love them with a sincere and wholehearted love (cf. Rom. 12:9–21).

An additional area that can be difficult to turn over to the Lord is their spouse's spiritual state of being. Nearly every unequally yoked spouse I have met struggles with the burden of their spouse's eternal destiny. The salvation of an unbelieving spouse is typically of utmost concern—something they pray for and agonize over regularly. Yet again, this is an area of suffering the believing spouse lives with daily. To know their spouse faces eternity separated from God is enough to lead even the strongest of people into despair and depression. Far from leaving things to chance, entrusting every circumstance to God leads not to subtle complacency or abject selfishness, but rather a robust agenda for love and good deeds.

While a spouse may have a hard time entrusting their unbelieving spouse to God, they may also struggle to entrust their own life as well. But we know that entrusting oneself to God in the midst of suffering is the model Christ chose to pursue: "If you suffer for doing good and you endure it, this is commendable before God. To this you were called, because Christ suffered for you, leaving you an example, that you should follow in his steps" (1 Pet. 2:20–21). It is important to remind your counselee that suffering and difficulty are not outside of God's plan for his beloved. Quite the opposite—for to this we have been called! However, whatever God calls us to, he will graciously empower and enable us to fulfill.

Help the spouse identify any unhelpful patterns of behavior.

Going back to our first story in this chapter, we are reminded that Suzanne is coming to us more from a world of despair and hurt rather than overtly sinful patterns of behavior. As such, remember that conversations like this need to happen in a wider context where a solid relationship exists between pastor and counselee and trust has been built. This is not a starting point, but a follow-up to a previous conversation. Whenever we are pointing out areas of sin or unhelpful patterns of behavior, truth must be spoken in love and in a spirit of gentleness. With this in mind, here are five areas to look for as you counsel men and women in unequally yoked marriages.

Gossip and slander

"Would you mind praying for Rob?" Sally sighs, "All he does is sit in front of the television. I can't get him to come to church to save my life!"

How often have we been in situations like this where prayer requests are veiled opportunities for venting rather than lamenting, for unhelpful gossip rather than a humble request for God's help? [8] Is Sally's motive good? Perhaps. But is there a discreet way she can ask for prayer for her husband without sharing unnecessary details about his sin? Don't allow spouses to defame or slander each other in front of others.

Critical spirit

The author of Proverbs highlights three types of women for us in his book: the adulterous woman (Prov. 5–7), the virtuous woman (Prov. 31), and the nagging/contentious woman. He writes,

> Better to live on a corner of the roof
> > than share a house with a quarrelsome wife . . . .
> Better to live in a desert
> > than with a quarrelsome and nagging wife . . . .
> A quarrelsome wife is like the dripping
> > of a leaky roof in a rainstorm.
> *Proverbs 21:9, 19; 27:15*

The message is clear—a man does not want to be married to a critical, nagging wife. The situations he presents as preferred alternatives serve as stark reminders that a contentious wife is the antithesis of a desirable partner.

But these admonitions are not only for wives; they apply equally to husbands. All of us would do well to take to heart Solomon's wisdom, "A gentle answer turns away wrath, but a harsh word stirs up anger" (Prov. 15:1). Believers, even in unequally yoked marriages, are still called to a life of behavior that is humble, gentle, patient, and that bears with others, seeking to build unity (cf. Eph. 4:1–3). All of us can be blind to our own sin, so as counselors we want to function as an instrument of sight, bringing perspective and encouragement. As you listen to the

---

8. I do believe there is a proper role for lamenting as opposed to complaining in cases like this. Helping the spouse rightly make use of the psalms can be a helpful assignment in counseling to help channel their thoughts and feelings. Walter Brueggemann categorizes the psalms into three categories: orientation, disorientation, and reorientation. The psalms of lament are essentially psalms that move the reader/listener from a place of disorientation (life is hard and not as it should be) toward reorientation (Lord, help me see my situation as you do).

counselee, is the other spouse frequently criticized over inconsequential matters? As you listen, is their tone of voice filled with disdain and contempt? Are their tone and posture adversarial in nature or collaborative in scope? If there is a pattern of undue criticism, bring this to their attention.

Nonverbal actions

It has been said that a picture is worth a thousand words. This is true of nonverbal actions in a marriage as well. From the well-placed eye roll to the exaggerated sigh of disappointment, we can all become masters at expressing our disapproval of another person.

Jared was a young man I had counseled several times. His wife was decidedly antagonistic. Not only to God and Jared's faith but also to Jared's extended family. Jared would attend church and Bible studies on his own, and he would find covert ways to spend time with his extended family. Over time he found himself growing embittered toward his wife. When she would ask him to help around the house, Jared would drag his feet, exhale loudly, and bang things around—all to ensure that his wife knew how inconvenienced he was. Why did he do this? In some ways he was trying to retaliate, to return evil for evil. Was he yelling and screaming? No, that's not the kind of guy he was. But he was not going to let an opportunity slip by where he could communicate how hurt he was by his wife's spiritual apathy. Thankfully, God convicted him of his attitude, and he began to make significant changes in his interactions with her.

Indifference

These types of marriages are not going to change overnight, and we don't want to promise that after a week of good behavior the spouse will come to faith in Christ (although we pray for that). As months and years pass, it is easy to grow weary of doing good. When weariness sets in, counselees may find themselves growing indifferent to their spouse's spiritual state. The conversation internally may go like this, "Well, I guess I've done everything I can. He's always going to be like this, and there's nothing I can do to change him. It is what it is."

One practical way indifference can affect a marriage is when the believing spouse views the entire marriage through the lens of spiritual vs. nonspiritual activity. Any attempt to share in the activities, common interests, hobbies, likes/dislikes of their unbelieving spouse is seen as "unspiritual" and thus not to be entertained or cultivated. Unequally yoked marriages can and should have an enjoyment of life together.

Believing spouses can separate their lives from their unbelieving spouses in a way that seems right to them: they're *prioritizing* the church. But this may prevent and preclude them from building and investing in the marital relationship with their unbelieving spouse. Some of the conflicts that arise in unequally yoked marriages come from the unbelieving spouse feeling neglected and abandoned. Each spouse handles the neglect in a variety of ways—some become angry while others withdraw. When spouses get to this place of indifference, a wise counselor can intervene and encourage. Life can be overwhelming, and change can seem elusive. Help the believing spouse remember and understand that their behavior before an unbelieving spouse is to be loving and gracious (cf. Matt. 5:16; John 13:35; Rom. 12:9; 1 Thess. 4:9–12). Help them to remain steadfast in prayer and not to yield to indifference.

Submission[9]

Peter is clear in 1 Peter 3:1 that submission is not a command only for a marriage between two believers.[10] Peter writes, "Wives, in the same way submit yourselves to your own husbands" (1 Pet. 3:1). The phrase *in the same way* refers back to Jesus's submission to the Father in the case of unjust suffering. Submission to their husbands, Peter argues, could result in husbands becoming believers: "they may be won over without words by the behavior of their wives, when they see the purity and reverence of your lives" (1 Pet. 3:1–2).

Are there ways the wife seeks to subvert or circumvent her husband's leadership? Let's say the unbelieving husband tells his wife he does not want her to tithe part of his paycheck to the church. What should the wife do in that situation? I would counsel her toward submitting and respecting her husband's wishes in this situation. Can she thoughtfully appeal to his decision? Yes, but ultimately on an issue like this, I would counsel her toward submission. Paul reminds us, "Each of

---

9. John MacArthur has helpful commentary on why the admonition to wives receives more attention from Peter than the admonition to the husband. "And Peter, I want you to understand, is not biased but he gives six verses to wives and one verse to husbands. Now somebody might say, 'That's a little out of balance.' But it isn't. And there's a very important reason why. And that is because when a wife became a Christian the potential for difficulty in the marriage was much greater than when a husband became a Christian because a husband was already in charge anyway. And in that society if a husband became a Christian, the wife would dutifully accept that since she had no mind of her own, at least that she was not allowed to have one. So the potential for conflict was greatly lessened. But when a woman who was viewed as a slave or an animal, and not much more, became a Christian independently of her husband, the potential for conflict and embarrassment and difficulty was much greater and that is why Peter gives much more attention to that particular problem." http://www.gty.org/resources/sermons/60-31/how-to-win-your-unbelieving-spouse.

10. In cases where abuse is happening, refer to chapter eleven, "My Spouse Is Abusing Me" for additional guidance. Additionally, Brad Hambrick has many helpful resources in similar situations: http://www.bradhambrick.com/my-favorite-posts-on-abusive-relationships/.

you should give what you have decided in your heart to give, not reluctantly or under compulsion, for God loves a cheerful giver" (2 Cor. 9:7). Are there other ways the wife can contribute her time, energy, and resources in a cheerful manner to her local church while still honoring her husband's request?

There will be situations like this that will demand further guidance and counsel. If the husband asks his wife to do something unbiblical, always counsel her toward obedience to God (Acts 5:29).[11] Carol Cornish advises, "Some husbands act like tyrants. They are excessively demanding and oppressive in effecting leadership in the family. Sometimes godly resistance to their idolatrous demands is appropriate."[12]

UNPACK THE WHOLE COUNSEL OF GOD

On this issue, like many others we have discussed, the whole counsel of God's Word must be brought to bear in the life of our counselee in order to helpfully and wisely provide help and hope. For example, are there times when spouses should be silent and not respond? Yes! (cf. 1 Pet. 3:4). Are there times when spouses should speak truth in love? Yes! (cf. Prov. 15:23). Good pastoral counseling will seek to equip spouses in unequally yoked marriages with a biblical mindset that is also sensitive and informed by their current context and situation.

Where might we go in Scripture to help someone who feels they are in relationship with a person who is opposed to them? Have you ever considered Psalm 3 and 4, commonly known as David's morning and evening psalms? The context of Psalm 3 and 4 is contained in the superscript, "A psalm of David, when he fled from Absalom his son." For a full retelling of the story, read the account in 2 Samuel 15–18. The context behind the psalms is that David has been forced out of his capitol city, Jerusalem, and is on the run because his son Absalom is mounting a *coup d'état* to wrest power from his aging father. In response, David flees to the forest of Ephraim and waits for his son to destroy him. Amid this turmoil and hardship, David pens these two intensely personal psalms.

---

11. John Piper offers a sample dialogue in a case like this, "I would love to follow your lead in this marriage, but when you ask me to do something that is sin, you are asking me to offend the one who has an even greater authority in my life than you have. I mean Jesus. And I cannot do it." http://www.desiringgod.org/interviews/hope-for-hard-marriages.

12. Fitzpatrick and Cornish, *Women Helping Women*, 226. "Any behavior that is *clearly* contrary to God's Word must be refused. At the same time, she needs to be careful that she doesn't abuse this principle and make issues out of things which are unclear in Scripture" (Fitzpatrick and Cornish, *Women Helping Women*, 222).

LORD, how many are my foes!

   Many are rising against me;

many are saying of my soul,

    "There is no salvation for him in God."

Psalm 3:1–2 ESV

Take this psalm, unpack the context with your counselee, and let them see how Scripture speaks to people who are in difficult or even hostile relationships. Help the spouse identify with David when he says in verse 2, "Many are saying . . . 'There is no salvation for him in God.'" Many times, spouses in this situation are mocked, ridiculed, and condescended to on a frequent basis for their faith in God.

What does David do in situations like this? He cries out to his Lord, "But you, O LORD, are a shield about me, my glory and the lifter of my head" (v. 3). David cries out to God and God hears his distress. God himself answers David from his holy hill. This is what enables David's actions in verse 5, "I lay down and slept; I woke again for the Lord sustained me." How can the psalmist trust in the Lord? Because the Lord is trustworthy and hears the cries of his children, just as he hears the cries and mourning of those in relationships like your counselee. So often, spouses in unequally yoked marriages experience isolation unlike any other kind of loneliness. While they are married and have the physical presence of a husband or a wife, they lack the spiritual unity the Spirit of God brings about through our common faith. My wife and I have conflicts and quarrels together, but what serves as a bedrock foundation in those conflicts is our common faith in God and focus on Christ. Spouses in unequally yoked marriages don't have this common foundation.

Counseling men and women who are married to unbelievers gives a pastor-counselor a significant opportunity to incarnate the loving presence of a Savior who knows what it is like to be rejected, mocked, and ridiculed by those closest to him. We promise no quick fixes, no speedy remedies. Rather, we come alongside them, listen to their situation, enter into their world, and offer steady and wise counsel that not only meets them in the moment but also prepares them for growth in ways that will undoubtedly stretch and mold them into the image of Christ.

And we all, who with unveiled faces contemplate the Lord's glory, are being transformed into his image with ever-increasing glory, which comes from the Lord, who is the Spirit.

2 CORINTHIANS 3:18

Counselor Fieldnotes

There are several complex issues that should be considered when counseling a spouse who is married to an unbeliever: (1) What are the expectations of both parties? Was the believer a professing Christian at the time of the marriage or did they become a Christian after marriage? Did the believer ignore advice not to marry an unbeliever? If so, was there any church discipline or admonition from a pastor or church leadership? Did the unbeliever make any promises about going to church with the believer, not giving the believer a difficult time in matters of faith and worship, or did they promise to explore the believer's faith? (2) What was the understanding the believer had of the marital covenant at the time of the marriage? Did the believer enter into this commitment unadvisedly? Did the unbelieving spouse agree with the marital vows or did they make a false vow, never having any intention of keeping the vows? (3) What kind of spouse is the unbeliever? Are they committed to marital fidelity or have they been unfaithful physically or emotionally? Are there grounds for desertion, such as physical or mental adultery (pornography), addictions, abuse, abandonment (lack of financial support or refusing to care for the family)? (4) What about children? Are they being properly nurtured and cared for, or is the unbelieving spouse hindering the covenantal responsibilities of healthy parenting? Are children being emotionally abused (sarcasm and ridicule), spiritually abused (kept from worship and Christian education and training), or sexually or physically abused by either overt action or negligence? (5) Does the believing spouse understand their identity in Jesus? While the believing spouse should not put intentional or unintentional hindrances to the gospel in the way of the unbelieving spouse (sarcasm, criticism, nagging, disrespectful language or tone, communicating the hardship of being married to the unbeliever), neither should they feel the weight of doing the work of the Holy Spirit in the unbeliever's heart. Speaking the truth in love at all times should mean that respect and kindness (the summation of the Fruit of the Spirit) are always present in the words of the believer.

Rod Mays, Senior Staff, Reformed University Fellowship;
Adjunct Faculty, Reformed Theological Seminary
and Westminster Theological Seminary

RESOURCES

Cindy Easley, *Dancing with The One You Love: Living Out Submission in the Real World* (ch. 3)

Elyse Fitzpatrick and Carol Cornish, *Women Helping Women: A Biblical Guide to the Major Issues Women Face*

Sarah Flashing, "Honoring God in an Unequally Yoked Marriage," June 19, 2012. https://www.thegospelcoalition.org/article/honoring-god-in-an-unequally-yoked-marriage

Brad Hambrick, *Self-Centered Spouse: Help with Chronically Broken Marriages*

Jennifer McGehee, "Going it Alone" http://biblicalcounselingcoalition.org/2016/06/03/going-it-alone-part-1/
http://biblicalcounselingcoalition.org/2016/06/06/going-it-alone-part-2/
http://biblicalcounselingcoalition.org/2016/06/08/going-it-alone-part-3/

Lee & Leslie Strobel, *Surviving a Spiritual Mismatch in Marriage*

Leslie Vernick, *How to Act Right, When Your Spouse Acts Wrong*

Chapter 10

I CAN'T GET NO SATISFACTION

I can't get no satisfaction
'Cause I try and I try and I try and I try
ROLLING STONES

Do nothing out of selfish ambition or vain conceit. Rather, in humility
value others above yourselves, not looking to your own interests but
each of you to the interests of the others.
PHILIPPIANS 2:3–4

I'm done. I can't take it anymore. I don't know why I keep staying in this marriage, expecting you to change. You've never cared about changing, you've never wanted to change, and I'm done trying!"

"Here we go again. She never stops. Nothing is ever good enough for her. If it's not my mom, it's how much TV I watch, or how lazy I am, or how I don't take the dog out. It's never enough. Her mom was like this too, you know? She constantly railed at her dad until he divorced her!"

"Are you kidding me right now? Do you want to talk about mothers? How about we talk about your mother? You can't go one day without talking to her on the phone. She's never liked me from the day I started dating her precious golden boy, and now she sits and talks about what a horrible wife I am."

"See—this is what I deal with. My mom doesn't hate you. She gave you a chance, and you pushed her out. You're threatened by her!"

Nikki lets a scream escape from her pursed lips, "I can't do this . . . I can't do this."

Welcome to your third session with Tom and Nikki. Welcome to counseling couples who are in the throes of chronic conflict. Marriage therapists John and Julie Gottman comment on how difficult it is to work with couples in conflict: "No wonder most therapists stay away from couples work! Even Sigmund Freud tried it once but dropped it with scalded hands. He thought he could individually psychoanalyze both spouses in separate sessions during the same week. Apparently, he hated the experience so much that in 1919 he wrote a paper condemning it and recommended that no psychoanalyst ever try to help any couple."[1]

Thankfully, you and I have something Sigmund Freud did not: the good news of Jesus Christ! At first, these sessions might seem impossible. The couple walks in hot, and before you can say a prayer, they are off to the races, tearing one another apart. Their words remind you of Proverbs 12:18, "The words of the reckless pierce like swords." You cannot even begin the session before both spouses are weary from battle. In sessions like this, the constant and chronic conflict may be overwhelming, and it presents you with an enormous challenge. Where do you begin? What do you address first?

In this chapter, we want to accomplish two goals:

1. Gain a biblical understanding of conflict
2. Give a biblical plan for handling conflict

THE PATHOLOGY OF INNER CONFLICT

During a class called Dynamics of Biblical Change, professor David Powlison once shared a visual illustration I will never forget. Speaking of couples in conflict, he took two books and began banging them together to illustrate the head-to-head conflict many couples engage in. He encouraged couples in situations like this to pause and open the books to see what was driving the conflict. I think this is a helpful picture of what often happens in head-to-head, face-to-face conflict. Instead of pushing against one another, couples need to understand *why* they are having conflict.

The apostle James gives us a straightforward pathology of conflict. In James 4:1–3, James reminds us that long before there is ever a war outside yourselves, there is a war going on inside yourselves: "What causes fights and quarrels among you? Don't they come from your desires that battle within you? You desire but do not have, so you kill. You covet but you cannot get what you want, so you quarrel

---

1. Julie Schwartz Gottman and John M. Gottman, *10 Principles for Doing Effective Couples Therapy* (New York: W. W. Norton & Company, 2015), 2.

and fight. You do not have because you do not ask God. When you ask, you do not receive, because you ask with wrong motives, that you may spend what you get on your pleasures."

There is a war on the outside because there is a war on the inside.

James tells us that at the root of our broken relationships are unmet desires or expectations.

- You desire and do not have → so you murder
- You covet and cannot obtain → so you fight and quarrel
- You do not have → because you do not ask
- You ask → do not receive
- You ask wrongly → to spend it on your pleasure

Internal desires and expectations lead to *external* conflict. James describes these frustrated desires as warring and battling each other. I believe it is helpful to understand conflict in the language James uses because it highlights what is at stake.[2] Peace in the home is not simply a desirable domestic goal; it exemplifies and embodies what we are made for. As human beings we were made to exist in *shalom*.

Paul puts it this way in Ephesians 4:3, "Make every effort to keep the unity of the Spirit through the bond of peace." A peaceful marriage enables couples to live out their calling before God. It is one of the most practical ways to live out the truth of the gospel. Jesus puts it like this, "Blessed are the peacemakers, for they will be called children of God" (Matt. 5:9).

You do not have because you do not ask God.

Tucked away in this inner pathology, James gives the reader a glimpse into how we are supposed to handle our desires that wage war. We are called to bring them to God in prayer! Encourage the couple to imagine the dynamic possibilities that could take place if they took their desires to God *before* they engaged in heated conflict. Unfortunately, in the heat of conflict, very few couples seek God in prayer.

War and love

James adds a few more metaphors to his vivid description of conflict. Not only is there a war going on inside, but there is also adultery. "You adulterous people, don't

---

2. "James chooses the vocabulary of war to express controversies and quarrels, animosities and bad feeling among Christians, not because there is no other way of saying it, but because there is no other way of expressing the horror of it." (Alec Motyer, *The Message of James* [Downers Grove: InterVarsity Press, 1985], 141).

you know that friendship with the world means enmity against God? Therefore, anyone who chooses to be a friend of the world becomes an enemy of God. Or do you think Scripture says without reason that he jealously longs for the spirit he has caused to dwell in us? But he gives us more grace. That is why Scripture says, 'God opposes the proud but shows favor (grace, ESV) to the humble'" (James 4:4–6).

If James did not have your attention before, his reference to adultery should have it now. James picks up on a metaphor that was familiar to his Jewish readers. The language of God's people being adulterous is a common theme in the prophetic books of the Old Testament. The full brunt of the phrase here in James reads simply as "You adulteresses!" James is saying that when you, the bride of Christ, try to fulfill your desires apart from God, you're committing adultery. When you pursue your desires over what God has designed for you, you are essentially loving yourself and what you want rather than God, the true and right object of desire and love.

When my oldest daughter was younger, she would bring a myriad of toys and Barbies to the dinner table with her. While we would pass dishes of mashed potatoes and peas, we would need to navigate a minefield of toys scattered everywhere. We told her over and over again that toys did not belong at the table, and yet every meal a stray toy would somehow make its way back to the table. One evening, as I was moving the toys to an adjacent counter, I caught her sneaking over and bringing them back.

I asked her, "Ava, why do you keep bringing these toys to the table after I've told you not to?" Her reply was simple and honest (and teary-eyed), "Because I love them!" In that moment, I had a snapshot of her heart. It was an honest answer. Why do you keep doing what you are doing? *Because I love to do it.*

This is exactly what James is describing. The reason you have these conflicts— these wars and quarrels—is because you love your own desires above and beyond what God has designed and created you for. God zealously and jealously yearns for us to be in right relationship with him and, by extension, right relationship with other people. David Powlison writes, "He is God, the jealous lover. God's jealousy is wonderful and an essential part of love; it is not petty or possessive. God's jealousy is meant to call us to the confidence that he loves us and gives us grace. As a result, the atrocity of betraying him heightens when we do not love him in return."[3]

A surprising answer to conflict and war

James does not leave us without a prescription for our chronic conflict: "Submit yourselves, then, to God. Resist the devil, and he will flee from you.

---

3. David Powlison, "Dynamics of Biblical Change," (lecture 7, Christian Counseling & Education Foundation, Glenside, PA, 2017), 30.

Come near to God and he will come near to you. Wash your hands, you sinners, and purify your hearts, you double-minded. Grieve, mourn and wail. Change your laughter to mourning and your joy to gloom. Humble yourselves before the Lord, and he will lift you up" (James 4:7–10).

Take the step of biblical repentance. To rescue us from this predicament of war and adultery, God does not judge and condemn, he offers us grace through his Spirit.

The ESV translates the end of verse 6 as "[God] gives grace to the humble." Could there be any sweeter news than that? In our conflicts, our never-ending pursuits of meaning and significance, God gives us grace. In this context, he gives us the grace to repent and turn back to him. What James does in these few short verses is show us a full-throated, embodied repentance that accesses every part of our humanity: emotional, spiritual, volitional, and cognitive.

James gives us ten imperatives, calling for immediate action.[4] This is James's long-hand for what authentic repentance looks like.

Addressing expectations in marriage

How do you as a counselor begin to sort through all of this in your marriage counseling sessions? If you have the time, I find that dedicating at least one session to understanding expectations in marriage proves to be very helpful. First, help husbands and wives understand how expectations are formed and influenced.

- *Family of origin*: Understanding the kind of family each spouse came from is helpful (not determinative) in understanding their current expectations. Spouses come from a variety of traditions and backgrounds:

Small, nuclear family	Large, extended family
A family who was punctual	A family who ran late
Lots of conflict	Suppressed conflict
Dinner on the go	Dinner with the family
Clean, neat, and organized	Messy, chaotic, and disorganized
Father was a spiritual leader	Father was absent
Mother ran the home	Mother was submissive

---

4. (1) submit to God (2) resist the devil (3) draw near to God (4) cleanse your hands (5) purify your hearts (6) be wretched (7) mourn (8) weep (9) let your laughter be turned to mourning and your joy to gloom (10) humble yourself.

This table simply presents contrasts. You are not making a statement on their merit or value but rather showing that husbands and wives come from different backgrounds.[5] Those backgrounds in turn shape their expectations. While I don't believe expectations are *determined* by their family of origin, I do find their family of origin plays a significant role in the development and expression of desires and expectations.

- *Personality and disposition*: It is also helpful to understand that each spouse has a unique personality and disposition that influences their desires and expectations. These personality traits are not issues of sin necessarily, but part of the way their humanity expresses itself:[6]

Introvert	Extrovert
Enjoys pets	Does not enjoy pets
Timely and punctual	Runs late
Adventurous and spontaneous	Safe and routine
Free-spirited	Cautious
Spender	Saver
Optimistic	Pessimistic

Again, like the previous table, these traits are contrasts, not statements of right and wrong. Yes, there are contexts where certain personality traits can morph into sinful expressions, but for our purposes they are listed here to show how each spouse is unique.

I find that most conflict arises in marriages when one spouse tries to conform their spouse into their own image. A husband can assume (because of his family of origin) that his wife should think and behave the same way he does, and vice versa. Let me offer a practical example from my own marriage. When Jen and I were first married, I decided one evening to make us a really nice dinner of roasted chicken. As we sat down to eat, I noticed she was politely picking away at the chicken. I asked her if there was something wrong it—was it done enough, was it too salty, was it too spicy? She replied that she did not like to eat chicken that had bones in it!

5. Conversely, many couples are very similar in these areas, which can present its own set of challenges. As in any counseling situation, each case is unique, which in the long run encourages the counselor to depend on the power of the Holy Spirit, and not their own talents, gifts, and abilities.

6. Brad Hambrick has a helpful worksheet to help couples assess these differences: http://bradhambrick .com/celebrating-non-moral-marital-differences/.

Well, based on how I reacted you might have thought she had just said something horrible. I immediately got angry and lashed out. I made a comment about how I didn't think she would make it on the mission field because people around the world eat bone-in chicken all the time. (Looking back, we can both laugh now, but in the moment, it seemed that this was the conflict to end all conflicts.)

Before we knew what was happening, we were embroiled in conflict—your everyday, garden-variety conflict. I was hurt—why didn't she like the chicken I *slaved* over? She was surprised at my anger—what's the big deal, I like boneless chicken breast, so what? After we both simmered down, we conducted a post-mortem, and it was clear what had happened. Was the problem the chicken? No! The problem was how I sinfully dealt with my unmet expectations:

1. I wanted Jen to be pleased that I had made her a chicken for dinner. (In my family, we could not afford boneless, skinless chicken breast, so we ate whatever was cheap or on sale.)
2. When Jen did not respond how I wanted her to, I lashed out in anger, sarcasm, and hurtful words.
3. Instead of calling out to God for help, I tried to get what I wanted (her happiness and pleasure) through my anger and manipulation.

When expectations in marriage go unmet, we typically have one of two reactions: we blow up or we clam up. Neither reaction moves couples toward the peaceful unity for which God created us. So what do we do in helping a couple deal with unmet expectations (a situation couples will experience scores of times over the course of marriage)? Instead of blowing up or clamming up, how can you encourage couples to *speak up*, to speak truth in love? A diagram is helpful to visualize this dynamic.

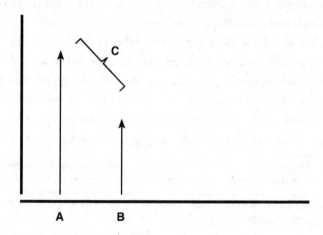

A. Stated desire or expectation
B. Actual situation or realized expectation
C. How do you respond when you don't get what you want?

This dynamic happens daily in almost every marriage. We consistently don't meet up to the expectations of our spouse. Conflict thrives and lives in that space between A and B.

Instead of blowing up or clamming up when we don't get what we want (letter C), how can couples speak the truth in love? How can couples handle conflict in a way that honors God? If you look at the diagram, there are at least two things spouses can do in times of conflict. First, spouses could reevaluate their expectations (A):

- Is this expectation of my spouse biblically informed and mandated or a personal preference? (e.g., I expect my spouse to love and pursue God [biblically informed mandate] vs. I expect my spouse to stay up late and enjoy watching TV with me [personal preference].)
- Is this expectation of my spouse unbiblical? If so, it needs to be removed.

Secondly, spouses can reevaluate their spouse's action that did not meet up to expectation (B):

- What is my spouse going through today that might inform my understanding of them?
- Am I being realistic of my context and environment (i.e., we live in a broken, fallen world, cf. Rom. 8:18–23)?
- Is this an opportunity to give grace? (1 Pet. 4:8)
- Would wisdom demand that I recalibrate and reorient my expectation?
- Will I choose to walk in the empowering grace of the Holy Spirit to deal with the disappointment of my unmet expectation?

A BIBLICAL PLAN FOR COUNSELING COUPLES IN CONFLICT

Remember Jim and Susan's fight at the beginning of the chapter? Where do you start in a situation like this? Armed with a biblically informed view of conflict, how do you minister truth and offer wise instruction? I use these helpful steps to navigate the remainder of the session:

1. Check your heart.
2. Pray silently and publicly.
3. Pursue a verbal commitment.
4. Plot out how the balance of the session will go.

Check your heart.

I'll confess that in the face of a situation like the one with Jim and Susan, I tend to withdraw and lose hope. In that moment, the mounting conflict seems so intimidating that I think to myself, "What in the world could I offer them in this moment that can change years of conflict?" Most of the time when I'm thinking this way, it indicates my lack of faith and hope in a God who does the impossible. I must remind myself in those moments that there is nothing I can offer them that will truly change how they interact. Can I offer some communication principles and techniques that might alleviate their conflict? Yes, but to what end? We must remind ourselves of who we are, and who really effects true change.

Not only do I need to remind myself that I'm an instrument in God's hands, but I must also remind myself that I'm a pastor-counselor, not an umpire. A frequent temptation in marriage counseling is to take the content the couple brings to you and to hold court, offering various opinions. A husband will come in hoping to relate a series of events—not to understand his heart or his wife's heart, but rather to receive validation for how he handled it. It's tempting for the counselor to affirm and validate the husband's experience, but be careful—as soon as you have offered an opinion on the husband's action, the wife has her own story to relate. She goes on to tell you how her husband lost his temper this past week because he could not find his golf clubs. As a result, the wife found herself in the path of her husband's anger, and the result was another blowup. What does she want from you right now? She wants to be validated. She wants to know that her subsequent irritation and simmering hostility were legitimate. After multiple rounds, you may step back and realize no real progress has been made, and in fact, there are still a dozen more stories left to be "called." Pastor, you are a counselor who is to bring the good news to this husband and wife, not an umpire who calls balls and strikes.

Pray silently and publicly.

Don't skip this. You might be thinking to yourself, "Yeah, I got it. Prayer is important. Next." Prayer is not only important in counseling, it's vital. Biblical counseling is not counseling unless prayer permeates the dynamics of the session.

Have you ever noticed that the prayers of the Bible seem to crop up all over the place? Some come to us during hardship and difficulty (David in Ps. 3 and 4). Some come to us in the middle of teaching (The Lord's Prayer in Matt. 6). Others come because the writer is overwhelmed with God's majesty and sovereignty (Paul in Rom. 11:33–36). Paul prays mid-letter for the Ephesian church and then continues with his teaching (Eph. 3:14–21). The model we see in Scripture is that prayer is unceasing and constant (cf. Eph. 1:16; 1 Thess. 5:17). The counseling room should be no different.

Prayer is and should be more than a session opener and closer. It is our very lifeline in counseling. It demonstrates the counselor's submission to God and their own inability to affect change in the hearts of the spouses. Prayer during session tells the couple that you cannot do this alone, but that you need the help of the Wonderful Counselor.

Practically, I find it resets the verbal dynamics of a session. Going from an environment of conflict to speaking with God in prayer leads to a dramatic shift in the tone and content of the session. A prayer might go something like this:

> *Father God,*
>
>   *We pause right now to ask for your help. Left alone to ourselves we can easily lose sight of the bigger picture. God, forgive us for the unkind words we have exchanged and for not believing your Word. God, instill in us a renewed hope and focus on your Son, Jesus Christ. May we use the next few minutes to address our hearts, our spouse, and our situation from your perspective. Help us, God, because we desperately need it. We cannot solve this on our own. In your Son's name, we pray.*
>
>   *Amen.*

Pursue a verbal commitment.

The next step is for the counselor to pursue a verbal commitment from the couple for three things:

1. To commit to following a biblical pattern of communication (e.g., no profanity, no name-calling, no screaming, no yelling, etc.)
2. To engage in active listening
3. To acknowledge personal responsibility

First, by seeking this verbal commitment to a biblical pattern of communication, you are reiterating Paul's command in Ephesians 4:1–3: "I urge you to live a life worthy of the calling you have received. Be completely humble and gentle;

be patient, bearing with one another in love. Make every effort to keep the unity of the Spirit through the bond of peace."

Essentially, you are asking the couple to live out their faith. "Jim and Susan, you both profess faith in Christ, so I'm asking you to conduct yourselves here in the session in a way that fulfills and discharges that calling. Do you agree to do that?" Robert Jones in his eminently helpful book *Pursuing Peace*, writes, "The twin gifts of God's reconciling peace through Christ's cross and God's inner peace through his Spirit lead to the third peace blessing, namely, relational peace with others."[7]

Jones goes on to write that because the gospel brings this peace to our relationships, it is incumbent on us to pursue peaceful living and relationships as a part of our calling as believers.

Secondly, you seek a verbal commitment to engage in active listening. This means spouses agree not to interrupt each other, walk out of the room while the other is sharing, or engage in dismissive nonverbal gestures (eye-rolling, loud sighs, etc.). Again, here is an opportunity for the counselor to model what they are looking for: eager and engaged listening. It is easy to underestimate how important active listening is. Here is a story of why listening is critical to resolving conflict:

> **Carol:** I told Michael I did not want a dog because I already have four children to clean up after (points at Michael aggressively), and the last thing I need is a pet!
>
> **Michael:** And what I told Carol is that if I want a dog, I'm going to get a dog! She can't stop me.
>
> **Carol:** You don't get it, and you don't listen! I don't have the time to take care of this house, get four kids to school, and take care of a new dog. I just can't do it.

When I asked Michael to tell me what Carol was seeking to communicate, he replied, "She is trying to control me again, and I'm not going down that path!" I gently pushed back and asked if that's what Carol *said*. It took a few exchanges for Michael to actually repeat back what Carol *said*, not his *interpretation* of what she said. You see, Michael and Carol had both failed to listen, and they immediately jumped to faulty interpretations. This led to a conflict that would last for days.

The final step in this process is to see if each spouse will commit to taking personal responsibility for their words and actions. Jesus tells us in Matthew 7:3–5, "Why do you look at the speck of sawdust in your brother's eye and pay

---

7. Robert D. Jones, *Pursuing Peace* (Wheaton, IL: Crossway, 2012), 23.

no attention to the plank in your own eye? How can you say to your brother, 'Let me take the speck out of your eye,' when all the time there is a plank in your own eye? You hypocrite, first take the plank out of your own eye, and then you will see clearly to remove the speck from your brother's eye."

Before a spouse points out the other's faults or sins, the spouse needs to take personal responsibility for their *own* faults and sins. What a basic truth, yet one that is so difficult to practice! Asking each spouse to take responsibility for their contribution to the conflict helps focus the spotlight squarely where it needs to be: their hearts before God.

Sinful conflict works two dynamics simultaneously: it shrinks the marriage to the conflict at hand and it shifts focus to the spouse rather than the individual's own heart. In the conversation we just looked at, I asked Michael if he realized he had escalated the conversation by accusing Carol of seeking to control him when that is not what she said. After a few excuses, Michael replied, "Yes, that's not what she said, and I know I need to listen better. She tells me I don't listen all the time."

Pivoting to Carol, I asked Carol if there was anything she could take responsibility for. After a pause, she replied somewhat quietly, "Well, I guess Michael isn't crazy for thinking I'm trying to control him. My life is so crazy right now, and this is just one more thing I can't control. So telling Michael he can't get the dog is one thing I can put my foot down on." When Michael heard this, his head began to nod vigorously as it seemed he had been validated. I held my hand up and asked him to wait until after I had spoken.

"Michael, what I think you're hearing Carol say is that the reason she doesn't want a dog is that her life feels like it is out of control, and this represents one area she can control. Michael, what would have been a better way for you to lead and love Carol in this moment, instead of jumping to this conclusion?"

Michael tilted his head, thought for a moment, and then responded, "I guess I could have just asked her why she didn't want the dog." I could have jumped out of my seat that moment. "Yes! That's exactly what you could have done," I said. "You could have pursued her heart. You could have asked a good question. You could have modeled our God who seeks to pursue and understand before he moves and acts."

The center of this conflict was not about a dog. (News flash: the actual problem is rarely the problem the couple wants to talk about.) The conflict was about warring desires that were not being fulfilled. Carol does not feel heard or understood, and she's finally taking a step to regain control of her life. Michael wants to be able to do what he wants and make decisions how he wants. James would tell us this is a recipe for disaster.

Getting each spouse to take responsibility for their own role in the conflict,

I was able to help them both see the real problem (not the dog, but their own hearts) and provide common ground for them to move forward. Michael can take personal responsibility for not responding biblically to Carol's anger and frustration. Instead of issuing a blanket ultimatum ("I'm going to get a dog! She can't stop her."), he can begin to pursue her heart. Carol can take personal responsibility for not communicating biblically with Michael. Instead of expressing her desires through anger and frustration, she can follow biblical principles of communication to make her appeal and reach out to Michael.

Plot out the balance of the session(s).

After securing a verbal commitment to listen and take responsibility, the counselor then has time (hopefully a few minutes left in the session) to make some forward progress. In a situation like Michael and Carol's, I will tell them we are going to use our remaining time to replay the previous conflict, but do it with the newly taught skills of active listening and personal responsibility. This accomplishes several goals; namely, reinforcing your teaching and identifying places where they could easily relapse into unbiblical patterns of conflict resolution. Here is a sample dialogue:

Counselor: Michael, will you ask Carol why she doesn't want to get a dog? Carol, after Michael asks you this question, I want you to pause and think about what you're going to say.

Michael: Carol, I really want to get a dog. Why don't you want one?

Carol: Michael, I'm so tired every day. Between taking Kate and Sam to soccer practice, cooking, and cleaning, I'm wiped out. The thought of adding a dog to the mix overwhelms me.

Counselor: Now Michael, last time you both had this conversation the wheels started to go off right about here because you didn't listen. What's a better, more gracious way to respond to what Carol said?

Michael: I guess I should try to understand where she is coming from.

Counselor: Right! Why don't you affirm her for sharing her heart with you, and then ask some follow-up questions?

Michael: Carol, thanks for sharing that with me. I should have known you are tired and busy. I really am thankful for all you do for me and the family. Given all that we're going through, maybe getting a dog right now isn't the best choice.

Carol: That's the first time in a long time I've heard Michael thank me. Michael, I hope you know that it's not that I don't want you to be happy, but I think I get nervous that a dog will just be one more thing that comes between you and me.

Michael: Really? I never thought of that at all, but I can definitely see why you would think that.

At this point, let them take the reins of the conversation. You can already begin to see some rays of light. You can see Carol seeking to move toward Michael and share heart-level issues. You can see that for Carol it's not necessarily about the dog but about a yearning for relationship with Michael. You can begin to see Michael grasp that his previous interpretation of Carol seeking to control him is not true at all. Carol actually wants a more intimate relationship with Michael, but she doesn't know how to communicate that. Michael, like Carol, is realizing that the conflict is not really about a dog, but about the priority of the marriage relationship.

At one level, this conversation represents a major step forward for them. They are able to reprocess the past incident without the invectives and anger that characterized the past situation. It took work and time, but they proved subsequently that they could recreate the situation in a way that honored God. If you have remaining time left (or another session), you will want to explain to them the reason why the conversation went better. It is incumbent on the counselor to instruct and remind the couple that the reason they were able to handle the conversation differently is not that they had magically become communication experts after fifteen minutes or that you're the best marital counselor they've ever seen. No, the reason the communication and conflict went better is that they believed and followed God's commands for communication. They rightly recognized that the biggest problem was not the dog (or whatever other situational circumstances are at hand), but their own heart's desires: Carol's desire for relationship and Michael's desire to not be controlled.

A good conclusion for the session might be rereading Ephesians 4:1–6. Be sure to remind them that God has given them what they need to resolve conflict biblically, but it is up to them to fulfill that calling and live in peace with one another. Conflict, far from being a bad thing, is actually an opportunity for them to glorify God and to grow closer to one another. Author Ken Sande says it well in his bestselling book, *The Peacemaker*: "Conflict always provides an opportunity to glorify God, that is, to bring him praise and honor by showing who he is, what he is like, and what he is doing. The best way to glorify God in the midst of conflict is to depend on and draw attention to his grace, that is, the undeserved love, mercy, forgiveness, strength, and wisdom he gives to us through Jesus Christ."[8]

---

8. Ken Sande, *The Peacemaker: A Biblical Guide to Resolving Personal Conflict* (Grand Rapids: Baker, 2004), 31.

CONCLUSION

Marriage counseling can be difficult, discouraging, and disheartening work. Even with a decade of marriage counseling experience, I must remind myself that I don't personally change anyone; only God can bring about the change that couples desperately need. Change that lines up with our biblical definition is only accomplished by God working through his Spirit. This fundamental understanding of my own limitations is a critical cornerstone of gospel-centered marriage counseling. The second I begin to believe that the couple's change depends on my personal ability is when I begin heading down a path that leads to despair and discouragement.

At times like this, we need to have a road map to help us navigate a path forward. That path begins with your own heart and your own beliefs. Nothing is more dangerous in biblical counseling than to sideline our trust in the Word of God to accomplish the work of God. As soon as a couple engages in heated conflict, it is tempting to think that what they need most lies outside the realm of biblical truth. We can be thankful we serve a God who enters the milieu of human conflict and redeems it for his glory and our good. May we offer this hope to couples who are engaged in conflict.

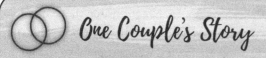

One Couple's Story

Many years ago we had to face the stark reality that our marriage was not in a good place. During the previous five years, we had added two babies to our family, changed jobs twice, and also relocated our family twice. The transitions were overwhelming, and Eric and I found ourselves in constant conflict. Though we tried to talk out the issues (sometimes loudly), we never could quite seem to get what we wanted out of the other person. We knew we needed the help of a third party and therefore went to counseling. Our first counselor was a person of faith but did not approach the conflict from a biblical perspective. He focused on strategies, tactics, and compromises that would reduce the conflict in our home. While some of these hints were helpful, they did not get to the root of our issues. It was like teaching someone how to bake a great pie by cutting the fruit a certain way while ignoring the fact that the fruit is rotten. Eric and I were working with rotten fruit.

The second time we attended marriage counseling, it was from a biblical counseling perspective. In this approach we did not emphasize the stresses or transitions of recent years, but instead we focused on the condition and alignment of our hearts. Focusing on the heart can seem scary, especially when your marriage is in conflict and there may be deep feelings of rejection, anger, or being unworthy of love. But because the gospel was at the center of our time together, the Spirit of grace, compassion, and forgiveness invited our true confessions. Biblical counseling led us to look at ourselves and see what we demanded of our spouses that can only come from God. We also identified what grace we had received from God but were withholding from one another. Rather than focusing on "baking pies" together, Eric and I had to focus on being people through whom God could bear much fruit. It was clear that our alignment with him was the key to alignment in our marriage. Christ is the cornerstone.

Since that time, we have experienced many more transitions, some deeply heartbreaking. Yet our relationship is stronger, and we have experienced the joy of personal and marital alignment with God. When we do experience conflict, it can always be traced back to one or both of us losing perspective of who we are in light of the gospel.

Eric and Liz Hehman

Counselor Fieldnotes

Ongoing interpersonal conflict can be exhausting, both for those embattled within it and for the counselors helping through it. The pathway to true change seems not only long but also daunting. We become disorientated and discouraged by the half-truths of the world that promise immediate comfort and peace. Unfortunately, those who look to find the "way out" of conflict instead of the "way through" conflict, find only more despair after the fleeting pleasures of immediate gratification subside.

Perseverance in the process of dealing with marital conflict is empowered only through hope in the words and works of our God. There is great capacity in the process of longsuffering, knowing that he will fulfill his promises and empower us by his grace one faithful step at a time. Galatians

5:16—6:10 guides our hearts to rely on the ongoing work of the Holy Spirit to do good through hard things. Our God empowers his people to make simple and clear choices of loving obedience to him while trusting that he will fulfill his promises even within the tension of ongoing marital conflict. Scripture reorients the journey of faith to everyday moments of walking in the Spirit and presents an eternal perspective and hope to the seemingly overwhelming challenges of the future.

If we are honest, there are many days when the heart of the biblical counselor becomes overwhelmed and weary from the ongoing work of helping marriages bound in conflict. What a humbling and everlasting joy it is to understand that our own hearts are also recipients of the same grace that we are presenting to others! Whatever the daunting journey before us, let us all place hope in our God who is who he says he is and will do what he says he will do.

Joe Keller, DMin, Council Member, Biblical Counseling Coalition

RESOURCES

Ernie Baker, *Help! I'm in a Conflict*

Brad Hambrick, Conflict-Resolution Online Evaluation: http://www.bradhambrick.com/wp-content/uploads/2014/06/GCMevaluation_Conflict-Resolution.pdf

Robert D. Jones, *Pursuing Peace: A Christian Guide to Handling Our Conflicts*

Ken Sande, *The Peacemaker: A Biblical Guide to Resolving Personal Conflict*

Paul David Tripp, *War of Words: Getting to the Heart of Your Communication Struggles*

Chapter 11

MY SPOUSE IS ABUSING ME

Domestic violence is a pattern of coercive, controlling, or abusive behavior that is used by one individual to gain or maintain power and control over another individual in the context of an intimate relationship.

JUSTIN AND LINDSEY HOLCOMB, *IS IT MY FAULT?*

I saw the tears of the oppressed—
and they have no comforter;
power was on the side of their oppressors—
and they have no comforter.

ECCLESIASTES 4:1

The first communication was brief.[1] Lucy told her Bible study leader she needed to talk to someone. The Bible study leader followed up, but Lucy said she had already figured out what she needed. The next communication came months later when Lucy asked for prayer for some difficulties in her marriage. The other women listened, nodded sympathetically, and moved on to the next need. Three months later, Lucy approached the Bible study leader again and asked if she could talk. The leader responded that she could and told her that she would call her to set something up. Lucy quickly replied, "No, please don't call me. I'll let you know when I can talk."

---

1. Lucy, like all the case studies in the book, is a composite.

Something did not seem right, so the Bible study leader pulled Lucy aside and pressed in a bit. "What's going on? Are you okay?" Lucy burst into tears but hurriedly brushed them aside while making the excuse that it had been a hard day. After a few gentle questions, Lucy confessed that her husband, Frank, was a "pretty angry man." When the leader pried a bit about the nature of Frank's anger, Lucy said, "Well, I mean I probably deserve it. I forget things easily, and the other day I forgot to pack Frank's lunch. He got really upset!"

By now the leader had grown concerned. She asked Lucy if they could talk alone sometime that week. Lucy told her it was very hard for her to meet outside of Bible study because Frank did not like her to be away from home too much. The leader offered that next time Bible study met, the two of them would excuse themselves and find a private room to meet. It was during that meeting that Lucy finally confessed that Frank was verbally and physically abusive. She pleaded with her leader, "Please don't be mad at Frank. He can't help himself most of the time. He has a ton of stress right now at work, and I think he's just taking it out on me."

Imagine that this Bible study leader comes up to your office after the Bible study and relays all of this to you. What do you do?[2]

By the time you finish reading this chapter, approximately 480 men and women will have been assaulted or beaten.[3] One in every three women and one in every four men, "will experience intimate partner physical violence, intimate partner sexual violence, and/or intimate partner stalking in their lifetime."[4] On a given day, over twenty thousand phone calls come into domestic violence hotlines.[5] Domestic abuse is a serious issue, and churches are not immune to this evil.[6]

Pastors and counselors must be equipped to deal with this pressing issue in a

---

2. At this point in conversation, you might need to reassure the Bible study leader (or whoever communicates to you) that they are doing the right thing in reaching out for help. Often, friends of the abused will feel guilty they did not spot the abuse or intervene earlier.

3. Based on this chapter taking you twenty-six minutes to read (thirteen pages at two minutes each). Approximately every minute, twenty people are physically abused. http://ncadv.org/learn-more/statistics.

4. Ibid.

5. https://ncadv.org/statistics.

6. The terminology I will use throughout the chapter is one of domestic abuse; however, other terms are frequently used as well: domestic violence or intimate partner violence. Examples of physical abuse include but are not limited to: having property damaged when the abuser is angry (thrown objects, punched walls, kicked doors, etc.); being pushed, slapped, bitten, kicked, or choked; abandonment in public or unfamiliar places; scaring a passenger while driving recklessly; using a weapon to threaten or intimidate; forcing the abused to leave their home; trapping the abused in their home or preventing them from leaving the home; preventing the abused from calling the police or seeking medical attention; hurting the children in front of the abused; using physical force in sexual situations. Emotional abuse includes but is not limited to: raging, criticizing, ridiculing, demeaning, belittling, withholding (money, sex, attention, and/or other necessities), restricting (freedom of movement, choices, or another person's emotional expression), isolating (from family, friends, and/or peers), threatening (to harm self, others, or objects of affection such as child, pet, or property), abandonment, coercing, accusing, ordering (ibid.)

biblically faithful manner. Justin and Lindsey Holcomb write, "Many victims believe clergy have the most potential to help them, when in reality they are too often the least helpful and sometimes even harmful"[7] because they are often uninformed on proper protocols and legal/ethical direction when it comes to counseling those who are in abusive relationships. The Holcombs note in their research that *direct* intervention helpers (lawyers, clergy, and police) are not as helpful compared to *less direct* intervention helpers (crisis hotlines, women's groups, social workers, and psychotherapists).[8]

What does the Bible have to say about abuse? Let's spend some time looking at the narrative of Sarai and her maid Hagar.[9] Because of her frustration with her infertility, Sarai has given Hagar to Abram, and Hagar conceives. "Then Sarai said to Abram, 'You are responsible for the wrong I am suffering. I put my slave in your arms, and now that she knows she is pregnant, she despises me. May the LORD judge between you and me.' 'Your slave is in your hands,' Abram said. 'Do with her whatever you think best.' Then Sarai *mistreated* Hagar; so she fled from her" (Gen. 16:5–6, emphasis added).

The ESV translates the last phrase of verse 6, "Then Sarai *dealt harshly* with her"[10] (Gen. 16:6, emphasis added). The Hebrew word here has a wide semantic range and is often translated according to its context. The word is often used to describe Israel's relationship with Egypt (cf. Ex. 1:11). Egypt frequently "mistreats," "afflicts," and "oppresses" Israel. Its Greek cognate, *kakoo*, means to inflict misery, to harm, or to injure. A common theme in its usage is the willful mistreatment of another person. It's the same word used in contexts of rape (cf. Gen. 34:2; Judg. 19:24; 2 Sam. 13:14).[11]

In the Genesis account, Sarai's plan backfires on her. She tries to circumvent God's plan to provide descendants for her and Abram by using Hagar as a surrogate mother. But Hagar, after becoming pregnant, begins to despise Sarai for reasons we do not know. Presumably, Hagar's success in giving Abram a child may have led her to aspire beyond her place as a servant and to treat Sarai as a rival competing for the heart of Abram and prominence in the household. Sarai complains to Abram, who gives her permission to do to Hagar as she pleases. Sarai, in turn, *abuses* Hagar, to the extent that Hagar is unable to take it and flees.

7. Justin S. Holcomb and Lindsey A. Holcomb, *Is It My Fault?: Hope and Healing for Those Suffering Domestic Violence* (Chicago: Moody, 2014), 16.

8. The Holcombs cite a study by J. Gordon, "Community Services Available to Abused Women in Crisis: A Review of Perceived Usefulness and Efficacy," *Journal of Family Violence* 11, no. 4 (1996): 315–29.

9. I'm indebted to a group of friends who discussed and researched this issue in depth with me online.

10. תִּרְבְּתוּ יֹרֵשׁ הֲנֶעְתוּ דְיָנְיֵעֲב בּוֹטָה.

11. Ludwig Koehler, Walter Baumgartner, M. E. J. Richardson, et al., *The Hebrew and Aramaic Lexicon of the Old Testament* (Leiden: Brill, 1994–2000), 1:853.

Throughout the Bible, there are stories like this of abusive relationships. The Egyptians kept the Israelite people in bondage and slavery for four hundred years. They used their power and position to inflict suffering and incite fear among the Israelites.[12]

Saul famously planned and attempted to kill David on several occasions (cf. 1 Sam. 19:1–2, 20:1). We know of at least two occasions when Saul hurled a spear at David, seeking to kill him (1 Sam. 18:8–11). Throughout the psalms, David and others would cry out to God to deliver them from their oppressors (cf. David in Psalm 57, fleeing from Saul).

Luke records in Acts 14:5–6 that the Jews were plotting to mistreat and stone Paul and Barnabas. Paul would later record his own mistreatment at the hands of his countrymen in 2 Corinthians 11:24–26.

There are also stories of sexual violence in the Bible. Potiphar's wife in Genesis 39 badgers Joseph day after day for sex. In today's environment, Potiphar's wife would have been written up for sexual harassment! The NIV translates the situation straightforwardly, "Joseph was well-built and handsome, and after a while his master's wife took notice of Joseph and said, 'Come to bed with me!'" (Gen. 39:6–7).

Potiphar's wife would not take no for an answer: "Though she spoke to Joseph day after day, he refused to go to bed with her or even be with her. One day he went into the house to attend to his duties, and none of the household servants was inside. She caught him by his cloak and said, 'Come to bed with me!'" (Gen. 39:10–12).

The crassness of her request is only exceeded by her theatrical naiveté: "'Look,' she said to them, 'this Hebrew has been brought to us to make sport of us! He came in here to sleep with me, but I screamed. When he heard me scream for help, he left his cloak beside me and ran out of the house'" (Gen. 39:14–15).

This story is an important reminder that abusers are often violent, controlling, and crass with their victim, while in public they may maintain a more respectable, convincing exterior.[13] While we often think of abuse being perpetrated by men, here is an example of a woman seeking to take sexual advantage in an abusive way against a subordinate.[14] Joseph is not the only victim of sexual assault and abuse in the Bible, however. You can find several other narratives detailing this evil, most notably the rape of Tamar in 2 Samuel 13.

---

12. Exodus 1:13–22 records the new Pharaoh's horrific command for the Hebrew midwives to kill every male Hebrew child—infanticide designed to wipe out an ethnicity.

13. This dynamic perpetuates to others that the abused is "crazy" or "making things up" and shifts the focus off of themselves [abuser].

14. She not only seeks to have sex with him but also uses her power, position, and authority to pressure him into this, which in and of itself is an abuse: an abuse of authority.

Clearly, abuse is not something new or modern. It has been one of the results of sin in our fallen world from the very beginning. Tim Lane and Paul Tripp write, "The Bible is not about an idyllic world full of noble people who always make the right choice. The Bible describes a world we recognize, where very good and very bad things happen, and where people make wonderful and horrible choices. The Bible describes a world that sometimes makes us laugh, but often makes us cry."[15]

The Bible condemns abusive violence of all kinds.

The Bible not only describes abuse and narrates tragic stories of abuse, it also clearly and unequivocally condemns abuse of all kinds (cf. Ex. 21:12–27).

Abuse of authority or power is always a sin. It is never an acceptable dynamic in any relationship, especially a marriage relationship. The psalmist writes, "The LORD examines the righteous, but the wicked, those who love violence, he hates with a passion" (Ps. 11:5). Does that language surprise you? Aren't we told hate the sin, not the sinner? Not always so. Here the Bible speaks loud and clear—God hates those who love violence.

The Bible speaks honestly of abuse, condemning abuse and those who practice violence. But most importantly—and what your counselee needs to hear—is this: God hears the cries of the abused, the oppressed, the torn down, the battered, and the beaten.[16] Psalm 10:17 states, "You, LORD, hear the desire of the afflicted; you encourage them, and you listen to their cry." The abused have a God who is never deaf to their cries for help.[17] Ed Welch writes, "If she [he] looks for words to say in the Psalms she will find that God especially invites those who have enemies and oppressors to come to him."[18]

Indeed, our Savior Jesus Christ is someone who understands what it means to be afflicted and oppressed: "He was despised and rejected by mankind, a man of suffering, and familiar with pain" (Isa. 53:3).

In marriage, all forms of abuse must be addressed and taken seriously by the counselor. As referenced in chapter three, when abuse is taking place in a marriage, the marriage counseling needs to come to an end. At this point, individual and separate counseling for the abused and the abuser is necessary.[19] Winston Smith writes, "It's important to identify the presence of abuse in marriage because, unde-

---

15. Timothy S. Lane and Paul David Tripp, *How People Change* (Greensboro, NC: New Growth, 2008), 98.

16. Cf. Abigail and Nabal in 1 Samuel 25:3, 17, 24–25, 38 and the Israelites in Jeremiah 50:33–34.

17. Cf. Psalm 5, 7, 10, 55–57, 140.

18. Edward T. Welch, "Living with an Angry Husband," *Journal of Biblical Counseling* 24, no. 4 (2006): 47.

19. The level of competency needed to address issues like domestic violence and abuse are most likely beyond the scope of the average pastor. That does not mean the pastor is absolved of responsibility, but in instances of abuse, pastors should probably help develop a network of care, accountability, and counsel.

tected, these patterns can sabotage the counseling process. A fundamental dynamic of marriage counseling is helping spouses examine their own behavior so that each understands his or her contribution to shared problems, but this very process can unwittingly play into patterns of abuse rather than stop them."[20]

In counseling husbands who are abusive, it must be made absolutely clear that biblical headship does not entitle a husband to treat his wife in a violent or oppressive manner. At the heart of most domestic abuse is the sinful use of a husband's leadership to exercise control over another individual.[21] Biblical headship is described as sacrificial servanthood, not unlimited authority (Mark 10:42–45). Let's not confuse terms—when a husband demands his own way or dominates his wife, we do not call this biblical headship, we call it what it is—selfishness and abuse of power.

In light of this, what should we do as counselors? Two immediate priorities emerge: *identify immediate needs* and *plan for long-term care*.

IMMEDIATE NEEDS

The first immediate need in any domestic violence situation is to prioritize the safety of the abused.[22] Often this is primarily a matter of physical safety. Make sure they have emergency contact numbers at hand. As a counselor or pastor, you should not be their first phone call in case of emergency.

- Emergency 9–1–1
- National Domestic Violence Hotline: 1–800–799-SAFE (7233)
- Local law enforcement
- If they are there in the office with you, offer to help make the call with them.
- I encourage pastors and ministry leaders to be familiar with local women's shelters and emergency personnel in their area.

---

20. Winston Smith, "When NOT to Do Marriage Counseling," *Journal of Biblical Counseling* 27, no. 1 (2013): 73–74.

21. One of the dynamics that can lead to outbreaks of domestic violence in marriages is an upside-down view of complementarian headship, i.e., that the husband is the head of the wife. A husband can wield such authority in an ungodly way. Jason Meyer states, "Hyper-headship is a satanic distortion of male leadership, but it can fly under the radar of discernment because it is disguised as strong male leadership. Make no mistake—it is harsh, oppressive, and controlling. In other words, hyper-headship becomes a breeding ground for domestic abuse." Jason Meyer, "Hyper-Headship and the Scandal of Domestic Abuse in the Church," April 28, 2015. *The Gospel Coalition*: https://blogs.thegospelcoalition.org/justintaylor/2015/04/28/hyper-headship-and-the-scandal-of-domestic-abuse-in-the-church/. Another dynamic that can lead to women being called to submit to such abusive headship is a high view of marriage that leads to a "marriages must be saved at all costs" mentality. Both must be balanced by a biblical understanding of Scripture.

22. Brad Hambrick has a helpful post on the triage of complex counseling cases: http://bradhambrick.com/triage2/.

If they are in an abusive relationship, help them develop a personal safety plan. Here are several helpful templates available online:

- Brad Hambrick: http://bradhambrick.com/safetyplan/
- Justin and Lindsey Holcomb: http://justinholcomb.com/wp-content/uploads/2014/05/IsItMyFaultAppendix2.pdf
- An example of a secular safety assessment: https://www.marincourt.org/PDF/LethalityRisk.pdf

Seek an assessment of the situation to differentiate abuse from everyday relational conflict. Using the definition of domestic violence provided by Justin and Lindsey Holcomb, a number of issues can help you understand the difference between abuse and everyday conflict:[23]

- Intentional: The abuser is willfully using abusive tactics to get what they want.
- Methodical: Abusers steadily increase abusive behaviors to get what they want.
- Pattern: Abuse is not a series of isolated events, but an overarching pattern of behavior designed to inflict harm on an individual.
- Tactics: Shaming, exploitation, threats, intimidation, and self-pity are all common tactics used by abusers.
- Power: The abuser uses power—physical, emotional, financial—to achieve control over their spouse or other victims.
- Control: By whatever means necessary, abusers want their spouse to be under their control—physically, emotionally, financially, and even at times, spiritually.
- Desires: The abuser wants what the abuser wants. Any outside needs or concerns are discounted at the expense of what they desire.

Understand that abuse typically escalates. Yes, there might be days and weeks when the abuse recedes into the background, but over the balance of the relationship, abuse tends to escalate and intensify without intervention. Make sure you are not sending the abused back into an environment unprepared.

In cases where physical safety is a concern, a physical separation is advised. However, encouraging the abused spouse to separate from their abusive spouse

---

23. Holcomb and Holcomb, *Is It My Fault?*, 57–58.

must not be done lightly. "When church leaders act too quickly, questioning or confronting the abuser before the victim is ready, they can cause more harm than good, even putting the victim in greater danger. The victim may be silenced and punished by the abuser who now knows she spoke to an outsider. Ensuring the immediate safety of the victim is essential, but so is securing her long-term safety."[24] Darby Strickland reminds us, "Keep in mind that the most dangerous time for a woman is when she is fleeing abuse. There is no room for optimistic and naive thinking when it pertains to safety issues. It is incumbent upon us to be educated."[25]

This is not a time to deliver a theological argument about divorce and remarriage. That can come at a later point. Right now the immediate need is the care and support of the abused.[26]

Yes, God calls us to endure suffering. Yes, he can redeem us through suffering and hardship, but those principles must be balanced and read in relationship to *all* of Scripture. God cares about the oppressed and seeks to deliver them. God cares for the individuals in marriage as much as he cares for the institution of marriage. You do not have a "high view of marriage" if you encourage spouses to endure abuse. This is actually a low view of marriage.

Ask questions to help you gain a better perspective and understanding of the situation.[27] At this point, some counselees might be fearful of retribution from the abusive spouse or feel they are betraying their spouse by answering your questions. Help the abused understand that sharing their story is not a betrayal of their spouse. Ed Welch notes, "It is *not* a betrayal of the perpetrator. Instead, one goal is to bring the perpetrator's sin to light so he has the opportunity to turn *to* God and, as a result, turn away from God's wrath."[28]

If the abused decides to leave the abuser, utilize all the resources at your disposal (e.g., benevolence fund, deacon fund, etc.) to help them find food and shelter. Remember that our faith is an active faith, so wise words should be accompanied by good deeds (James 2:14).

---

24. Bruce Ashford, J. D. Greear, and Brad Hambrick, "4 Myths about Responding to Spousal Abuse," May 2018, *Christianity Today*: https://www.christianitytoday.com/pastors/2018/may-web-exclusives/4-myths-about-responding-to-spousal-abuse.html.

25. Darby Strickland, "Counseling in the Brambles: How to Help Oppressive Marriages," *Journal of Biblical Counseling* 30, no. 3 (2016): 37.

26. For additional reading on the topic of divorce in abusive marriages, I would recommend Jim Newheiser, *Marriage, Divorce and Remarriage: Critical Questions and Answers*, 259–65; and David Instone-Brewer, *Divorce and Remarriage in the Church: Biblical Solutions for Pastoral Realities*, 93–106. The scope of this chapter does not allow for questions related to the biblical arguments for/against divorce/separation in cases of abuse.

27. The Holcombs have a list of questions in their book *Is It My Fault?* on pages 32–35. Leslie Vernick has a downloadable survey you can use at her website: http://www.leslievernick.com/pdfs/Relationship-test.pdf.

28. Edward T. Welch, "Living with an Angry Husband," *Journal of Biblical Counseling* 24, no. 4 (2006): 48.

Do not handle this situation on your own. Early on, you will need to identify and get help from a variety of people, including: medical professionals, legal professionals, counselors, law enforcement, etc.

Pray with your counselee. It might seem inconsequential to you, but this powerful act of prayer is most likely something they haven't experienced before. Pray specifically, powerfully, and expectantly for God to draw near to the abused.

Heavenly Father,

I come to you this afternoon and ask for your help in the midst of Lucy's trouble. Father, you know her, you created her, and you love her. Help her right now in this moment to sense your presence and care. I pray that she knows that you see her, hear her, and have a plan to rescue her from evil.

Amen.

What should you do with spouses who choose to remain in abusive relationships? First, do not condemn or shame. The dynamics of seeking to separate from an abuser are incredibly complex. Leaving an abuser does not necessarily mean that the abuse ends. Justin and Lindsey Holcomb note, "Domestic abuse does not end immediately with separation from the abuser. Over 75% of separated women suffer post-separation abuse."[29] While separation from the abuser is recommended, that is not always what the abused chooses. Chuck DeGroat writes, "A decision to stay in a relationship with an abuser requires significant spiritual/emotional strength. They have an internal strength and sense of identity (rooted deeply in Christ, not in the devastating "arrows to the heart" from the abuser). This choice often comes after significant self-assessment in relationship with wise counselors and pastors. It also comes in the context of community looking in on her well-being. When or why she should stay is not answered by filling out a checklist, but by working through some pretty heavy questions and with very wise counsel."[30]

LONG-TERM CARE

Counselors need to understand that the process of helping the abused and the abuser will most likely be a long-term process. This is not a situation where you offer a few words of care and then pass them off to another individual. Stay the

29. Holcomb and Holcomb, *Is It My Fault?*, 64.
30. Chuck DeGroat, "Identity, Abuse, and Cruciformity: Does 'Being Like Jesus' Mean Staying with an Abuser?," May 25, 2005. https://chuckdegroat.net/2009/05/25/identity-abuse-and-cruciformity-does-being-like-jesus-mean-staying-with-an-abuser/.

course, be steady, and offer wise care to the abused. I would also encourage individual counseling for the abuser, if they are willing. Additionally, I would encourage pastors and counselors to wait for a significant amount of time to allow for a period of authentic repentance and change. Abusers are manipulative, cunning, and comfortable with patterns of deceit. Beware of supporting the abuser at the expense of your care for the abused too early in the process.[31]

Those who have been victims and survivors of abuse will need counseling as well. Necessary elements of this counseling journey will include helping them understand their true identity in Christ, offering validation and belief of their story, and clarifying the abused individual's responsibility as it relates to their abuser.

Identity

An abuser is extremely adept at belittling and bullying. Often this leads to a complete loss of identity. As a pastor, you need to help them see that their story matters to God and that they are more than their abuse. The abuse they have suffered should not be the primary lens through which they view themselves. They are created and loved by God. That's what matters most.

Many spouses who are in abusive relationships feel like they are going crazy. This is due to the incessant and often subtle patterns of abuse and oppression that their spouse puts them through. This classic *turning of tables* creates a sense of disorientation. Darby Strickland writes, "Their oppressors convince them they are the ones to blame for the problems in the marriage and even the cause of their own abuse. Victims hear things like: 'You don't know what you are doing,' 'You're crazy,' 'I had to keep you in line!,' or 'If you listened to me, I wouldn't have had to get your attention this way.' To survive, they must placate the endless demands and whims of the oppressor."[32]

The experience of shame is a powerful one for those who have been abused. Many have endured this abuse for a long period of time and have felt too powerless and embarrassed to come forward. Display the powerful love of Christ by moving toward them and affirming their decision to expose the evil deeds of the abuser (Eph. 5:11).

Validation and belief

In many contexts of abuse, the abused spouse can encounter situations where their story is not believed or validated. In counseling, I find many pastors are averse to the victim mentality common in our culture. An unintended consequence

---

31. http://bradhambrick.com/manipulative-repentance-8-red-flag-phrases/.
32. Strickland, "Counseling in the Brambles," 31–32.

of this dynamic is that pastors and counselors may evidence skepticism when people share stories of abuse. Pastor, when someone comes and shares their story of abuse, this is not the time to express skepticism or disbelief. Comments like "I can't believe _____ would act like that. He seems like such a nice guy" or "Do you think you might be overreacting?" or "What did you do that brought on this reaction?" are harmful. Holcomb explains, "Blaming victims for post-traumatic symptoms is not only erroneous but also contributes to the vicious cycle of traumatization because victims who experience negative social reactions have poorer adjustment. Research has proven that being believed and being listened to by others are crucial to victim's healing."[33]

Here is a sample dialogue of what this validation might look like:

Lucy, I'm sincerely sorry for what has happened to you. I cannot even imagine the suffering and the hurt you have been through. I believe you, and I want you to know that what happened to you was not your fault. You did not do anything to deserve this. I also want you to know you have not been forgotten by God. You are not getting what you deserve. The evil that was done to you will be held accountable by God. I want you to hear that from me and know that today. I'm thankful you had the courage to come and share this with me. Thank you.

Clarify responsibility

Once you have addressed a number of the immediate needs discussed earlier in the chapter and conducted a thorough assessment of the abused person's situation, part of your long-term care is caring for their soul. Part of that long-term care is helping the abused spouse clarify their responsibility in relationship to their spouse. Many spouses who have experienced abuse will seek to understand *why* their spouse did what they did. In many cases, they will continue to believe they did something to bring on the abuse, perhaps believing the lie that they deserved it. Pastoral counseling must draw their gaze to Christ. The abused is *not* responsible for their spouse's controlling and abusive behavior. Darby Strickland explains how this misunderstanding finds its way into the mind of the abused:

Sometimes, an oppressed wife will make excuses for her husband's brutality—especially at first. Or she might take responsibility for the oppression. This might baffle you, but remember she may have been deceived and manipulated into thinking that the abuse is her fault. Help her reframe her story, but do not expect her to see her spouse's behavior with the same clarity you

---

33. Holcomb and Holcomb, *Is It My Fault?*, 202.

have. Be patient as she oscillates between seeing her husband's domination and defending his behavior. The guilt and responsibility laid upon her for his sin or happiness ensnares her. Therefore, we need to help her see key truths about the reality of her situation. She needs to learn that she is not responsible for her husband's sin.[34]

Abuse of any kind—emotional, spiritual, physical, sexual, economic—is evil and wrong. Pastors and counselors must be unequivocal in condemning such behavior as it is entirely opposed to the sacrificial love of our Savior. Counseling those in abusive relationships is one of the most difficult situations we encounter in counseling, and it requires a pastoral counselor to marshal all the resources at their disposal to bring help, hope, and healing to bear. May God equip us well for this task.

Counselor Fieldnotes

As Jonathan has already said, marriage counseling should at least pause, if not end, when a pattern of abuse is present. Abuse undermines marriage counseling because one of the people in the room (the abuser) will use the counseling relationship itself to abuse, manipulate, humiliate, or otherwise wound the other party. The abusive spouse might attempt to form an alliance with the counselor against the other spouse, may quote the counselor out of context outside the counseling session to manipulate or control (counselors call this "weaponizing" their words), or may subtly intimidate through words or body language that wouldn't even be noticeable to the counselor, but would send an extremely clear message to their partner. Until a perpetrator of abuse is able to recognize, own, hate, and completely reject these patterns of coercive control, marriage counseling is unsafe and inadvisable. Further, marriage counseling at this point in the relationship reinforces the myth that the problem is a marriage problem, when it is really a sinful oppression problem.

Marriage counseling should generally only resume if and when *both* counselees and their counselors agree that safety has been restored and there is little likelihood of the counseling relationship being subverted by the previously abusive partner. Typically, this is accompanied by the acknowledged repentance of the perpetrator, including the abuser's recognition and

---

34. Strickland, "Counseling in the Brambles," 34.

ownership of abusive patterns of behavior, and his or her hatred and rejection of that behavior. Usually, this fruit of repentance is evidenced over a relatively prolonged period of time in the context of community. There are no shortcuts to repentance, but the Scriptures remind us that the difference between godly sorrow and worldly sorrow becomes evident over time (Prov. 26:24–26, Luke 6:43–45, 2 Cor. 7:10–13).

> *Greg A. Wilson, MA, LPC-S; Lead Counselor, Soul Care Associates;*
> *Care Deacon, The Village Church, Flower Mound, Texas*

Abuse is a difficult topic to discuss and teach, but more awareness is needed. Abuse is very personal and laced with shame that leaves scars— both seen and unseen. Some church leaders seem more focused on the semantics of abuse versus the presence of abuse in a marriage. For instance, I've met pastors who question whether the term "abuse" is appropriate or whether emotional abuse exists. As Christians, I agree that we should be theologically accurate, but are we keeping the letter of the law and missing the gospel message by not loving others as God has loved us? Let's not debate on whether a certain type of abuse exists. Abuse of any form is sin, and we can rest in God's knowledge of all things.

Counselors should confront signs of a controlling relationship early on, rather than waiting until physical bruises appear. I know false allegations occur, but I find that men or women who are being abused will not easily call it abuse. In my experience, the women had become accustomed to being mistreated and were not aware of the severity of their marriage problems until their husband threatened to hurt them or actually did. In our initial conversations, we must teach a biblical understanding of leadership and submission, which has been critical for women who believed submission meant accepting whatever treatment they received without complaint. In some instances, the husbands knew how to use the Bible in their favor, so the wives thought their husbands were being biblical. I've also met men who were abused by their wives. Believing their words is a simple but powerful response.

As a church, God tells us to care for the whole body of Christ (1 Cor. 12). We follow Christ's example in being merciful (Matt. 9:10–12). May we not be guilty of enabling sin and instead notice those who are weak.

> *Lilly Park, PhD, Assistant Professor of Biblical Counseling,*
> *Southern Baptist Theological Seminary*

RESOURCES

Bruce Ashford, J. D. Greear, and Brad Hambrick, "4 Myths About Responding to Spousal Abuse" https://www.christianitytoday.com/pastors/2018/may-web-exclusives/4-myths-about-responding-to-spousal-abuse.html

*Chuck DeGroat, "Identity, Abuse and Cruciformity" https://chuckdegroat.net/2009/05/25/identity-abuse-and-cruciformity-does-being-like-jesus-mean-staying-with-an-abuser/

Brad Hambrick, http://bradhambrick.com/abuse/

John Henderson, *Abuse: Finding Hope in Christ*

Justin S. Holcomb and Lindsey A. Holcomb, *Is It My Fault? Hope and Healing for Those Suffering Domestic Violence*

Chris Moles, *The Heart of Domestic Abuse: Gospel Solutions for Men Who Use Control and Violence in the Home*

Lilly Park, https://www.biblicalcounselingcoalition.org/2013/10/01/responding-to-emotional-abuse-in-marriage/

———, https://www.biblicalcounselingcoalition.org/2015/06/23/responding-to-abuse-part-ii/

David Powlison, *Why Me: Comfort for the Victimized*

Darby Strickland, "Counseling in the Brambles: How to Help Oppressive Marriages," *Journal of Biblical Counseling* 30, no. 3 (2016): 24–46

———, "Identifying Oppression in Marriages," *Journal of Biblical Counseling* 30, no. 2 (2016): 7–21

———, *Domestic Abuse: Help for the Sufferer*

———, *Domestic Abuse: Recognize, Respond, Rescue*

Leslie Vernick, *The Emotionally Destructive Marriage: How to Find Your Voice and Reclaim Your Hope*

Edward T. Welch, "Helping the Victim of Domestic Abuse," *Journal of Biblical Counseling* 15, no. 2 (1997): 51 53

———, "Living with an angry husband," *Journal of Biblical Counseling* 24, no. 4 (2006): 46–53

———, *Shame Interrupted: How God Lifts the Pain of Worthlessness and Rejection*

*This book/resource is not written from a biblical counseling perspective.

Chapter 12

WE DON'T TALK ANYMORE

Half the world is composed of people who have something to say and can't, and the other half who have nothing to say and keep on saying it.

ROBERT FROST

When there are many words, transgression is unavoidable,
But he who restrains his lips is wise.

PROVERBS 10:19 NASB

Peter walked into the house after a stressful day at the office eager to sit down and relax on the couch. As he unlocked the door, he could hear the kids fighting over an iPad, but he quietly ignored their perennial argument. Coming in the door, he yelled a quick, "I'm home!" to Sandra and got a faint reply from upstairs. Peter plopped on the couch, turned on the TV, and began mindlessly scrolling through ESPN scores.

Meanwhile, Sandra was upstairs folding laundry. She knew she should not have procrastinated on the kids' laundry, but here she was on a Friday night folding six loads of laundry. She heard Peter come in from work, and she was secretly hoping he would come upstairs so they could talk about the fight they had earlier in the week.

"Peter! Can you come up and give me a hand for a second?" Sandra yelled.

"What? I can't hear you." Peter replied half-heartedly.

Sandra trudged downstairs, "Well if you turned off the TV for a second you could hear me!"

"Oh, not this again!"

"What's that supposed to mean?" Sandra fumed.

"I just got home from work, and you're already on me about something. Can't you just give me a break for a few minutes?"

"Oh, that's right, because I have been taking breaks all day while you've been working," Sandra retorted.

Peter replied, "That's not what I said, but that's your specialty right? Putting words in my mouth." At this point, Peter looked down at his phone, pretending to ignore Sandra, who was now standing right in front of him. Sandra glared back, "Fine. Go spend time with your real lover."

Peter rolled his eyes and grunted something unintelligible to Sandra. Sandra stomped upstairs, holding back hot tears. How did this escalate in minutes? Why couldn't she and Peter have a simple conversation without it devolving into a fight? Sandra shook her head and headed back to folding laundry, wondering how they had gotten to this place in their relationship.

COMMUNICATION PROBLEMS ARE HEART PROBLEMS

In ten years of marriage counseling, almost every single case I have counseled involved communication problems. From couples who have no communication to couples who have horrible communication, couples struggle to know how to communicate. You are undoubtedly counseling couples on issues related to this as well. Communication is a staple of premarital counseling for a reason—so many marriage problems are communication problems. Building on the foundation we laid in chapter two, it will not surprise you that communication problems are ultimately heart problems.

James addresses this topic in his brief letter when he writes,

The tongue is a small part of the body, but it makes great boasts. Consider what a great forest is set on fire by a small spark. The tongue also is a fire, a world of evil among the parts of the body. It corrupts the whole body, sets the whole course of one's life on fire, and is itself set on fire by hell. All kinds of animals, birds, reptiles and sea creatures are being tamed and have been tamed by mankind, but no human being can tame the tongue. It is a restless evil, full of deadly poison. With the tongue we praise our Lord and Father, and with it we curse human beings, who have been made in God's likeness. Out of the same mouth come praise and cursing. My brothers and sisters, this should not be.

James 3:5–10

James wants the reader to understand clearly that the tongue is a powerful instrument. Toward the end of the section, James acknowledges a hypocrisy that should not be present amongst his readers: a tongue that can bless God but curse people. It's a clear allusion to Jesus's teaching in Luke 6:43–45: "No good tree bears bad fruit, nor does a bad tree bear good fruit. Each tree is recognized by its own fruit. People do not pick figs from thornbushes, or grapes from briers. A good man brings good things out of the good stored up in his heart, and an evil man brings evil things out of the evil stored up in his heart. For the mouth speaks what the heart is full of."

Both James and Jesus acknowledge two incontrovertible truths:

1. What is inside the heart will come out in speech, and
2. good communication cannot come out of an ungodly heart.

This teaching goes directly against what most spouses will tell you in marriage counseling.

- "If Kyle actually listened to what I said, I wouldn't have to yell."
- "If Laura didn't keep nagging and pressing me to talk, I wouldn't lose my patience with her."
- "I have to get angry with Carolyn so she actually pays attention to what I have to say."
- "Stephen only understands one language: condescending. You get what you give, so I don't know why he's so surprised when we fight."

Notice the implicit theology in each scenario I just mentioned: a lack of godly communication is *because* of their spouse's ungodly communication. There is a passing of responsibility. What each spouse fails to recognize is that their spouse's ungodly communication is only the *occasion* and not the *cause* of their own ungodly communication.

Here is one way I will illustrate it for couples: I'll take a water bottle and squeeze it until water gushes out the top. Then I'll ask them why water came out of the bottle, and inevitably they will respond, "Because you squeezed it." To which I will reply, "No, the reason water came out of the bottle is because water was *inside* the bottle. The squeezing is only the occasion or the catalyst to release what was already inside.[1] The reason why husbands and wives have ungodly communication is that there is a heart problem.

---

1. I'm not sure where this illustration originated, but I'm indebted to both David Powlison and Paul Tripp for their use of this practical visual.

Until couples understand this principle, any attempts at providing communication principles and techniques will be like stapling fresh, vibrant, healthy fruit on a rotten, dying, unhealthy tree. Yes, you can do some speaker-listener exercises or role-playing, but until couples understand that communication begins in the heart, you will not make any lasting headway into their communication problems. Winston Smith summarizes, "We must realize that the war against sin is not simply *inter*personal, but *intra*personal. Our first responsibility in battling against sin is in waging war against ourselves."[2]

COMMUNICATION PROBLEMS ARE IDENTITY PROBLEMS

Once you've taught a biblical theology of communication—that it comes from the heart—you can begin to address the *why* of communication problems. *Why* do couples have communication problems? To answer and address this issue, we turn to the letter to the Ephesians, where the apostle Paul spends a significant amount of time discussing our speech and communication. He spends the first three chapters grounding our identity, which flows out of our union with Christ. Because we are in Christ, we should live lives worthy of that identity and calling (cf. 4:1–3). He goes on to say that our communication plays a critical role in our spiritual maturity. "Speaking the truth in love, we will grow to become in every respect the mature body of him who is the head, that is, Christ. From him the whole body, joined and held together by every supporting ligament, grows and builds itself up in love, as each part does its work" (Eph. 4:15–16).

As Paul continues, it becomes clear that this lofty vision of God's people being built up in Christ does not always happen. He acknowledges not only the possibility of living like our old selves but also the reality that this often happens! Because we slip into living like our old selves, we must proactively *put off* the old ways associated with the old nature, and *put on* new ways and patterns of life, which flow from our relationship and union with Christ: "You were taught, with regard to your former way of life, to put off your old self, which is being corrupted by its deceitful desires; to be made new in the attitude of your minds; and to put on the new self, created to be like God in true righteousness and holiness" (Eph. 4:22–24).

The reason husbands and wives have communication problems is because they have identity problems. *If communication problems are heart problems, then*

---

2. Winston T. Smith, "Getting the Big Picture of Relationships," *Journal of Biblical Counseling* 22, no. 3 (2004): 12.

communication problems are also identity problems. Paul is helping us see that you cannot fulfill and live this new life in Christ while still trying to hold on to your old way of life. It's one or the other.

COMMUNICATION PROBLEMS LEAD
TO RELATIONAL PROBLEMS

Paul loses no time in illustrating what this putting off and putting on will look like in Christian relationships and, by extension, Christian marriages. It should not surprise us that the mix of issues he describes in the latter half of Ephesians 4 are overwhelmingly related to our communication.

> Each of you must put off falsehood and speak truthfully to your neighbor, for we are all members of one body. "In your anger do not sin": Do not let the sun go down while you are still angry, and do not give the devil a foothold. Anyone who has been stealing must steal no longer, but must work, doing something useful with their own hands. . . . Do not let any unwholesome talk come out of your mouths, but only what is helpful for building others up according to their needs, that it may benefit those who listen. . . . Get rid of all bitterness, rage and anger, brawling and slander, along with every form of malice. Be kind and compassionate to one another, forgiving each other, just as in Christ God forgave you.
>
> *Ephesians 4:25–29, 31–32*

Paul gives us insight into several communication issues that will be imminently useful to you in marriage counseling. First, he identifies the problem of deceitfulness in our communication. Paul commands us to speak truthfully to our neighbor (and our spouses are most definitely our neighbors). It sounds so simple, but truthfulness between husband and wife doesn't always happen. Here are a few ways couples fail to practice truthfulness with one another:

Outright lies: This happens in marriage more than most couples let on. Think of this common one with couples in crisis: "Are you mad at me right now?" How many times do spouses respond dishonestly to this question? Instead of answering in the affirmative, husbands and wives lie and say no simply to avoid conflict.

Half-truths: A wife asks her husband where he has been since he got off work at 5:30 p.m. and now it's 9:00 p.m. The husband replies, "Oh I stopped by to get some drinks with guys at work." What he does not tell his wife is that part of the time he was also having drinks with his secretary with whom he's begun an emotional affair.

Distorted truths: A husband tells his wife that they have enough money in their bank account to purchase a new vehicle, but what he doesn't tell her is that he has taken out a high-interest loan to finance the payments.

Exaggerations: A wife locked in perennial conflict with her husband lobs off an exaggerated statement, "You're the laziest person I know! You're just like your father." Is it true that her husband is lazy? Yes. Is he the laziest person she knows? Probably not.

If couples want to make progress in their communication, they must resolve to speak the truth in love with one another.

Anger is another problem that can exacerbate our struggle with communication. The NIV translates verse 26 well, stating clearly that it is possible to be angry without sin (cf. Ps. 4:4). James elaborates, "My dear brothers and sisters, take note of this: Everyone should be quick to listen, slow to speak and *slow to become angry*" (James 1:19, emphasis added). But according to Paul, anger presents a particular temptation to the Christian, and thus must be attended to diligently.

What is anger? A simple equation I use in marriage counseling is: disappointment + time = anger.

Put another way, when disappointment is not dealt with in a biblical, godly way and time is added, the inevitable result is anger. The breeding ground for anger, as with most marital issues, begins with unmet expectations and disappointment. Add a bit of time, and one can see how anger begins to germinate. Add years of marriage, and one can see how anger becomes the default method of dealing with disappointment.

Anger in our marriage affects our communication in two ways: it can intensify our communication or it can stifle our communication. I've seen one spouse's anger provoke their spouse's anger in horrific ways. I've also seen as one spouse's anger grows and intensifies, the other spouse recoils and withdraws. Either way, godly communication is truncated. What Paul advocates is neither a blowing, hot anger, nor is it a lack of anger, but an anger which knows how to express itself in a righteous, godly manner.[3] Ed Welch writes of anger, "Anger specializes in indicting others but is unskilled at both self-indictment and love."[4]

---

3. For more on this topic, I recommend David Powlison's *Good and Angry*, Ed Welch's *A Small Book About a Big Problem*, and Robert Jones's *Uprooting Anger*.
4. Edward T. Welch, *A Small Book About a Big Problem: Meditations on Anger, Patience, and Peace* (Greensboro, NC: New Growth, 2017), 11.

Third, Paul hits the communication problem head-on: the issue of unwholesome or ungodly communication. The old adage of "if you don't have something nice to say, don't say anything at all" owes a great debt to the apostle Paul. It's not simply that we miscommunicate sometimes, but our communication is often unwholesome and does not build each other up. As we saw earlier, unwholesome communication stems from a sinful heart. Imagine if people applied the following litmus test to *every* word that came out of their mouths: "Am I building up or am I tearing down?"[5] Paul's admonition toward godly communication means we must be attentive to not only the content of our words but also how we communicate, how much we communicate, and when we communicate.

A fourth problem that contributes to our relational problems is one that is often overlooked. It is the problem of grieving and ignoring the Holy Spirit in our communication. New Testament scholar F. F. Bruce explains, "Conversation that helps to build up the common life in Christ is a congenial instrument for the Holy Spirit to use to this end. On the other hand, conversation (or any other activity) that endangers the unity of the body of Christ 'grieves the Holy Spirit'."[6] Paul has already drawn our attention to how important the unity of the body of Christ is to God's plan for the church (Eph. 4:3–5). On a smaller scale, couples contribute to the overall unity of the body of Christ by being in unity with one another. That unity is disrupted when spouses don't walk in the power of the Holy Spirit to fulfill and discharge their calling before God. Ask couples in crisis this question and watch for their response (or lack thereof): What role does the Holy Spirit play in how you speak with one another?

In Galatians 5:22–24, Paul makes it clear the fruit believers are called to display in their lives is fruit of the *Spirit*. This means the fruit is not something we conjure up in and through our own abilities, but it grows through the power of the Holy Spirit. This is why Paul commanded believers to *walk by the Spirit* (cf. Gal. 5:16). The power of the Holy Spirit enables spouses to evaluate their words in light of our calling in Christ. The power of the Holy Spirit gives us a new power to respond biblically to problems in our marriage. The power of the Holy Spirit pours out the love of God in our hearts, reminding us that we don't have to be so needy of our spouse's affirmation and love because we are firmly rooted in the love and approval of God (cf. Rom. 5:5).

In verse 31, Paul identifies additional problems that complicate our communication: bitterness, rage, anger, brawling, slander, malice. One of these—bitterness

---

5. Julie Lowe, "Nurturing Family," 2017 CCEF National Conference.
6. F. F. Bruce, *The Epistles to the Colossians, to Philemon, and to the Ephesians* (Grand Rapids: Eerdmans, 1984), 363.

—plays a recurring role in most communication struggles. If our earlier equation of anger looked like this: disappointment + time = anger, then the "bitterness equation" looks like this: anger + time = bitterness.

All the problems Paul mentions play a significant role in our communication struggles. Whether it is sinful anger or a lack of Spirit-filled living, all of these issues prevent us from communicating to our spouses in a biblical way.

So how does a counselor address them? Is it enough to tell spouses to *put off* these behaviors and *put on* their corresponding opposite? I would maintain that it is possible but not wise. Hear me out. A couple comes in to meet with you and it's clear they are harboring bitterness against one another. You hear it; you can feel it in their voices. You open up Ephesians 4 and tell them bitterness has no place in the life of a Christian, and therefore must be eliminated. You tell them they need to forgive each other for whatever they are bitter about and move forward. Done, right? Not so fast.

I believe many couples can do this put off/put on for a period of time, but ultimately couples need a better, more weighty rationale for putting off sinful behaviors and putting on godly behaviors. The knowledge of what you *need* to do does not always lead to a transformed life. Couples need something to draw their gaze outside of the confines of their marriage to a larger vision of Christian flourishing. If you read Ephesians 4 closely, Paul gives us a fitting motivation for abandoning each ungodly habit he has identified. Below, notice a few of the reasonings or motivations (in italics) for his commands:

- Each of you must put off falsehood and speak truthfully to your neighbor, *for we are all members of one body* (v. 25).
- Anyone who has been stealing must steal no longer . . . *that they may have something to share with those in need* (v. 28).
- Do not let any unwholesome talk come out of your mouths, but only what is helpful for building others up according to their needs, *that it may benefit those who listen* (v. 29).
- Be kind and compassionate to one another, forgiving each other, *just as in Christ God forgave you* (v. 32).

These motivations provide a holistic vision for couples seeking to live out their calling together. It's not simply a better, higher-functioning marriage; it's about couples living life together in a way that helps them live the life for which they were saved.[7]

---

7. Common motivators in marriage: threat, guilt, and manipulation.

PUTTING TOGETHER A PLAN FOR HEALTHIER, BIBLICAL COMMUNICATION

Once you feel that the couple has a solid foundation on which to build—they know that communication problems are both heart problems and identity problems— you can begin to erect a structure, a plan to help couples communicate in a way that honors God. What I've included below represents relational commitments to which you are calling couples to engage.

A commitment to communicate according to biblical principles

I will not expand on this extensively, but as a counselor, you are seeking a commitment from both spouses to communicate in a way that embodies the teaching we highlighted at the beginning of the chapter. Couples should commit to not blaming their sinful communication on each other, but rather take personal responsibility for sinful words and actions.

A commitment to say something good about the other spouse

One of the patterns we learn from Paul is that even when he has something critical or difficult to say to his audience, he always includes something good about them at the beginning of the letter. Think of the church at Corinth, a church rife with problems. Even there, Paul acknowledges at the beginning that they have been given grace in Christ Jesus (1 Cor. 1:4), enriched in every way with knowledge and speech (1:5), and do not lack any spiritual gift (1:7). Encourage couples to begin their conversations with encouragement and affirmation. I find even couples at the absolute bottom of the barrel can find at least one ray of encouragement. For some couples it's as simple as, "Thank you for coming to counseling with me." At the beginning don't be surprised if the encouragements or affirmations are more superficial or boilerplate (e.g., "You're a good mom" or "You're a good dad"). Over time, as the relationship strengthens, I find there is more depth and richness to the encouragement.

A commitment to talk about communication

This commitment may seem redundant. Talk about how you talk? Exactly. Most couples don't have a plan or any sort of framework to guide their communication. To help couples begin this process, I assign what I call the Communication Covenant (CC). The CC is created by the couple after spending time in the book of Proverbs and paying attention to what the authors have to say about communication. At the start, I typically narrow their focus to Proverbs 15–18 and ask them to develop fifteen CC principles that, by God's grace and the Spirit's power, they will seek to embody.

For example, CC Principle 1: We will seek to choose a time that is wise and appropriate for our communication. We will seek to learn what time is best to approach our spouse. This takes investigation and patience on our part. "A person finds joy in giving an apt reply—and how good is a timely word!" (Prov. 15:23).

After couples have formed their CC, I ask them to type it up or even get it professionally printed so that they can post it somewhere in their home where its visibility will serve as a helpful visual reminder to them.

A commitment to look inward before looking outward

Before couples engage in conversation that is oriented toward conflict resolution, each spouse must commit to taking personal responsibility for their words and actions. Matthew 7:1–5 describes the folly of seeking to pick out a speck in someone else's eye when you have a huge log jutting out of your own eye. The image is ridiculous for a reason. You can imagine the damage done as a spouse stumbles around the house with a gigantic log in their eye. This type of relational damage happens when spouses don't look inwardly and acknowledge their part in relational conflict.

Ed Welch insightfully writes, "Imagine it—reserving our harshest judgment for ourselves. We submit to being judged before we judge."[8] How might spouses do this? Encourage them toward times of self-reflection and contemplation. Give them Psalm 139:23–24 as a template to pray to God asking for wisdom.

A commitment to stay away from communication grenades

What are communication grenades? Communication grenades are phrases we say in anger to purposely cause harm. Grenades not only decimate their target, they also often cause significant damage to the nearby environment. What are some common communication grenades couples need to stay away from?[9]

- Grenades of hate
  - I'm done with you.
  - Go to hell.
  - I don't love you anymore.
  - I want a divorce.

---

8. Welch, *A Small Book About a Big Problem*, 14–15.

9. If and when any of these "communication grenades" are used during a counseling session, I immediately stop and seek to address it. While you want to provide a place for spouses to speak openly and honestly, you do not want to allow such unbiblical communication to happen in front of you without some sort of intervention. Sometimes couples have become so accustomed to using some of these phrases that they fail to recognize how sinful their communication has become.

- ○ I hate you.
- ○ You're stupid.
- Global grenades
  - ○ You've never loved me.
  - ○ We don't have anything in common.
  - ○ You always run away from the conversation.
  - ○ You never stand up for me.
  - ○ I'm the only one who puts up with your crap, and I'm done with it.
- Catastrophic grenades
  - ○ You're ruining my life!
  - ○ You're suffocating me!
- Generalizing grenades
  - ○ You're such a lazy person.
  - ○ You're a bully!
  - ○ You're an insufferable human being.

A commitment to be a good listener[10]

This is a topic for another book, but we are quickly becoming a culture that is losing the art of conversation, the art of truly listening to other people. In an age of technology, we have lost the ability to connect with another human being. Everything comes to us in sound bites and blog posts. Author and MIT sociologist Sherry Turkle writes,

> During the years I have spent researching people and their relationships with technology, I have often heard the sentiment "No one is listening to me." I believe this feeling helps explain why it is so appealing to have a Facebook page or a Twitter feed—each provides so many automatic listeners. And it helps explain why—against all reason—so many of us are willing to talk to machines that seem to care about us. . . . We expect more from technology and less from one another and seem increasingly drawn to technologies that provide the illusion of companionship without the demands of relationship. Always-on/always-on-you devices provide three powerful fantasies: that we will always be heard; that we can put our attention wherever we want it to be; and that we never have to be alone. Indeed, our new devices have turned being alone into a problem that can be solved.[11]

---

10. Adam McHugh has a helpful article on "How to Be a Bad Listener": https://www.quietrev.com/be-a-bad-listener/.

11. Sherry Turkle, "The Flight from Conversation," April 21, 2012. *The New York Times*: http://www.nytimes.com/2012/04/22/opinion/sunday/the-flight-from-conversation.html.

The irony here captures one of the most consistent dynamics that comes up in marriage counseling. It's the "he doesn't talk to me/she doesn't listen to me" dynamic. Imagine if couples put their phones down for a moment and spoke face-to-face (not text-to-text). Sounds a bit scary, right?

Part of committing to being a better listener includes asking questions in response to what your spouse says. I try to give husbands and wives a few sample phrases they can learn to help sharpen their listening skills:

- Thank you for sharing that.
- Did I hear you correctly?
- Is there anything you'd like to add?
- Tell me more!
- Am I making a fair observation based on what you just said?
- Do you mind if I summarize what I believe I heard you say?
- How can I grow in our communication?

Communication problems arise out of our hearts and our identity. When we use our words sinfully, they come from a heart that is living out an old identity, not the new way of Christ. Our words are powerful; James calls our tongue the most powerful part of our body. What we speak about shows us what we love, what we value, and what we are fundamentally about as a couple. Couples must not only unlearn bad communication principles, they must also embody what the Bible has to say about our communication. When couples infuse their words with grace, they will often find that "gracious words are a honeycomb, sweet to the soul and healing to the bones" (Prov. 16:24).

One Couple's Story

When we reflect on the biblical marriage counseling we received, we recall when our eyes, ears, and hearts were opened to better comprehend that instead of pointing fingers at one another for what each of us felt the other was doing wrong in our marriage and focusing on all of his or her faults, we each needed to prayerfully consider our own relationship with God.

We learned we needed to ask ourselves, "What isn't right in my own walk with the Lord?," which was not always an easy question to ask or answer.

We learned if our own walk with Jesus wasn't where it should be, then our marriage wouldn't be all that God intended it to be and wouldn't glorify God.

Considering our own walk with Jesus was eye-opening and proved to be true. Over the years, we have often prayed about Matthew 7:1–5, and we have to continually pray to ask God to help each of us look at our own self when we become frustrated with one another and only want to focus on his or her flaws. These verses and teachings have improved not only our marriage but more importantly our relationships with Christ.

Jim and Kristina Risk

Counselor Fieldnotes

Good communication is always hard work. It's tempting to want to offer couples "techniques" for better communication. It's easy to understand why this is so commonly done. Most couples seeking help want a quick fix that will solve our problems, and as counselors we want to be the hero of those seeking help. Jonathan has well pointed out that the problem in communication is mostly a problem of our hearts and motivations. Unfortunately, we can often communicate something we meant to hide—our internal bitterness, anger, resentment, fear, malice, or disrespect. While we all communicate, we don't always communicate well.

I find it very helpful, both personally and professionally, to approach communication problems in marriage with great weakness and humility. The difficulty of trying to understand what someone else is saying and to communicate our own thoughts and feelings is one of the unending reminders that we are profoundly finite and self-centered. Therefore, if understanding is to come to us, we must rely on the supernatural resources available to us through the Holy Spirit in order to get what only comes through him: truth, a knowledge of someone else's spirit, and an ability to become a selfless servant. I had Philippians 2:1–7 engraved in my wife's wedding ring as my commitment to her. Obeying Paul's charge offers a great guideline for communication. Oh, that I would remember it more often.

As counselors we have a unique privilege and responsibility to help the couples we serve discover how to listen carefully and seek clarity. Modeling for the couple how to listen well and draw out understanding can be one of our greatest contributions and an act of service as we seek to love well the couples God entrusts to us.

Greg Cook, Soul Care Pastor, Christ Chapel Bible Church,

Fort Worth, Texas

RESOURCES

Brad Hambrick, http://bradhambrick.com/wp-content/uploads/2016/12/240-Marital-Conversations.pdf

Adam S. McHugh, *The Listening Life: Embracing Attentiveness in a World of Distraction*

Ken Sande, *The Peacemaker: A Biblical Guide to Resolving Personal Conflict*

Paul David Tripp, *War of Words: Getting to the Heart of Your Communication Struggles*

———and Timothy S. Lane, *Relationships: A Mess Worth Making*

Chapter 13

THE KIDS ARE NOT ALL RIGHT

Watch yourselves closely so that you do not forget the things your eyes have seen or let them fade from your heart as long as you live. Teach them to your children.

DEUTERONOMY 4:9

The key to being used by God with your children is to start with your own heart.

PAUL DAVID TRIPP

Hi Pastor Holmes, it's Pam. Do you have a few minutes to talk about Kyle?"

We've all been there. As soon as they call, you get that sense that something is not right. As you talk to Pam, she shares how Kyle, her sixteen-year-old son, sneaked out of the house with some friends from high school. The next day when Pam and her husband, Rocky, confronted Kyle about what happened, it came out that Kyle and his friends were drinking. Rocky was furious, and immediately told Kyle he was grounded and that he had to quit the basketball team. Pam, while supportive of Rocky, wasn't sure this was the right path and tried to intervene on Kyle's behalf. But that only made the situation worse.

While there are many issues that put pressure on marriages, I find that issues related to the couples' children present a unique opportunity for heartbreak and trouble. A noted clinical psychologist writes, "For around 30 years, researchers have studied how having children affects a marriage, and the results are conclusive: the relationship between spouses suffers once kids come along. Comparing couples with and without children, researchers found that the rate of the decline in relationship satisfaction is nearly twice as steep for couples who have children than for childless couples. . . . The irony is that even as the marital satisfaction of new parents declines, the likelihood of them divorcing also declines. So, having children may make you miserable, but you'll be miserable together."[1]

This doesn't sound too encouraging, does it? For years, husband and wife invest time, energy, resources, and love into their kids, only to find themselves heartbroken when their children make decisions that put them at odds with the family's values and faith.

I have sat with couples who have wept over their children and the choices they are making. I have sat and listened as couples have been embroiled in conflict over how best to deal with their children. In some cases I have seen marriages fall apart over disagreements on how to parent and handle consequences. Longtime biblical counselor and author Wayne Mack identifies the irony: "Strange as it may seem . . . children can be a magnetic force drawing married people together or a wedge that drives them apart."[2]

As a pastor, caregiver, or friend, we all need principles from God's Word to guide our counsel. Without these foundational principles, couples can feel unmoored and hopeless. Your tendency as a counselor may be to offer a solution or quick fix to the problem, but don't miss an opportunity to encourage and strengthen parents in their God-given calling.

GOD CALLED YOU TO BE A PARENT[3]

After their relationship with God, the married couple's primary responsibility is to their relationship as husband and wife; however, husbands and wives with children also bear the callings of father and mother. In Ephesians 4, Paul starts off with the broadest and most general of the callings, that of a believer, and slowly narrows it down—husbands and wives (5:22–33), then parents and children (6:1–4). He gives encouragement and instructions for such relationships based on the confidence that God never calls us to a task without also giving us the grace to fulfill it.

What does God's calling as a parent entail exactly? Listen to what Moses commands of parents in Deuteronomy: "Love the LORD your God with all your

---

1. Matthew D. Johnson, "Decades of Studies Show What Happens to Marriages after Kids," May 9, 2016. *Fortune*: http://fortune.com/2016/05/09/mothers-marriage-parenthood/.

2. Wayne A. Mack, *Strengthening Your Marriage* (Phillipsburg, NJ: P&R, 1999), 139.

3. The scope of this chapter does not allow us to cover a biblical theology of parenting. For resources on that, consult the list at the end of the chapter. The goal of this chapter is to address difficult and complex parenting issues that can negatively impact marriages.

heart and with all your soul and with all your strength. These commandments that I give you today are to be on your hearts. Impress them on your children. *Talk* about them when you sit at home and when you walk along the road, when you lie down and when you get up. Tie them as symbols on your hands and bind them on your foreheads. Write them on the doorframes of your houses and on your gates" (Deut. 6:5–9, emphasis added).

What Moses tells parents here is critical. Teaching our children involves two key principles out of which everything else flows: who God is and what it means to love him. Moses says these two things are to be impressed on our children.

How do we do this, you might ask? By taking them to church and Sunday school? Getting them into a good youth group? Homeschooling them? No. Moses says parents should *talk* about God's truths *all the time*. The implication is that the home life should be oriented toward teaching children about God. The actual conversations in the home have this as their goal. This has radical implications for parents and their everyday conversations. There is no such thing as "spiritual" talk and "nonspiritual talk." In fact, the book of Proverbs is a prime example of this holistic approach to teaching our children. The book of Proverbs comes to us essentially as a dialogue between a father and mother and their son.[4] One common proverb on teaching and training children is Proverbs 22:6: "Start children off on the way they should go, and even when they are old they will not turn from it."

A variety of interpretations attend this verse, ranging from some saying this means you should parent children according to their personality, to others who maintain you should parent your children according to biblical principles. Tim and Kathy Keller write that the ambiguity might be purposeful: "One of the great mysteries is why some children when they are old embrace their parent training and others do not. Whose fault is it if a child's life goes 'off the rails'?"[5] The Kellers go on to note that sometimes the foolish adult is the result of parental neglect (Prov. 29:15) while others simply choose not to heed their parents' instruction (Prov. 13:1; 17:21).

Tim and Kathy conclude, "So according to Proverbs, there are three factors that determine the way a child grows up—the hearts they are born with (nature), the quality of the parenting they receive (nurture), and their own choices. The three interact in complex ways that no one can control, except God himself (cf. 21:1). A parent's final but most powerful resource, then, is prayer to the God who opens hearts."[6]

---

4. Timothy and Kathy Keller, *God's Wisdom for Navigating Life: A Year of Daily Devotions in the Proverbs* (New York: Viking, 2017), 249.

5. Ibid., 279.

6. Ibid.

As parents consider the Mosaic imperative to *talk* about the commandments of the Lord, what is a good place to begin? Several months ago, author Tedd Tripp came to our church to conduct a seminar on parenting. There were many things he shared over the course of the weekend that impacted how my wife and I evaluate our own parenting. Tedd had one line, though, that made an indelible impact on my thinking. He said that one of our goals in parenting is to help our children *joyfully live under authority*.

Tedd went on to unpack what he meant, namely that we live life as dependent, created beings. One of the reasons why children and teens often find it hard to live under parental authority is because authority itself is generally seen as a negative, not a positive. Yet according to God's Word, living under God's authority is not only our duty but also our joy as his creatures. As a parent, I want to communicate this principle as often as I can.

DON'T BYPASS THE HEART (YOURS OR THEIRS)

Parenting is hard work, which explains why it is easier to focus on behavior and short-term results at the expense of the heart. Think of your everyday parenting struggles. Imagine your kids are yelling and fighting over the iPad. As you're trying to get dinner prepared, you yell at both kids to get along or you'll take away screen time from both of them for a week. The kids quickly quiet down, and you finish making dinner. It's a win, right? Sure, you get dinner on the table, but over time, if this is the predominant pattern of your parenting, you will miss a valuable opportunity to shape their hearts.

Heart work is hard work. This is one of the reasons why it seems easier to utilize external motivators when parenting: manipulation, guilt, and threats seem to get quick results. Paul David Tripp pinpoints the problem with this solution: "If I could turn the human heart by the force of my voice, the strength of my personality, the logic of my argument, or the wisdom of my parenting strategies, then Jesus would never have needed to come."[7]

Not only do we feel the urge to bypass the hearts of our children, we simultaneously bypass our own desires and motives. Let's go back to the mother making dinner in the scene above. What is going on in her heart? What motives, desires, or expectations does she need to examine? Perhaps it is a desire for peace and quiet, which is a good desire, but one that can come at the expense of loving her children

---

7. Paul David Tripp, "What is 'Success' in Parenting Teens?" *Journal of Biblical Counseling* 23, no. 3 (2005): 19.

well. It could be a desire for ease, and the children's fighting is making it harder for her to concentrate and get dinner on the table in a timely manner.[8]

Many couples might not be prepared for you to ask *them* questions about their hearts and motives when they come with questions about parenting. They are looking for help with their child, not a counseling session for their marriage. In a spirit of gentleness and humility, when the time is right, it's good to ask some of these questions about *their* hearts. You're not trying to blame them for their children's problems; you are seeking to help them see the problem from an angle they might not have considered. Additionally, they, not their children, are likely the ones sitting in your office, and thus the most progress can be made initially with them.

ENTRUST YOUR CHILDREN TO GOD

Peter writes in 1 Peter 2:23, "Instead, [Jesus] entrusted himself to him who judges justly." Contextually, Peter is saying that Jesus, in the midst of circumstances that were hard and downright unfair, ultimately entrusted himself and his future to God. This in no way minimized the pain and suffering Jesus encountered as he made his way to the cross, but there was a profound submission to the Father's will, which enabled him to stand up under that suffering (cf. John 6:38).

This principle is one I seek to teach and leave with my couples who are in difficult parenting situations. A diagram, which I have adapted from Paul Tripp, helps husbands and wives conceptualize this principle.

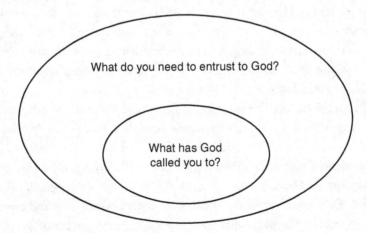

What do you need to entrust to God?

What has God called you to?

---

8. Paul David Tripp identifies a number of idols that can drive parents, including but not limited to: comfort, respect, appreciation, success, and control (Andreas J. Köstenberger with David W. Jones, *God Marriage, and Family: Rebuilding the Biblical Foundation*, 2nd ed. [Wheaton, IL: Crossway, 2010], 150).

First, you want to help husbands and wives discern what God has created them for and subsequently called them to do. Their calling comes from Scripture, and God gives them grace to fulfill their calling (not someone else's calling). You can help couples list their callings in life, starting with their primary role. For example, someone would list their callings as:

1. Child of God (Eph. 4:1–3)
2. Husband (Eph. 5:26–27)/Wife (Eph. 5:22)
3. Father[9]/Mother[10] (Eph. 6:1–4)
4. Employee at work (Eph. 6:5–9)[11]

Notice that each of these callings is not only sequential but also builds on the others. In Paul's thinking, a godly husband is a godly Christian. A godly father is first a committed Christian and husband. Often in times of parental crisis, it will be tempting for couples to neglect their *primary* calling (husband and wife) to fulfill their *secondary* calling as parents.

Time after time, I find that parents do best by their children when they are each committed to and in unity with each other. Couples, you will not do your children any favors by prioritizing your children above your spouse, whom God has given you. That does not mean that parents will not have disagreements, but couples should endeavor to work through those disagreements in a way that honors and pleases God, thus telling a powerful story of unity to their children.

I cannot tell you how many times I have seen marriages fall apart because the pressure point of children bears down on the fault lines that were *already present* in the marriage relationship. Fault lines form when couples don't actively seek to be unified in the Spirit and by the Spirit. Let me say that again—wayward, rebellious children do not cause marriages to fall apart. What they do is reveal the sinful bent of our human hearts.

Back to the circles! The inner circle shapes and informs our callings. With each calling there are duties and obligations. To neglect those responsibilities is not to fulfill the calling God has given us. Unfortunately, we often choose to *shrink* the outer circle of entrusting things to God and artificially *expand* the inner circle of calling and responsibility into areas for which we are not designed, called, or equipped. This simultaneous shrinking of the outer circle of trust and expansion of the inner circle of responsibility can cause a significant number of issues.

9. Cf. 2 Cor. 12:14; Col. 3:21; Heb. 12:6.
10. Cf. 1 Tim. 2:15; 5:14.
11. Not everyone is called to work outside the home.

Think with me for a moment of things related to our children that ultimately need to be placed in the outer circle of trusting God:

- Will people like my children?
- Will they have friends?
- Will they be smart? Will they be athletic? Will they be musical?
- Will they get married?
- Will they have children?
- Will they profess faith in and have a relationship with Jesus Christ?
- Will they come back to church?
- Will they get sober? Will they come out of rehab?
- Are they always going to be an addict?
- When will they get their life back on track?
- How many times are they going to do this to us?

These are all real and serious questions ranging from the everyday concerns of life to the more serious crises a person can experience. Are parents able to be influential in some of these areas? Absolutely, and they should be! (cf. Prov. 22:6) However, parents cannot control the outcomes of these areas, but must prayerfully and *practically* submit these concerns to God.

I'm convinced that part of the reason God entrusted children to our care is to teach us to submit humbly to him. If parents could determine the outcomes for their children (even good outcomes) on their own, there would be no need to rely on the power of the gospel. The author of Proverbs says,

> Trust in the LORD with all your heart
>   and lean not on your own understanding;
> in all your ways submit to him,
>   and he will make your paths straight.
> *Proverbs 3:5–6*

This proverb illustrates the dual dynamic of actively trusting the Lord to help us be obedient within the areas of our calling while actively entrusting *all* things to his care. When we put our trust in the Lord—we can trust his faithfulness, sovereignty, care, goodness, and power—then we not only fulfill our calling faithfully but also rightly place all our concerns at his feet.

This is not a "let go, let God" model by any means. Quite the opposite in fact, because to trust in the Lord means we actively submit our will to his. We actively reach out to God in prayer and dependence. We admit and confess our inability to change anyone apart from his intervention. No, this is not a passive shifting of responsibility but a proper alignment of who we are in relationship to God. Carol Floch writes, "When we entrust ourselves [and our children] to the One who is ultimately in control, and find our peace there, that is a place of great security."[12]

Take parents to places like Psalm 131, where David writes of his need to entrust things to God and find security in God:

> My heart is not proud, LORD, . . .
> I do not concern myself with great matters
>   or things too wonderful for me.
> But I have calmed and quieted myself, . . .
>   like a weaned child I am content.
> *Psalm 131:1–2*

In fact, David takes it a step further and notes that the expansion of his inner circle of responsibility into things he cannot control is actually a manifestation of pride and haughtiness! David is illustrating the need to situate himself in such a way that he is able to rest in God. The visual is striking in its portrayal. Amid "great matters" that surround David, he can calm and quiet himself like a weaned child with its mother.[13] What an amazing picture of God's tender love and care for his children![14]

Most couples you see in your office are likely exaggerating their personal circle of responsibility in a way that justifies their attempts to control, manipulate, or create outcomes they desire in their children.[15] I don't say this by way of condemnation but as an observation. Most couples don't even know this dynamic is happening.

---

12. Kathy Leonard, "Helping Parents Avoid 3 Understandable Parenting Mistakes," May 17, 2016. *Care Leader*: https://www.careleader.org/helping-parents-avoid-3-understandable-parenting-mistakes/.

13. David writes elsewhere of this in Psalm 22:9, "You made me trust in you, even at my mother's breast."

14. Job says something similar in Job 42:3, "Surely I spoke of things I did not understand, things too wonderful for me to know."

15. Harvey and Gilbert note that many parents confuse godly influence with controlling the actual outcomes of their children. "This realization that your influence and engagement with the wayward has been laced with your own sin and imperfections can then provide an opportunity for your own repentance and change. The key word here, however, is *influence*. Too many Christians unconsciously confuse the ability to influence with the power to determine an outcome. They [parents] believe that faithfully and obediently honoring your role as a parent or spouse does not merely influence but actually *determines* the outcomes of the family. This assumption makes much of humans and seriously underestimates other substantial influences such as God, the world, individual choices, and personal suffering to name a few." Dave Harvey and Paul Gilbert, *Letting Go: Rugged Love for Wayward Souls* (Grand Rapids: Zondervan, 2016), 59–60.

They have a good desire—they want their kids to be healthy, flourishing, and walking with the Lord—and they don't know that this good desire has taken over their life. Remember, a good desire becomes a bad desire when it becomes a ruling desire.

Jeff and Morgan were a couple who dearly loved one another, but their recent conflicts over their youngest son, Tyler, were causing friction. Tyler was twenty-four years old. He had been in and out of college classes with little academic (or any kind of) success. Consistently late to classes and work, he would enroll, then drop out by the end of the semester, costing Jeff and Morgan thousands of dollars in lost tuition money.

The disagreement between Jeff and Morgan did not follow the usual story of a sympathetic mother and an enforcer-of-the-rules dad. In fact, their roles were the opposite in relation to Tyler. Jeff was far more lenient with Tyler and less concerned about the funding for college. After each failed semester, they would have a serious "talk" about his future, with Tyler offering some sort of commitment to "turn things around." Meanwhile, Morgan had to find a job to help pay for Tyler's tuition. She felt her voice was not heard when she tried to set boundaries and thresholds for his academic performance. Jeff would respond, "You just need to give him some time. He's a boy trying to become a man and find himself." Morgan was tired. She could feel her heart growing bitter, not toward Tyler but toward Jeff.

When Jeff and Morgan came to me for counseling, the goal was superficial at best. Jeff wanted Morgan to be more lenient with Tyler, and Morgan wanted Tyler to stop being lazy, get a job, and pay for his own college. After spending time with them, listening to their concerns, and asking questions, we were able to reach clarity on a number of things. First, Tyler and his college tuition were not their biggest problems! (For many couples, this concept, alone, is somewhat revolutionary.) The biggest problem in marriage is always the couple's own hearts. What Jeff wanted from Morgan was more grace, more leniency, more wiggle room for error. When he didn't get that, he would get irritated and frustrated with Morgan, resorting to guilt and shame tactics to get what he wanted.

Morgan wanted to be heard. She wanted to know that she mattered to Jeff, and that her sacrifice at work mattered. When she felt her sacrifice was ignored, she became angry. Over years of mounting college tuition bills, that anger had turned to bitterness that was slowly killing their marriage. Through counseling, Jeff and Morgan were able to see that in trying to control each other and Tyler, they had neglected their primary responsibilities as believers. They needed to get back to their calling to be humble, gentle, patient, and to bear with one another in love.

By entrusting Tyler to God, Jeff and Morgan were able to realize that their gaze and their energies had been misplaced. They were better able to see that Tyler's situation needed to be entrusted to God and that their primary responsibility was to one another. Jeff and Morgan reached an agreement that was not only practical but biblically rooted. Jeff and Morgan realized that the strain on their finances was actually keeping them from (a) tithing and giving to their local church and (b) requiring Morgan to work outside the home, something she did not feel called to do. After reaching agreement and unity through prayer and conversation, Jeff and Morgan told Tyler they were cutting back on paying his tuition, but more importantly, they explained why they were cutting back.

When dads and moms live their lives as God created and intended them to be lived, they often experience a great deal of clarity. Clarity of calling is critical in situations like this. Otherwise, the counselor and pastor will be forced into arbitrating solutions and creating outcomes pragmatically but not biblically. John Piper writes eloquently yet honestly about what happens when we practice this principle of entrusting our children to God:

> This is your calling this morning. It's not merely a rule to be followed. It's a miracle to be experienced, a grace to be received. It's a promise to be believed. Do you believe, do you trust, that God sees every wrong done to you, that he knows every hurt, that he assesses motives and circumstances with perfect accuracy, that he is impeccably righteous and takes no bribes, and that he will settle all accounts with perfect justice? This is what it means to be "conscious of God" in the midst of unjust pain. If you believe this—if God is this real to you—then you will hand it over to God, and though nobody in the world may understand where your peace and joy and freedom to love is coming from, you will know. The answer is God. And sooner or later, they will know, too.[16]

NAVIGATING PARENTAL CRISIS

The couples we have discussed in this chapter have had what you might call "garden-variety" parenting struggles. These troubles are significant but not severe or critical. They are not crises. As a pastor you will encounter couples who are enduring the crisis of a prodigal child and whose hope is fading. What can you offer to couples at this stage? How does the gospel bring hope and comfort? Dave Harvey and Paul Gilbert write of the weariness of parenting a prodigal,[17] "Parents

---

16. John Piper, "He Trusted to Him Who Judges Justly," August 25, 1991. *Desiring God*: https://www.desiringgod.org/messages/he-trusted-to-him-who-judges-justly.

17. For our purposes, I will define a prodigal child as one who consistently over a prolonged period of time rejects and turns away from the biblical counsel and love of their parents. Harvey and Gilbert

of prodigals live in a world of battle fatigue. Disoriented by the stress and assaulted daily by a nameless enemy, they need time to talk their way forward through the fog of war. My job, at least at this stage, was [is] to listen."[18] This weariness—physical, emotional, and spiritual—is one of the number one characteristics I find when counseling couples who have a prodigal child. Harvey and Gilbert continue, "Few things crush the life out of us more than experiencing the remorseless rejection of someone we love."[19] This rejection often has a double sting to it: rejection of the parents and rejection of God. When couples come in with a crisis related to their child, they don't need judgment and guilt (most parents are experts in that area). They need a listening ear and biblical hope.

Couples cannot be expected to bear the burden of caring for wayward, prodigal children on their own. Pastors can and should offer care and support to parents in crisis, either directly or through someone else. Often you may know of other couples or families in your congregation who have been through similar situations. These couples' stories might not be entirely the same, but they can provide spiritual and emotional support for weary parents. Parents are going through a roller coaster of emotions, ranging from anger and frustration to numbness and fatigue.

Help couples know when to speak and when to walk away.

Couples will need the wisdom of wise people in their life to help them resolve the tension of knowing when to intervene and when to walk away. Each situation is unique and different. As a pastor, start with what you do know. Where does Scripture speak clearly and honestly?

In Jesus's interaction with the rich young man in Mark 10:17–22, it is interesting to note that after speaking the truth to the young man's question, Jesus leaves it there. Verse 21 reads, "Jesus looked at him and loved him. 'One thing you lack,' he said. 'Go, sell everything you have and give to the poor, and you will have treasure in heaven. Then come, follow me.'" The young man hears the truth and understands what is entailed, but ultimately refuses the counsel Jesus offers and walks away. Jesus does not chase him down. He looks on him with compassion and lets him leave.[20] Many times you will be encouraging parents to follow the example of Jesus—to love deeply but to walk away when appropriate.

note four characteristics of prodigals: personal irresponsibility, victim-centeredness, a declaration of independence, threat of flight (Harvey and Gilbert, *Letting Go*, 38–39). Additionally, they want choices without consequences, autonomy without accountability, and leaving without loss (Ibid., 56–58).
18. Harvey and Gilbert, *Letting Go*, 29.
19. Ibid., 32.
20. Harvey and Gilbert talk about this compassion or "rugged love" in their helpful book *Letting Go*. "Rugged love is the way God engages and reaches sinful people. We are all wayward, dead, and trapped in

At other times, an ongoing conversation is in order. Godly rebuke and confrontation might be what is needed to bring children and teens out of their rebellion. There are times when the most merciful thing parents can do is speak the truth in love.

Don't let the couple become addicted to their children's crisis.

A common theme I find when counseling couples in parental crisis is that they often become addicts. What do I mean? Some couples have been traveling the road with their wayward child for so long that their entire life is wrapped up in their child's problem or addiction. It has become their new identity.

David Sheff, a well-known journalist, published a moving memoir titled *Beautiful Boy* that relates his son's battle with meth addiction. Sheff writes, "My addiction to his addiction has not served Nic or me or anyone around me. Nic's addiction became far more compelling than the rest of my life. . . . Now I am in my own program to recover from my addiction to his."[21] How can you help couples identify whether they are becoming addicts themselves?

- Are they neglecting their primary roles as husband and wife?
- Is marital unity suffering as a result of their child?
- How much time is dedicated to discussing their child's addiction or problem?
- Is a significant amount of money and resources being poured into the problem to the point where it is adversely affecting the couple?
- Is their joy and happiness dependent on the choices their wayward child makes?
- Is their spiritual growth dependent on the decisions their child makes or does not make?
- Are they withdrawing from relationships and friendships in the church?

If the answer to many of these questions is affirmative, as a pastor you can help them see that they might need to take a step back from the situation to pause, pray, and evaluate.

---

our sin. So the way we love prodigals must be patterned after the rugged love of God. What is this rugged love? Love is rugged when it's
strong enough to face evil;
tenacious enough to do good;
courageous enough to enforce consequences;
sturdy enough to be patient;
resilient enough to forgive;
trusting enough to pray boldly" (Harvey and Gilbert, *Letting Go*, 68).
21. David Sheff, *Beautiful Boy* (Boston: Mariner, 2009), 305.

God makes no mistakes. He is sovereign, good, and wise. There will be times when couples feel they are in over their heads and that the situation with their child is impossible. They may begin to fear it is beyond the scope of God's power. During a time of trial with a couple remind them of these truths. It's your privilege to "encourage the disheartened, help the weak" (1 Thess. 5:14).

Counselor Fieldnotes

The email arrived, dripping with pain. *"Does loving my wayward addict basically mean guarding my heart from bitterness and anger?"* My answer—yes and no—may have landed like double-minded lameness, at least at first. Hopefully, this mom kept reading.

By yes, I explained, we get radical with the predictable resentment that attacks those who love a prodigal, particularly prodigals locked in substance abuse. Addiction is a world where temptations abound. For instance, it's common for addicts to blame those closest to them as the cause for their condition. Addiction, after all, is the soul's escape from reality and culpability in the pursuit of a false love. Those that love the addict—the spouses, parents, and siblings—often get thrown under the bus in the addict's self-justifying quest for indulgence. For the addict, it's a 'low-risk' disloyalty since the people they love are less apt to reject them for their betrayal. But it's painfully defiling stuff, and clearly illustrates how loving a prodigal becomes a daily battle against resentment.

When left unaddressed, bitterness dulls the experience of grace. God calls us to fight against it. "See to it that no one falls short of the grace of God and that no bitter root grows up to cause trouble and defile many" (Heb. 12:15).

But love is more than avoiding evil. This is why my yes was followed by an equally strong no.

Love means sacrificial acts of kindness. Is your addict ungrateful and doing great wrong? "Love your enemies, do good to them, and lend to them without expecting to get anything back. Then your reward will be great, and you will be children of the Most High, *because he is kind to the ungrateful and wicked*" (Luke 6: 35, emphasis mine). This means we love our prodigals not simply in how we tend our souls, but in how we actively express our love. Do we express kindness without expectations of reciprocity? Can we love through nonagenda communiqués such as expressions of affection, reminders that you are praying, or perhaps a helpful Scripture? Offers of money may not be wise, but love does not withhold relationship because of sin. Remember, it was "while we were God's enemies, we were reconciled to him through the death of his Son" (Rom. 5:10).

But there was one last thing that seemed important to say. Love does not enable evil. Addicts can often manipulate those they love because their family is more emotionally invested in the relationship. Quite frankly, they are loved more than they love, which arms them with a kind of power—an ability to exert certain controls over those who love them. This imbalance becomes the ecosystem for enabling. I told this mom that love must resist her child's leverage through the superior potency of gospel love—a love that is strong enough to face evil, courageous enough to enforce consequences, yet tenacious enough to do good.

I finished, prayed, and then sent the email. With it went my hope that God would supply resilience to the mom, repentance to her prodigal, and my prayer that I would better apply the very love of which I wrote.

Dave Harvey, President, Sojourn Network; Teaching Pastor,
Summit Church; Chairman of the Board of Directors, CCEF

RESOURCES

Nick Batzig, "Hope When Your Children Stray," https://www.thegospelcoalition.org/article/hope-when-your-children-stray/

Richard A. Burr, *Praying Your Prodigal Home: Unleashing God's Power to Set Your Loved Ones Free*

Dave Harvey and Paul Gilbert, *Letting Go: Rugged Love for Wayward Souls*

Rick Horne, *Get Outta My Face! How to Reach Angry, Unmotivated Teens with Biblical Counsel*

———, *Get Offa My Case! Godly Parenting of An Angry Teen*

Robert D. Jones, *Prodigal Children: Hope and Help for Parents*

Julie Lowe, "Seeing Relationships Through the Eyes of a Child," *Journal of Biblical Counseling* 26, no. 1 (2012): 40–45

Jim Newheiser and Elyse Fitzpatrick, *You Never Stop Being a Parent: Thriving in Relationship with Your Adult Children*

Paul David Tripp, *Parenting: 14 Gospel Principles that Can Radically Change Your Family*

———, *Age of Opportunity: A Biblical Guide to Parenting Teens*

Tedd Tripp, *Shepherding a Child's Heart*

Tedd and Margy Tripp, *Instructing a Child's Heart*

Chapter 14

SURVIVING MISCARRIAGE, INFANT LOSS, OR INFERTILITY

Death, be not proud, though some have called thee
Mighty and dreadful, for thou art not so; . . .
One short sleep past, we wake eternally
And death shall be no more; Death, thou shalt die.
JOHN DONNE

Before I formed you in the womb I knew you.
JEREMIAH 1:5

Facebook was fairly new ten years ago, but even at that time news traveled quickly. I had just posted an update, one I had dreamed of posting for a long time: "Jen and I are expecting! New baby due for arrival ____." I came into church the following Sunday, and people were giving Jen and me high fives, hugs, and congratulations. We were ecstatic. On top of the world. What we did not know was how quickly our world would come crashing down just a few weeks later.

We went to our first ultrasound appointment eager to see our baby. That moment will forever be ingrained in our memories. The ultrasound technician grew quiet. Then she excused herself to go find the doctor. After what felt like an eternity, the doctor told us they could not locate the baby's heartbeat. Time seemed to slow down. The doctor was talking, but we weren't hearing or comprehending everything he was saying. He used phrases like "This is nature's way of handling chromosomal abnormalities" and "You'll need to get a D&C to remove fetal tissue."

We were heartbroken and in tears. We called Jennifer's mom to share the news. She cried and comforted us both, assuring us that everything would be okay. We drove back home somewhat in a fog, preparing for the D&C later that day.

There are some things in life you are simply not prepared for, and I can honestly say I was not prepared for the loss of our first child. Some have said that miscarriage changes you, and I know the truth of that firsthand. Our miscarriage fundamentally reshaped me, Jen, and our relationship. We traveled through a season of depression to a season of joy again when we learned we were pregnant yet again, this time with our daughter, Ava.

One dynamic comes up again and again in conversations we have with others about miscarriage: the loss that every couple experiences. I remember being astounded by the number of couples who came to us and shared their own story of miscarriage and infant loss. Ultimately, our miscarriage deepened our faith and love for one another and for God. Sadly, for some marriages a miscarriage or infant loss can set the stage for marital discord.

In a groundbreaking study done in 2010, a team of doctors tracked the effects of miscarriage on couples who were either married or living together (cohabitating).[1] They studied 7,700 pregnancies—16 percent of which ended in miscarriage and 2 percent in stillbirth. The study showed that "couples who experienced a miscarriage or stillbirth were still more likely to split up."[2] Indeed, couples who experienced a miscarriage were 22 percent more likely to break up and those who experienced a stillbirth were more than 40 percent more likely to break up. Additionally, the researchers found that time did *not* heal all wounds. Couples who experienced miscarriage noted seeing the effects for at least two to three years, and couples who experienced a stillbirth experienced effects for up to a decade after the birth.[3]

Dr. Katherine Gold and her team, who put together the study, positively noted that in some cases miscarriage and infant loss can bring couples together. Gold and her team advised that couples who have experienced such loss could benefit from counseling.[4] In this time of grief and loss, how can pastors and church leaders create an environment where hurting parents are willing to seek counseling?

---

1. Katherine Gold, Ananda Sen, and Rodney A. Hayward, "Marriage and Cohabitation Outcomes After Pregnancy Loss," April 5, 2010. https://www.ncbi.nlm.nih.gov/pmc/articles/PMC2883880/.
2. Amanda Gardner, "Couples at Greater Risk of Breakup after Pregnancy Loss," April 5, 2010. *CNN*: http://www.cnn.com/2010/HEALTH/04/02/breakup.miscarriage.pregnancy/index.html.
3. Ibid.
4. https://www.ncbi.nlm.nih.gov/pmc/articles/PMC2883880/. "Understanding how a fetal loss affects the stability of the parental relationship has important implications for counseling and supporting

As you preach Sunday after Sunday, it is important for you to know that there are families who have gone through this loss, are going through this loss, or will at some time go through this loss. Statistics range from miscarriages happening in one in seven pregnancies to one in three pregnancies.[5] Furthermore, after a couple experiences a miscarriage, their probability of experiencing another miscarriage rises 20 percent the first time, 28 percent after the second, and 43 percent after the third miscarriage.[6]

Church and ministry leaders, we must speak up about miscarriage and infant loss! Whether it is incorporating it into our sermons and teaching illustrations or corporately gathering around those who have lost infants, the church cannot be silent on this all too common experience. The silence that often surrounds the suffering of those who have had miscarriages only increases their hurt and sense of isolation. Jessalyn Hutto, an author who has experienced the pain of miscarriage discusses the culture of silence: "What did surprise me, however, was the silence that seemed to surround these topics on the part of the church. Rarely were these particular tragedies—which are so strikingly common—being addressed by pastors or women's ministries. Suffering women simply were not getting the biblical counsel they desperately need. Instead, as they suffered in isolation, they would often turn to the internet for answers and comfort."[7]

During times of loss, how can we as counselors and pastors best come alongside couples who are suffering? How can you counsel couples who have suffered a miscarriage or infant loss?

MISCARRIAGE AND INFANT LOSS

Be there.

There are a few ministry situations where I will drop anything I have in order to be with someone in need. Miscarriage and infant loss is one of those situations.

---

couples after pregnancy loss. Although many parents find that a loss brings them closer together, the event also may create significant relationship stress. This study finds that married and cohabiting parents are at significantly greater hazard for separation after miscarriage, and this risk is even higher after stillbirth. Providers who care for bereaved families should recognize that, for some families, the stability of parental relationships may be at increased risk after loss, and they should consider whether selected parents would benefit from relationship support or counseling."

5. Markham Heid, "You Asked: What Causes a Miscarriage?," October 19, 2016. *Time*: http://time.com/4535226/miscarriage-fertility-pregnancy/.

6. Sue Nicewander, "Walking through the Dark Valley of Miscarriage," *Journal of Biblical Counseling* 24, no. 1 (2006): 49.

7. Trillia Newbell, "Mother's Day and Miscarriages: An Interview with Jessalyn Hutto," May 5, 2016. *The Ethics and Religious Liberty Commission*: https://erlc.com/resource-library/articles/mothers-day-and-miscarriages-an-interview-with-jessalyn-hutto.

Wherever or whenever a couple needs help, you should try to be with them in their time of suffering. I know schedules can be difficult to rearrange, but as a friend told me once—you will never regret being with your people during their time of grief. In those initial moments, the myriad of emotions and decisions are overwhelming. Having someone who cares makes a difference.

In your ministry of presence, allow the couple to grieve and express their pain. Like most loss there will be a multitude of emotions, and each couple's story of loss will look different. Couples will experience anger, depression, suicidal thoughts, confusion, theological questioning, numbness, shock, and much more. Hutto discusses what she seeks to do:

> Initially, the most important thing I want to convey to a woman who has miscarried is that her pain has merit. What I mean by this is that I want her to know that what has happened to her truly is as terrible as it feels. I don't want her to feel burdened to "get over" her loss quickly simply because it is hard for those around her to understand. She has lost a child—death has robbed her of one of the sweetest gifts we can experience in this life!—and that is worth mourning. The pain she is experiencing is justified, and I want her to know that I am willing to walk through those dark valleys with her.[8]

During these first few days and weeks, the couple will likely hear a variety of voices of counsel, some good and some bad. Stay away from disembodied platitudes like "God is always good, and he has a plan for your loss" or "God wanted the baby in heaven with him" or "Don't worry, God will give you another baby to replace this one." Sue Nicewander writes, "Don't say something just to make yourself feel useful or helpful."[9]

I asked a dear couple whom I had married and counseled to share what was helpful and not helpful to them in the aftermath of their miscarriage. Matt and Natalie wrote, "In our experience with miscarriage, I vividly remember the response of the people around me who knew what we went through—their words or lack thereof and the thoughtfulness we were shown through cards, gifts and messages sent even 10 months later on my first Mother's Day. I will never forget the people who stepped up just to show they cared without trying to fix anything or the awkwardness of people who looked away like nothing had happened."

---

8. Ibid.
9. Nicewander, "Walking through the Dark Valley of Miscarriage," 52.

Don't put a timeline on grief.

There is always talk about closure surrounding any sort of death, but particularly in the loss of a child through miscarriage or stillbirth. Well-meaning individuals will speak of things like "Time heals all wounds," or "You'll be pregnant again in no time," or even worse yet, "At least you know you can get pregnant." Implicit in these phrases is a rushed timeline of grief. There is an expectation that such a loss will affect you for a time but not for all time. Jesus reminds us of the goodness of grieving when he writes, "Blessed are those who mourn, for they will be comforted" (Matt. 5:4). It is important to note what this doesn't mean; it doesn't mean those who mourn are blessed because God will help them get over it immediately. It does mean that those who mourn will be blessed with the Lord's own comfort and presence in their mourning, no matter how long it lasts. It also means that Christ's empathetic companionship in the process of grief is a blessing and comfort that makes the mourning sacred, even though it hurts.

Kyle and Laura, another couple who recently lost a child in miscarriage, wrote, "When I found out I lost my baby at ten weeks, I was heartbroken and overwhelmed by the many feelings that followed, some of which confused me and left me conflicted and guilty. I am so thankful a relative suggested talking to someone about what my husband and I were facing. I really just needed to hear that what we were feeling was absolutely normal."

Encourage them to feel free to remember their child.

A loss is a loss is a loss. Stillbirth is a loss of a child. Miscarriage is a loss of a child. Many times, couples suffer through miscarriage in silence because there is not always an intact body to bury and to grieve over, as there is during a stillbirth. This can cause a great degree of shame, a sense that those who have suffered a miscarriage did not experience a "real loss." Even if the woman was unaware of the pregnancy prior to the miscarriage, it still hurts. Both miscarriage and stillbirth are very real and legitimate losses.

In counseling, encourage the couples to find ways to remember their child. Sometimes there is a rush to move forward or find closure. Remind them there is nothing wrong with remembering their baby. Counselors should understand that for many husbands and wives, their emotions and feelings are all they have of their lost child. To simply "move on" or "get closure" translates to them forgetting their child. "If I let go of these emotions, then I let go of the memory of this child. . . . Am I somehow agreeing that this child did not exist?"[10]

---

10. Ibid., 51.

Here are some ways you can help couples remember their child:

- Set a reminder on your calendar or in your planner of their loss to remind you to reach out on the anniversary of their loss. The first anniversary of a family's loss is a potent marker of grief, and often after twelve months have passed many people have forgotten. Sue Nicewander writes, "The one-year marker is a particularly critical time for most, and memorials seem to soften the pain."[11]
- Send flowers to the grieving couple. Put their names on the church prayer list or include them in the bulletin for prayer if the couple is comfortable with this level of disclosure. Bring a meal to their doorstep.
- Offer to have a memorial service or some sort of remembrance for their child. Author Dan Doriani acknowledges that miscarriage is a "strange kind of death . . . where is the funeral, the gathering of family . . . it is the death of someone whom no one knew, except perhaps the mother."[12] For those desiring some sort of memorial service, pastor and counselor Brad Hambrick has a helpful template you can follow.[13]
- Many families choose to name their babies lost in miscarriage even if the gender was not known to them. This can help couples grieve practically and put a name with a face they haven't seen.
- Keep an open-door policy where they have the freedom to reach out to you to talk, but also make sure to follow up on your own since many couples might not feel comfortable reaching out again for help.
- Additional ideas include but are not limited to: getting a piece of jewelry with their baby's birthstone, planting a tree or plant in their baby's honor, buying a Christmas ornament for their baby, creating or purchasing artwork to remember their baby.

Answer questions honestly and biblically.

Some couples come into counseling with a variety of questions. Some just want to spend time *not talking* about their loss because that's all they have talked about the past week or month. Whatever the situation is, seek to answer questions or concerns honestly and biblically. A common question that arises is whether the mother did something during pregnancy to cause miscarriage: "Did I drink too

11. Ibid., 54.

12. Dan Doriani, "Miscarriage: A Death in the Family," *Covenant Theological Seminary Online Resources*, 2.

13. http://bradhambrick.com/memorial-ceremony-for-an-unborn-child-2/.

much caffeine?" or "Maybe I should not have worked out at the gym last Friday." *Time* magazine columnist, Markham Heid writes, "What you won't hear from fertility experts, at least when it comes to miscarriage, are warnings about caffeine, stress, poor sleep or any of the other behavioral factors people often point to when trying to explain a lost pregnancy. While living a healthy lifestyle is linked to better odds of becoming pregnant and healthier babies, the ties between unhealthy behaviors and miscarriage are absent or dubious."[14]

When there are questions about medical issues surrounding the couple's loss, be sure to direct them to a medical professional.[15] Following miscarriage and infant loss, there are many physiological and hormonal issues that may need attention and care. While commending them to the help of medical doctors, be sure to let them know you are also there to help in any way you can.

Other questions are easier to answer, such as, "Am I a mother?" The answer is a resounding *yes*. Mothers who have experienced miscarriage or stillbirth often struggle to know how to celebrate Mother's Day. A practical way we can care for women on Mother's Day is to acknowledge women who have experienced the pain of miscarriage or infant loss. The loss of a child does not take away the fact that they are a mother.

For questions to which you do not have an answer, don't be afraid to say, "I don't know, but I'm willing to look into that for you and get back to you." There is no shame in not having the answers to every question.

Offer theological hope, not just platitudes.

Every parent who has lost a child has one question they want answered: Where does my baby go when they die? While sentimental answers are easy to offer: "Of course, your baby is in heaven," I find most parents want something more stable than sentimental, more secure than superficial. Jessalyn Hutto noticed this dynamic in her own conversations: "Much of what they would find there [the internet] focused on the emotional aspects of losing a baby rather than on how the truth of God's Word applied to their loss. They were receiving empathy from

---

14. Heid, "You Asked: What Causes a Miscarriage?," http://time.com/4535226/miscarriage-fertility-pregnancy/.

15. Glenda Mathes writes of the complications that arise when medical professionals do not approach these issues with similar convictions as the couples. She writes, "What do you do when you are in an emotional upheaval, you need medical advice, but you don't trust the advice you are getting, as they obviously have no understanding of the sanctity of life?" Into this dilemma, Mathes encourages couples to seek the advice of medical professionals who hold views similar to theirs (Glenda Mathes, *Little One Lost: Living with Early Infant Loss* [Grandville, MI: Reformed Fellowship, Inc., 2015], 39–41).

the articles they were reading, but not necessarily the hope that could be found in the glorious gospel of Jesus Christ."[16]

What does the Bible have to say about where babies go when they die? Admittedly, theologians have a diversity of opinions on the topic, with some believing that only elect, baptized babies go to heaven (Augustine and Ambrose)[17] while others hold the view that babies are already of the elect and thus, go to heaven (Calvin and Spurgeon).[18] Spurgeon wrote, "Now, let every mother and father here present know assuredly that it is well with the child, if God hath taken it away from you in its infant days"[19] and "I rejoice to know that the souls of all infants, as soon as they die, speed their way to paradise. Think what a multitude there is of them."[20]

John Calvin's view on this was not theoretical for him, but deeply personal. Calvin married a widow, Idelette, who had two children; he and his new wife lost their only child, a son named Jacques, two weeks after his birth. Calvin grieved the loss deeply and wrote to a fellow minister and friend, "God have pity on us. God has indeed dealt us a heavy blow by the death of our son, but He is our Father and knows what is good for his children."[21] Grief would visit John and Idelette again, as three years later they had a daughter die at birth, and two years following a third child was born prematurely and died.[22]

While this issue is not explicitly discussed in detail by the Scriptures, wise theologians who have read the full counsel of Scripture have marshaled what I believe is a convincing argument that children who die in miscarriage and stillbirth are with God in heaven. In holding to this view, we are not denying that children are born with original sin (cf. Ps. 51:5), but we understand that the Bible makes a distinction between original sin and volitional sin (volitional sin flows from our sin nature, cf. James 4:17). Daniel Akin explains, "While all are guilty of original sin, moral responsibility and understanding is necessary for our being accountable for actual sins (Deuteronomy 1:39; Isaiah 7:16). It is to the one who knows to do right

16. Newbell, "Mother's Day and Miscarriages," https://erlc.com/resource-library/articles/mothers-day-and-miscarriages-an-interview-with-jessalyn-hutto.

17. Alan Bandy, "Do Children Go to Heaven When They Die?" May 26, 2017. *Christianity Today*: http://www.christianitytoday.com/ct/2017/june/do-children-go-to-heaven-when-they-die.html.

18. Ibid. Many well-known theologians and church leaders throughout history have lost infants: Martin Luther, John Bunyan, George Whitfield, Charles Wesley, Horatius Bonar, and C. H. Spurgeon (Mathes, *Little One Lost*, 30).

19. Charles H. Spurgeon, "Infant Salvation," a sermon preached September 29, 1861. *The New Park Street and Metropolitan Tabernacle Pulpit* (London: Passmore and Alabaster, 1862), 7:505.

20. Daniel L. Akin, "Why I Believe Children Who Die Go to Heaven," http://www.danielakin.com/wp-content/uploads/2004/08/Why-I-Believe-Children-Who-Die-Go-to-Heaven.pdf.

21. Mathes, *Little One Lost*, 30.

22. William J. Peterson, "Idelette: John Calvin's Search for the Right Wife," Christian History, Issue 12. 1986. *Christianity Today*: http://www.christianitytoday.com/history/issues/issue-12/idelette-john-calvins-search-for-right-wife.html.

and does not do it that sin is reckoned. This is the teaching of what happens at the Great White Throne in Revelation 20:11–15 when those who are cast into hell are judged out of the books of works, 'according to what they had done' (vs. 12, 14). Infants are incapable of such decisions and actions."[23]

A verse often quoted in support of this argument is 2 Samuel 12:23, where David speaks of going to see his deceased infant son, "But now that he is dead, why should I go on fasting? Can I bring him back again? I will go to him, but he will not return to me." In light of David's confession, it seems that he knew he couldn't bring his baby back to life, but that he expected to go to be with him in heaven.

In the New Testament, it is clear Jesus has a particular love for children (cf. Matt. 18:1–6, 19:13–15). John MacArthur writes, "Those verses don't state that children go to heaven, but they do show God's heart toward children. He created and cares for children, and beyond that, He always accomplishes His perfect will in every circumstance."[24] In Luke 18, "People were also bringing babies to Jesus for him to place his hands on them. When the disciples saw this, they rebuked them. But Jesus called the children to him and said, 'Let the little children come to me, and do not hinder them, for the kingdom of God belongs to such as these. Truly I tell you, anyone who will not receive the kingdom of God like a little child will never enter it'" (Luke 18:15–17).

Albert Mohler and Daniel Akin conclude,

> "When we look into the grave of one of these little ones, we do not place our hope and trust in the false promises of an unbiblical theology, in the instability of sentimentalism, in the cold analysis of human logic, nor in the cowardly refuge of ambiguity. We place our faith in Christ, and trust Him to be faithful to his Word. We claim the promises of the Scriptures and the assurance of the grace of our Lord. We know that heaven will be filled with those who never grew to maturity on earth, but in heaven will greet us completed in Christ. Let us resolve by grace to meet them there."[25]

Don't forget the husbands.

While the primary focus in miscarriage and loss is on the wife, and rightly so, don't overlook the care of the husband. Again, Jessalyn Hutto is helpful,

---

23. Akin, "Why I Believe Children Who Die Go to Heaven."

24. https://www.gty.org/library/questions/QA101/do-babies-and-others-incapable-of-professing-faith-in-christ-automatically-go-to-heaven.

25. R. Albert Mohler Jr. and Daniel L. Akin, "The Salvation of 'Little Ones': Do Infants Who Die Go to Heaven?," July 16, 2009. https://albertmohler.com/2009/07/16/the-salvation-of-the-little-ones-do-infants-who-die-go-to-heaven/.

I think it is important to understand that husbands are in a very difficult position when their wives miscarry. They, too, experience intense grief when their babies die, but at the same time, they know that their wives are grappling with the loss on a whole other level. These men need to grieve themselves, but are simultaneously seeking to comfort their distraught wives. They need good, faithful friends who will walk alongside them, check in on them consistently, pray with them and simply listen to them as they grapple with the deep emotions and questions they are confronted with at the loss of their children.[26]

Often, we find that husbands and wives tend to grieve differently. Whereas the wife's process of grieving can last longer, the husband can appear to move forward more quickly, at least externally. This can cause a marital disconnect where either the wife feels hurried in her grief or left behind in her grief. Neither dynamic is good, and as a counselor, you can encourage husbands to engage in the grieving process with their wives. Encourage husbands to be present physically and emotionally for their wives.

One husband, Matt, shares a sentiment common among husbands who are grieving with their wives, "Because I felt helpless to make things better, anything I did try (comforting, praying for/with her, etc.) felt trite to me. I discovered over several months that I simply didn't understand how profoundly this miscarriage had impacted and hurt Jodi. Because there was not the same physical bond between me and the baby as there was between Jodi and the baby, I frankly didn't perceive how deeply she was hurt by the miscarriage. I was confused when she wanted to give the baby a name. That probably made me appear indifferent/distant from her and her needs."[27]

From personal experience, I know that my wife and I handled the loss of our child differently. While I tended to stuff and compartmentalize my grief, Jen needed to process and share her grief. Shamefully, I look back and realize how at times my lack of care and compassion communicated a lack of love and care for her and our child.

While fathers may grieve differently, they still grieve. Blogger Laura Thigpen writes,

Another common misconception people often have is the assumption that miscarriages only affect women. Men desire to be fathers. Men get excited about being daddies. Men grieve when their babies die. Men need to be

26. Newbell, "Mother's Day and Miscarriages," https://erlc.com/resource-library/articles/mothers-day-and-miscarriages-an-interview-with-jessalyn-hutto.
27. Nicewander, "Walking through the Dark Valley of Miscarriage," 50.

comforted. Watching my husband grieve gave me a greater appreciation for him, for fathers and even for brothers who chose to grieve with my husband. To expect a man not to grieve the loss of his baby, no matter what stage of gestation, is to suggest this child is somehow unworthy of fatherly grief. Our Heavenly Father demonstrated grief so great over the brokenness of His image bearers that He sent His only Son to redeem us.[28]

Use Scripture wisely, but use Scripture!

Scripture is a comfort to the soul. It restores us and it re-stories us. Our tears mean something to God.

> You keep track of all my sorrows.
> You have collected all my tears in your bottle.
> You have recorded each one in your book.
> *Psalm 56:8 NLT*

He is a refuge to those who are suffering. He weeps with us. He grieves and is angry at death. There is only one book that is honest about the pain of this world but also offers us a hope that is durable and sane amid such pain. The apostle Peter writes, "And the God of all grace, who called you to his eternal glory in Christ, after you have suffered a little while, will himself restore you and make you strong, firm and steadfast" (1 Pet. 5:10).

During a time of miscarriage and infant loss, be wise about how you use Scripture. Do not move too quickly to passages like Romans 8:28, James 1:2–4, or 2 Corinthians 1:3–7. I once tried to explain to a grieving couple that God was going to use their suffering to one day help another couple, and the spouse replied, "That's nice to know, but I don't want to help anyone else right now. I need help!"

It shouldn't surprise us, but the psalms will be a natural place for suffering couples. The psalms of lament (cf. 39, 44, 55, 102) are a good starting point.[29] Psalm 23 is universally comforting for those in the painful valley of the shadow of death. The prophet Isaiah brings words of comfort and hope in Isaiah 42:1–17. Ask couples to find a metaphor for God that they can draw comfort from. Perhaps it is God as shepherd (Ps. 23), God as rock and refuge (Ps. 18), or God as defender (Ps. 43). Personally, I've drawn comfort from two other psalms as well. Psalm 27:5:

28. Laura Thigpen, "A Pro-Life Ethic: Miscarriages and Misconceptions," May 4, 2016. *Intersect*: http://intersectproject.org/faith-and-culture/pro-life-ethic-miscarriages-misconceptions/.

29. For an extended and comprehensive treatment on the psalms of lament, I recommend *The Psalms as Christian Lament* by Bruce Waltke, James M. Houston, and Erika Moore.

> For in the day of trouble
>> he will keep me safe in his dwelling;
> he will hide me in the shelter of his sacred tent
>> and set me high upon a rock.

And Psalm 91:4:

> He will cover you with his feathers,
>> and under his wings you will find refuge;
> his faithfulness will be your shield and rampart.

What's your image or metaphor of God that brings you a measure of comfort and peace? Expanding your couple's gaze beyond their everyday understanding has the potential to bring robust comfort to their hurting souls.

INFERTILITY

There is yet another loss that affects couples as it relates to children and family. Whereas the pain and suffering of miscarriage is the loss of a child, infertility's pain and suffering is the *inability* to have a child.[30] Again, both are losses. Both represent real forms of suffering. As my friend Brad Hambrick frequently says, "Suffering is not a competitive sport."

Pastors and counselors need to understand that the church, a place where God's people can gather for mutual edification and encouragement, can often be a place of hardship and difficulty for couples who are battling infertility. Think of how many activities and programs at your church or place of worship revolve around children. The church, in seeking to uphold the family, can create an uncomfortable and at times shameful dynamic for those who don't match the typical husband-wife-children paradigm.[31] Professor and author Karen Swallow Prior writes, "There is an unspoken assumption that this failure to fit the pattern is just that—a failure."[32]

---

30. Amy Baker and Dan Wickert write, "Medically, infertility is defined by a couple unsuccessfully trying to conceive for a year. Statistically about 15% of couples who try for a year will not conceive" (Amy Baker, *Infertility: Comfort for Your Empty Arms and Heavy Heart* [Greensboro, NC: New Growth, 2013], 5).

31. The Bible consistently draws our gaze toward people who do not fit the mold of this nuclear family (e.g., orphans, eunuchs, widows, infertile couples, etc.).

32. Karen Swallow Prior, "Called to Childlessness: The Surprising Ways of God," March 6, 2017. *The Ethics & Religious Liberty Commission*: https://erlc.com/resource-library/articles/called-to-childlessness-the-surprising-ways-of-god.

Prior goes on to write, "I believe that the church and the world need more of the particular gifts that infertile (and childless and unmarried) women (and men) can offer. I can't help but wonder how different the church and the world would look if infertility were viewed not as a problem to be solved, but a calling to serve God and meet the needs of the world in other ways."[33] Scripture again is our honest guide and draws our attention to barren couples like Sarah and Abraham (Gen. 16:1), Rachel and Jacob (Gen. 30:1–2), Hannah and Elkanah (1 Sam. 1:5), Michal and David (2 Sam. 6:23), and Elizabeth and Zechariah (Luke 1:6–7).

Again, infertility is something with which I am directly familiar. My own parents were not able to have children, and so they pursued adoption with both my sister and myself. For them, adoption presented another pathway to having children that, in God's sovereignty, was not Plan B for them, but rather God's Plan A. As a pastor, you will undoubtedly have the joy and privilege of coming alongside couples to explore several issues related to infertility:[34] adoption, IVF (In Vitro Fertilization), surrogacy,[35] embryo adoption,[36] and foster care. Dr. Megan Best offers five morally permissible options for infertile couples to pursue:[37]

- It's okay to pursue no further treatment.
- It's possible to wait.
- The couple can seek a diagnosis to determine the cause of infertility.
- After diagnosis it's increasingly common for the couple to receive a recommendation to go straight to Assisted Reproductive Therapy (ART) treatment rather than to try treating the underlying problem.[38]
- Couples may consider adoption at any point in their journey.

---

33. Ibid.

34. Joe Carter, "38 Ways to Make a Baby," September 28, 2011. *First Things*: https://www.firstthings.com/web-exclusives/2011/09/38-ways-to-make-a-baby.

35. Joe Carter, "9 Things You Should Know About Surrogacy," June 6, 2014. *The Gospel Coalition*: https://www.thegospelcoalition.org/article/9-things-you-should-know-about-surrogacy/.

36. Aaron Wilson, "What Christians Should Know About Embryo Adoption," February 16, 2017. *The Gospel Coalition*: https://www.thegospelcoalition.org/article/what-christians-should-know-about-embryo-adoption/.

37. Megan Best, "Your Options in Infertility," March 19, 2014. *The Gospel Coalition*: https://www.thegospelcoalition.org/article/your-options-in-infertility/.

38. Megan Best, "At this point I'd particularly urge Christian couples to stop, pray, collect information, think carefully, and not just agree to anything that will help them achieve their desire for a baby. Ethical problems are avoided by looking ahead. In some ways, the advent of assisted reproductive therapies—in vitro fertilization (IVF), for example—has increased the anguish of infertility since these treatments can prolong the struggle for years. Moreover, pressure from other family members, such as potential grandparents, can make it even harder to choose. Someone familiar with the process needs to be involved in order to make sure decisions are based on facts. Costs are not just medical but also emotional, relational, and spiritual" (ibid).

This short chapter does not allow us to study the full scope of the various options for couples who are struggling with infertility. All options must be examined carefully and put up against the full weight and wisdom of Scripture. In situations like this, decisions are best made in community and through a great deal of prayer.[39]

CONCLUSION

As I reflect on my own counseling experience, I realize what a privilege it is to come alongside couples at every stage of life. From womb to tomb, pastors play an integral role in the life of families. This is not an opportunity for boasting in any way, but rather complete and utter amazement that God uses frail jars of clay (2 Cor. 4:7) to minister to his people. Pastor and counselors should not miss the opportunity to incarnate the active, personal, and deep love of our Savior and Redeemer Jesus Christ to couples who are suffering.

 One Couple's Story

Stephanie and I never expected to experience infertility and miscarriage. Infertility surprised us because we had heard many times "have sex, get pregnant." We were more concerned about preventing a pregnancy than having one. However, we soon learned that it was not so simple. There are almost five years between each of our three children. People compliment us on our family planning—only one in diapers at a time . . . only one in college at a time. In reality, we did not plan the timing of any of our children.

After the Lord provided our first child, we lost our second child. We had no idea a miscarriage club existed until we joined it. In the first seven years of our marriage, we tasted the bitter pills of both infertility and miscarriage. We grieved, became envious, and struggled with bitterness and anger.

Thanks be to God that these struggles were not the final chapter to our story. God's grace, the kind that abounds over sin and suffering, met us right where we needed it most. The Lord helped us to see the broader picture of

---

39. For more on this topic, I recommend Andreas J. Köstenberger's, *God, Marriage and Family: Rebuilding the Biblical Foundation,* 2nd ed., chapter seven, for its breadth and scope and commitment to biblical wisdom and discernment.

life. We could pray and seek him because he cared (1 Pet. 5:7), he knew our pain (Heb. 4:14–16), he would be a source of strength and shelter (Ps. 46), and a rock on which to stand (Ps. 61:1–4). The Lord met us in our need and strengthened us. He used this suffering to help us be more compassionate to others (2 Cor. 1:3–4), to help us develop a deeper theological well, to strengthen our faith through trial (1 Pet. 1:7), and to show us that ultimately, we live for the glory of God (John 9) rather than for our own glory.

Infertility and miscarriage are painful, but God's work and Word provide what is needed to use the suffering to make a difference for the cause of Christ.

Rob and Stephanie Green, Pastor of Counseling and Seminary Ministries, Faith Church, Lafayette, Indiana

RESOURCES

Daniel L. Akin, "Why I Believe Children Who Die Go to Heaven" http://www.danielakin.com/wp-content/uploads/2004/08/Why-I-Believe-Children-Who-Die-Go-to-Heaven.pdf

Amy Baker, *Infertility: Comfort for Your Empty Arms and Heavy Heart*

Megan Best, *Fearfully and Wonderfully Made: Ethics and the Beginning of Human Life*

Elizabeth B. Brown, *Surviving the Loss of a Child: Support for Grieving Parents*

Cameron Cole, *Therefore I Have Hope: 12 Truths That Comfort, Sustain, and Redeem in Tragedy*

Dan Cruver, ed., *Reclaiming Adoption: Missional Living through Rediscovery of Abba Father*

Dave Furman, *Being There: How to Love Those Who Are Hurting*

David and Nancy Guthrie, *When Your Family's Lost a Loved One: Finding Hope Together*

Nancy Guthrie, *What Grieving People Wish You Knew About What Really Helps (and What Really Hurts)*

————, *Hearing Jesus Speak into Your Sorrow*

Brad Hambrick, "Memorial Service for an Unborn Child" http://bradhambrick.com/memorial-ceremony-for-an-unborn-child-2/

Jessalyn Hutto, *Inheritance of Tears: Trusting the Lord of Life When Death Visits the Womb*

Robert W. Kellemen, *God's Healing for Life's Losses: How to Find Hope When You're Hurting*

Timothy Keller, *Walking with God Through Pain and Suffering*

John MacArthur, *Safe in the Arms of God: Truth for Heaven About the Death of a Child*

Glenda Mathes, *Little One Lost: Living with Early Infant Loss*

Albert Mohler and Daniel Akin, "The Salvation of the 'Little Ones': Do Infants Who Die Go to Heaven?" https://albertmohler.com/2009/07/16/the-salvation-of-the-little-ones-do-infants-who-die-go-to-heaven/

Russell Moore, *Adopted for Life: The Priority of Adoption for Christian Families and Churches*

Sue Nicewander and Jodi Jewell, "Walking through the Dark Valley of Miscarriage," *Journal of Biblical Counseling* 24, no. 1 (2006): 49–57

David Powlison, "Thinking Rightly About Recurrent Miscarriages" https://www.ccef.org/resources/video/how-do-i-think-rightly-about-recurrent-miscarriages

Karen Swallow Prior, "Called to Childlessness: The Surprising Ways of God" https://erlc.com/resource-library/articles/called-to-childlessness-the-surprising-ways-of-god

Aaron Wilson, "What Christians Should Know About Embryo Adoption," https://www.thegospelcoalition.org/article/what-christians-should-know-about-embryo-adoption/

Nicholas Wolterstorff, *Lament for a Son*

Chapter 15

FROZEN INTIMACY

May you ever be intoxicated with her love.
PROVERBS 5:19

Love you? I *am* you.
CHARLES WILLIAMS

Would you rather be single and lonely or married and bored?"[1] So asks one well-known comedian. From the world's perspective, these are the choices when it comes to marriage and relationships. This suggests that the way to avoid both loneliness and boredom is to date but never commit to marriage. Sounds descriptive of our culture, doesn't it?

A study done in 2000 noted that only 15 percent of movie scenes involving sexual intercourse occurred between a married couple. A whopping 85 percent of scenes involve intercourse that happens outside of marriage.[2] The authors of the study conclude, "This and other findings suggest that sexual behavior among married characters is rare and rather mundane compared to those having unmarried sex."

If the culture glorifies sex outside of marriage, making it *the* human experience, then the church can go the opposite pathway of disparaging sex altogether. In an effort to condemn sexual activity outside of marriage, we throw the proverbial baby out with the bathwater. Then we are surprised to find newly married couples ill-equipped to navigate not only their wedding night but sexual intimacy in general.

---

1. Timothy and Kathy Keller, *The Meaning of Marriage* (New York: Dutton, 2011), 22.
2. J. M. Dempsey and T. Reichert, "Portrayal of Married Sex in the Movies," *Sexuality and Culture* 4, no. 3 (2000): 21–36.

Author Christopher Ash writes, "Christians tend to focus on the epidemic of sexual activity outside marriage, but I suspect we ought to devote at least equal attention to the epidemic of sexual *in*activity within marriage. It is important to remember not only that the Bible forbids sex outside marriage, but that it commends sex within marriage."[3]

Many youths growing up in the church have heard conflicting messages about sex. They've been told it's immoral, something not to be discussed, and yet on their wedding night, they are expected to suddenly become experts with their only frame of reference being scenes from movies, television, or—worse yet—pornography. I'm not saying this is the sole reason couples struggle with sexual intimacy, but pastors and counselors would be well served to see the larger framework in which we teach, instruct, and train future husbands and wives as it relates to sex.

Pastors who do any amount of marriage counseling will likely encounter couples struggling with sexual intimacy. While most couples don't come in to see a pastor specifically for help with their sex life (at least in my experience), their sex life inevitably has suffered or is suffering from whatever has brought them in that day. While some couples might be more reticent to discuss issues surrounding sexual intimacy, I'm often surprised by how honest and vulnerable couples are in sharing their struggles. Couples who are struggling with intimacy need to know the Bible has something to say that is worthwhile and encouraging.

GOD'S PLAN FOR SEXUAL INTIMACY

Here are a series of four principles you can work through with married couples who are experiencing marital intimacy issues. Whether addressed within a session or as part of assigned homework, these principles will enable you and the couple to have a fruitful discussion on this important issue.

1. Sexual intimacy in marriage is for God's glory.
2. Sexual intimacy in marriage unites couples.
3. Sexual intimacy in marriage is to be regular.
4. Sexual intimacy in marriage is to be other-oriented.

Sexual intimacy in marriage is for God's glory.

As with most subjects in marriage counseling, it is best not to assume the couple has a biblical foundation until you have asked good questions. Ask a couple

---

3. Christopher Ash, *Married for God* (Wheaton, IL: Crossway, 2016), 67.

what they think God's purpose is for sexual intimacy and you are liable to get a variety of answers: pleasure, procreation, love. Those are all true, but what is the larger vision that guides and orients sexual intimacy in marriage? What lifts married sex out of the cultural cesspool in which it so often resides?

If humanity's *raison d'être* is to bring God glory through everything, then it should not surprise us that this applies to sex too. God created Adam and Eve in his image, placed them in the garden, and told them to be fruitful and multiply, bringing him glory in everything.

God not only made Adam and Eve in his image, he created them as gendered, sexual beings. Dwight and Margaret Peterson write, "Sexuality is an intrinsic aspect of what it means to be a human being. People don't exist as androgynous, sexless beings. They exist as men and as women, bringing their gendered selves into every situation they encounter."[4] This means your sexuality is not a mistake. There is a goodness to how God created and designed man and woman.

Adam and Eve were specially created to bring their Maker the glory he deserved in every activity, in every conversation, with no dichotomy between the sacred or secular, with no division between the soul and the body, and all for God's glory. The apostle Paul brings this concept home in his letter to the Corinthians. In 1 Corinthians 10:31, Paul instructs them that even the most mundane of activities—eating and drinking—should be done to God's glory. If God has a plan for our eating and drinking to be done for his glory, should it surprise us that he would provide a way for sexual intimacy to be good and glorifying too? Earlier, Paul goes to great lengths to teach them about glorifying God with their bodies. Paul writes, "The body, however, is not meant for sexual immorality but for the Lord, and the Lord for the body. . . . Do you not know that your bodies are temples of the Holy Spirit, who is in you, whom you have received from God? You are not your own; you were bought at a price. Therefore honor God with your bodies" (1 Cor. 6:13, 19–20).

The body, far from being an afterthought in God's creation plan, is purposefully built to allow us to glorify and enjoy God. When he created Adam and Eve and joined them together in marriage, it was his express intent that this union would bring him glory in every aspect of their union. Ed Welch elaborates, "Our Christian task is to remember that every sexual union is profound. It always points to the deeper union that we have with Christ by faith. Sex mirrors the glory of God in the gospel. It exists because it expresses God's oneness with His people,

---

4. Margaret Kim Peterson and Dwight N. Peterson, *Are You Waiting for "The One"?: Cultivating Realistic, Positive Expectations for Christian Marriage* (Downers Grove, IL: InterVarsity Press, 2011), 129.

His fidelity to us, His ownership of us, His self-sacrifice, and the pleasure we can take in this relationship."[5]

Tim Savage says it succinctly, "Sexual union is an expression of the glory of God."[6]

Sexual intimacy in marriage unites couples together.

Sexual intimacy in marriage is not only designed to bring God glory but also unites husband and wife in a one-flesh relationship. Listen to the words of Genesis 2:22–25:

> Then the LORD God made a woman from the rib he had taken out of the man, and he brought her to the man.
>
> The man said,
>
>> "This is now bone of my bones
>>   and flesh of my flesh;
>> she shall be called 'woman,'
>>   for she was taken out of man."
>
> That is why a man leaves his father and mother and is united to his wife, and they become one flesh.
>
> Adam and his wife were both naked, and they felt no shame.

This intimacy between man and woman was always designed to happen within a particular context. It wasn't supposed to happen between just *anyone*, but between a man and a woman committed together in a covenantal relationship with God. Tim and Kathy Keller write, "Indeed, sex is perhaps the most powerful God-created way to help you give your entire self to another human being. Sex is God's appointed way for two people to reciprocally say to one another, 'I belong completely, permanently and exclusively to you.' [Sex] . . . is your covenant renewal service."[7]

As husband and wife are joined together in marriage, something unique happens in their relationship. Two become one flesh. This union is more than just sexual intimacy. Kevin DeYoung writes, "The *ish* [man] and the *ishah* [woman] can become one flesh because theirs is not just a sexual union but a *reunion*, the

---

5. Edward T. Welch, "The Apostle Paul: On Sex," *Journal of Biblical Counseling* 23, no. 4 (2005): 17.

6. Tim Savage, *No Ordinary Marriage* (Wheaton, IL: Crossway, 2012), 105.

7. Keller, *The Meaning of Marriage*, 223–24.

bringing together of two differentiated beings, with one made *from* and both made *for* the other."[8]

The final phrase of Genesis 2 records for us that Adam and Eve could stand before each other completely naked but not ashamed. What a difference from the way in which couples often view sexual intimacy in marriage! Of all the topics to be discussed in marriage, sexual intimacy is most often the one that gets shrouded in shame, secrecy, and guilt. Sex is spoken of in hushed tones and with blushing complexions. The goodness of sex is quickly obscured by the brokenness of the world and the sinful bent of our flesh.

Sexual intimacy in marriage is to be regular.

Sexual intimacy is for God's glory and serves as an embodied reminder of a couple's one-flesh relationship. Thus, it makes sense that sexual intimacy should be a regular part of married life. Denny Burk states, "The conjugal bond of marriage is not merely for consummation. It is intended by God to be the ongoing affirmation of the husband and the wife's unique union."[9] To understand the biblical teaching on this topic, we must read and understand the apostle Paul's teaching in 1 Corinthians 7:2–5:

> Each man should have sexual relations with his own wife, and each woman with her own husband. The husband should fulfill his marital duty to his wife, and likewise the wife to her husband. The wife does not have authority over her own body but yields it to her husband. In the same way, the husband does not have authority over his own body but yields it to his wife. Do not deprive each other except perhaps by mutual consent and for a time, so that you may devote yourselves to prayer. Then come together again so that Satan will not tempt you because of your lack of self-control.

In-depth explanations of this passage can be found in several commentaries. To understand the impact of Paul's teaching, it's helpful to note that Paul is seeking to combat erroneous teaching that delegitimized the role of intimacy within marriage.[10] Paul is replying to something the Corinthians had written to him earlier and is now seeking to correct it ("It is good for a man not to have sexual relations with a woman.") Many scholars have noted this kind of asceticism was in the ideological air in Paul's day.

---

8. Kevin DeYoung, *What Does the Bible Really Teach About Homosexuality?* (Wheaton, IL: Crossway, 2015), 28.

9. Denny Burk, *What is the Meaning of Sex?* (Wheaton, IL: Crossway, 2013), 111.

10. Not only sexual relations within marriage but sex of any kind.

There is no hint of such asceticism in Paul's teaching to married couples. They are to fulfill their marital duty through engaging in sexual activity together. This sexual activity is to be consistent unless both parties agree to a time of abstinence for prayer. Denny Burk writes, "Paul teaches not that couples *may* come together in regular conjugal union but that they *must* come together. Sexual intimacy is not merely a privilege of marriage but also a duty. This sexual intimacy within marriage becomes a touchstone for the spiritual and emotional vitality of marriage."[11] Paul is not explicit with a specific amount of time or frequency, but it is clear that couples should not enter lightly into a time of marital abstinence.

Devoting oneself to prayer and by mutual agreement is the framework he sets up in order to help protect couples from the temptation of the Evil One. Regarding frequency and regularity of sex in marriage, Brad Hambrick has a good word, stating, "A satisfying sex life is not created by frequency. A satisfying sex life creates frequency. If you put your energy (which you protected with your schedule) into anticipating and satisfying your spouse, then you (plural) will mutually enjoy your intimacy enough that frequency will take care of itself."[12] Questions surrounding frequency will be addressed later in the chapter.

Sexual intimacy in marriage is to be other-oriented.

Paul goes on in verses 3–4 to describe sexual intimacy within marriage in terms which would have probably been surprising and somewhat alarming to his readers.[13] Neither husband nor wife possess authority over their own body. R. C. Sproul notes the implications: "Here also is one place where the man and the woman have equal authority in marriage."[14] For Paul's female readers, this would have been downright revolutionary. Women at this time were considered the legal property of their husbands. "Paul was teaching that each partner, male and female, had the right to mutual sexual relations. Nothing like this had ever been said before."[15]

The wife is entitled to sexual relations with her husband! This mutual reciprocity completely reoriented the one-sidedness of sex for husband and wife in the first century. Both husband and wife are to give to one another; they are to willingly yield their bodies to one another. Biblical sexual ethics fly in the face of not only

---

11. Burk, *What is the Meaning of Sex?*, 111.

12. Brad Hambrick, "10 Pre-Marital Questions on Sex (Part 10)," http://bradhambrick.com/premaritalqonsex10/.

13. The NLT translates verse 3 in easy-to-understand language, "The husband should fulfill his wife's sexual needs, and the wife should fulfill her husband's needs."

14. R. C. Sproul, *The Intimate Marriage* (Phillipsburg, NJ: P&R, 2003), 122.

15. Keller, *The Meaning of Marriage*, 232.

first-century Corinthian culture but also twenty-first-century Western culture. The Bible tells us sex is not solely about you and your needs. Sex is not about self-actualization or authenticity. Sex is meant to be about bringing pleasure and love to your spouse. Tim and Kathy Keller write, "Each partner in marriage is to be most concerned not with getting sexual pleasure but with giving it. In short, the greatest sexual pleasure should be the pleasure of seeing your spouse getting pleasure."[16]

When husbands and wives practice this principle in their sexual intimacy, couples tell a cruciform story of self-denial and self-sacrifice. Joel Beeke adds a necessary word here, "Making love is hardly bearing a cross," a sentiment I believe most would agree with. He continues, "But making love, if it is truly an act of love, involves self-denial."[17] No longer is the focus on the person and their needs, but on the other and their needs and desires. When this sort of reciprocity is present, the opportunities for mutual pleasure, enjoyment, and joy are endless. Savage is helpful again, "[Sex] is maximally enjoyed when it is exclusively given."[18] When sex becomes less about *what you owe me* and moves to *how can I serve you*, sexual intimacy is completely transformed from a mere physical act to an actual display of the gospel story.

ADDRESSING SEXUAL INTIMACY STRUGGLES IN MARRIAGE

With a solid foundation laid, how can you begin to address intimacy struggles in marriage? Where do you begin? Is it true that sex leads to greater intimacy? Or does greater intimacy lead to more sex? Based on my experience in marriage counseling, I find both statements to be true, but I find the latter statement has greater weight. When a couple can grow in intimacy in other areas of their marriage, it often has a positive effect on their sex life. Tim and Kathy Keller write, "Unless your marital relationship is in a good condition, sex doesn't work."[19] Beeke concurs, "Sex does not *make* a good marriage; it is the *fruit* of a good marriage."[20]

That being said, what are some possible ways you can help couples address sexual struggles? I suggest starting with conversations that help you ascertain why sexual intimacy presents a struggle for them. Here are some possible reasons you may hear.

---

16. Ibid., 233.

17. Joel R. Beeke, *Friends and Lovers: Cultivating Companionship and Intimacy in Marriage* (Adelphi, MD: Cruciform, 2012), 71.

18. Savage, *No Ordinary Marriage*, 114.

19. Keller, *The Meaning of Marriage*, 235.

20. Beeke, *Friends and Lovers*, 50.

Biological/physiological factors

In some situations, the husband will struggle with ED (erectile dysfunction) or male impotence. ED is defined as "the inability of the husband to achieve or keep an erection sufficient for intercourse."[21] Dr. Ed Wheat is helpful in addressing underlying issues associated with male impotence: anxiety or fear of failure, which leads to more anxiety and fear of failure.[22] As a counselor, these are areas you are well positioned to address. If the condition persists though, Dr. Wheat encourages seeking medical professional help.

Another physiological factor that might inhibit sexual intimacy is that for some couples, sex is painful—physically so. Pastor and counselor Brad Hambrick counsels, "When sex is painful it means something is wrong; not with you morally but physically. Pain is the alarm system of the body like guilt is the alarm system of the soul. When you're hurting go to the doctor like you go to God when you feel guilty. There is no reason for you to feel shame. Allow God to care for you through the expertise of an OBGYN or other relevant physician."[23] Hambrick goes on, quoting Christian psychologist Doug Rosenau, "Painful sex does not get better by ignoring it or trying to play through it. Often, it further traumatizes and creates more sexual difficulties."

Some couples might not have received proper premarital counseling, which should address sexual intimacy as a part of the overall curriculum. A lack of basic anatomical knowledge, positions, hygiene, etc. might hinder a couple's ability to be intimate. Dwight and Margaret Peterson note the lack of preparation with which many couples enter marriage:

> On the subject of marital sex beyond the wedding night, the sex education received by most Christian young people falls completely silent. The assumption seems to be that if the bride and groom can be brought safely virgin to the altar, then married sex will just take care of itself. If they're not virgins, it's their tough luck. And in any case, there is really nothing to say. There is nothing to be said about married sex to the unmarried because it might put ideas into their heads. As there is nothing to be said about married sex

---

21. Ed and Gaye Wheat, *Intended for Pleasure: Sex Technique and Sexual Fulfillment in Christian Marriage*, 3rd ed. (Grand Rapids: Revell, 1997), 123. Impotence, medically speaking, is not a one-time occurrence of a man losing an erection. The criterion for impotence is failed intercourse at 50–75% of his attempts. Dr. Wheat adds, "Occasional failures should *not* be viewed as impotence."

22. Ibid., 124.

23. Brad Hambrick, "Common Challenges to a Healthy Marital Sex Life," October 26, 2013. http://bradhambrick.com/common-challenges-to-a-healthy-marital-sex-life/.

to the married because once the ring is on your finger, sex comes perfectly naturally—right?[24]

In his helpful book *Marriage Matters*, author and pastor Winston Smith identifies other contributing biological and physiological factors:[25]

- Hormonal imbalances
- Conditions that affect blood flow (cardiovascular diseases and diabetes)
- Conditions that affect nerve functioning (neurological disorders)
- Chronic problems, such as kidney or liver diseases
- Abuse of medication (particularly antidepressants)
- Menopause
- Alcohol abuse

When these sorts of issues are complicating sexual intimacy, I find that the holistic approach to counseling, self-care, medical, and professional treatment is best.

Aging

As some couples get older, their intimacy increases in both frequency and pleasure. The Petersons write, "Bodies change over time, and sex changes over time too. But that change does not have to be from good to bad—it can be from the goodness of youth to the goodness of maturity. Sex is not just a matter of plumbing and hormones. Sex is about relationship and vulnerability and openness to intimacy. These aspects of marriage only get better with age, and as a result, more mature couples can find their sexual satisfaction increasing as the years go by."[26] Tim and Kathy Keller agree: "It took years for us to be good at sexually satisfying one another. But the patience paid off."[27]

That is not always the case, however, as you contrast the above experiences with roughly two-thirds of couples who experience a decrease in sexual activity in midlife. In many of these cases surveyed, that limitation in frequency is put in place unilaterally by one spouse without the consent or engagement of the other spouse.[28] Often a mixture of physiological factors (impotence, decreased libido) and psychological factors (feelings of failure, rejection) lead to one spouse cutting off intimacy.

---

24. Peterson, *Are You Waiting for "The One"?*, 136.
25. Winston Smith, *Marriage Matters* (Greensboro, NC: New Growth, 2010), 229.
26. Peterson, *Are You Waiting for "The One"?*, 148.
27. Keller, *The Meaning of Marriage*, 226.
28. Peterson, *Are You Waiting for "The One"?*, 147.

Dr. Ed Wheat has a helpful chapter (13) in his well-known book, *Intended for Pleasure*, where he addresses some of these factors that can hinder sexual intimacy in marriage. While very honest about some of the struggles the aging and elderly will encounter in marital intimacy, he maintains a robust optimism: "Sex after sixty can be better than ever. . . . The couple who keep active sexually can continue to enjoy lovemaking after sixty . . . seventy . . . and even eighty."[29]

Historical factors

Another barrier to sexual intimacy can be childhood or even adult trauma/abuse.[30] A history of sexual abuse in childhood can adversely affect both men and women in their ability to be sexually intimate. David Powlison notes, "The experience of violation can leave the victim self-labeled as 'damaged goods.' Sex becomes intrinsically dirty, shameful, dangerous. Even in marriage, it can become an unpleasant duty, a necessary evil, not the delightful convergence of duty and desire."[31]

Additionally, if a spouse was sexually active prior to marriage, there can be inhibitions surrounding intimacy in marriage. Feelings of guilt, embarrassment, and shame can abound surrounding previous sexual interactions. These are issues to work through in community. When spouses keep these feelings private and internal, the accusing voice of the Evil One can counter the truth of the gospel. Passages like Hebrews 10:1–18 can be helpful. The author of Hebrews concludes this section, writing, "And where these have been forgiven, sacrifice for sin is no longer necessary." Spouses who are struggling to reconcile a past history of sexual regret need to hear this truth repeated often.

Paul Maxwell offers hope to those struggling with an embarrassing past, "A sexual history only complicates matters. It can make us nervous, cautious, withholding, unsparing, unforgiving, and bludgeoning. But, by God's infinite and mysterious grace, it can also be an event for mending, for excavating, for cherishing, for learning—if we have the courage."[32]

In marriages where there has been infidelity, sexual intimacy can be a struggle.

---

29. Wheat, *Intended for Pleasure*, 214, 224.

30. For spouses who have been raped, sexual intimacy can present profound and difficult dynamics. Careful concerns and caution should attend the way we counsel, care, and advise in situations like this. Heath Lambert, Executive Director of ACBC (Association of Certified Biblical Counselors) has a brief podcast where he addresses this, among other issues: https://biblicalcounseling.com/2017/04/til-095-spouse-doesnt-want-sex/.

31. David Powlison, *Making All Things New: Restoring Joy to the Sexually Broken* (Wheaton, IL: Crossway, 2017), 41.

32. Paul C. Maxwell, "You Are Not Damaged Goods," January 23, 2016. *Desiring God*: https://www.desiringgod.org/articles/you-are-not-damaged-goods.

Ironically, some couples experience a season of sexual activity post-affair. The reason is usually that the offended spouse views sex as one way they can physically reconcile their spouse's misplaced and misguided sexual affections. However, long-term struggles will persist in a couple's relationship if the marital infidelity is not biblically addressed.

Finally, I will ask couples if there were struggles during their dating and engagement story. Physical boundaries that were crossed during this time in a couple's relationship can often lead to physical struggles in marriage. Guilt surrounding lapsed boundaries sow the seeds of sexual dysfunction for a couple. Tim and Kathy Keller write, "If we do something sexually that is wrong, we should use the gospel of grace on our consciences. That gospel will neither take the sin lightly nor lead you to flagellate yourself and wallow in guilt indefinitely. It is important to get the gospel's pardon and cleansing for wrongdoing. Often it is unresolved shame for past offenses that stirs up present, obsessive fantasies."[33]

Use of pornography

A common struggle I find that produces sexual intimacy struggles in marriage is the ongoing use and indulgence of pornography and masturbation. A husband who experiences the rejection of his wife may be tempted to use this as an excuse and turn to pornography to satisfy his needs. After time, the use of pornography and the gratification of masturbation enslaves him. It's so much easier to log onto a website to be sexually satisfied than to do the hard work of investing in your marriage. There is no room for accommodation here: the use of pornography in marriage is in direct contradiction to the Bible's commands for sexual conduct in marriage. A spouse's sexual abstinence or frigidity is never an excuse for the use of pornography or masturbation in marriage.

One spouse's use of pornography sometimes causes another problem: a couple's use of pornography to catalyze sexual intimacy. The thinking goes that the use of pornography, if agreed upon between husband and wife, can produce and introduce sexual excitement and spontaneity into the marriage bed. In most cases, however, one spouse is typically pushing this as a solution over the objections and quiet hesitancies of the other. The use of pornography in marriage not only creates unrealistic expectations of what sexual intimacy is, it also distracts the focus of the spouse from his/her partner during lovemaking. I vividly remember a young couple with whom I was working giving voice to the negative impact pornography had played in their marriage. The wife tearfully confessed to her husband, "I feel

---

33. Keller, *The Meaning of Marriage*, 234.

like a prostitute in bed, not like a wife whom you love." In this situation, the husband proved pastor Matt Chandler's statement true: "This is [another] reason pornography is so dangerous. It makes men sexually stupid."[34]

(Un)Biblical views of sex

In some situations, an unbiblical view of sex can cause marital intimacy struggles. If the story of marriage is to be a story of the gospel-embodied life, again it stands to reason that this applies to every facet of marriage, including our sex lives. As we have seen, the apostle Paul had remarkably positive views on sex within marriage, and as such he stands in contrast to Gnostic attitudes toward sex.

The church, perhaps in reaction to culture, has often downplayed sex altogether. In the early church, abstaining from sex completely was seen as a way to increased holiness. In fact, Paul quotes a saying to that effect: "It is good for a man not to have sexual relations with a woman," (1 Cor. 7:1) and then goes on to correct it. Christopher Ash writes that the people quoting this saying in the Corinthian context were "falsely spiritual people who were encouraging married couples to avoid sex, because they thought sex was dirty or unspiritual."[35] Richard Hays concurs: "Sexual abstinence was widely viewed as a means to personal wholeness and religious power."[36] Ironically, Paul's quotation was misunderstood and this mistaken view persisted in the early church. Many church fathers, including Augustine, had negative views on sex, except when it was used for procreation.[37] An extended quote from Gary Thomas is enlightening:

> In the 2nd century, Clement of Alexandria allowed unenjoyed and procreative sex only during twelve hours out of the twenty-four (at night), but by the Middle Ages, preposterous as it now seems, the Church forbade it forty days before the important festival of Christmas, forty days before and eight days after the more important festival of Easter, eight days after Pentecost, the eves of feast days, on Sundays in honor of the resurrection, on Wednesdays to call to mind the beginning of Lent, Fridays in memory of the crucifixion, during pregnancy and thirty days after birth (forty if the child is female), during menstruations, and five days before communion! This all adds up to 252

---

34. Matt Chandler, *The Mingling of Souls: God's Design for Love, Marriage, Sex & Redemption* (Colorado Springs: Cook, 2015), 125.

35. Ash, *Married for God*, 65.

36. Richard B. Hays, *First Corinthians—Interpretation: A Bible Commentary for Teaching and Preaching.* (Louisville, KY: Westminster John Knox, 2011), 114.

37. Ash, *Married for God*, 62. Augustine taught that sexual intercourse transmitted original sin . . . thus, entangling sex and sin for centuries. Ambrose called marriage honorable but chastity "more honorable."

excluded days, not counting feast days. If there were thirty of those (a guess which may, in fact, be on the conservative side), there would have been eighty-three remaining days in the year when couples with the permission of the Church could have indulged in (but not enjoyed) sexual intercourse.[38]

Tim and Kathy Keller make the point that unfortunately, "this view is still very influential in the world."[39] Consequently, as Joel Beeke writes, "The root of much sexual dysfunction is a lingering doubt whether marital sex is pure and acceptable in God's sight."[40]

At the opposite end of the spectrum are marriages where the Bible is misinterpreted to serve one spouse's sinful desires. From husbands who demand sex in order to control wives who withhold sex to punish, unbiblical views of sex lead to unbiblical uses of sex in marriage. Misinterpreting Scripture to suit your desires, particularly sexual desires, is wrong. I counseled a couple where the husband demanded sex from his wife as part of her marital duty. He had twisted Scripture to the point where he believed he could have sex with his wife apart from her consent.[41] Sex without consent is rape. There must be mutual consent, even in a marital relationship.

(RE)BUILDING SEXUAL INTIMACY IN MARRIAGE

After spending some time discerning the cause of intimacy struggles in marriage, what are some practical ways a pastor or counselor can help a couple resume a healthy, mutually satisfying sex life?[42]

---

38. Gary Thomas, *Sacred Marriage* (Grand Rapids: Zondervan, 2000), 202.

39. Keller, *The Meaning of Marriage*, 220.

40. Beeke, *Friends and Lovers*, 45. Compounding this is the tradition embedded in Roman Catholic thinking that sexual intercourse in marriage was a venial sin. R. C. Sproul writes, "Within Neo-Platonism, the physical world is regarded as being at best an imperfect copy of the spiritual world. Consequently, anything of a physical nature is imperfect. Deeply imbedded in the Roman Catholic tradition is the idea that people sin at least venially when they engage in sexual intercourse within marriage" (R. C. Sproul, *The Intimate Marriage* [Phillipsburg, NJ: P&R, 2003], 117).

41. Doug Rosenau writes, "Please don't use God's loving guidelines as weapons against each other. Some husbands and wives club their mates with this passage and say things like, 'If you don't have sex with me tonight, you are sinning.' The real sin is theirs because they usually have never taken the time, loving kindness, and energy to make changes needed to appeal to their mates romantically. . . . Remember, making love is about giving—not demanding. . . . On the other hand, are you too fatigued or busy or inhibited to have sexual relations regularly? You two are missing God's plan for marriage and the enjoyment of one of His avenues for increasing intimacy" (Doug Rosenau, *A Celebration of Sex: A Guide to Enjoying God's Gift of Sexual Intimacy* [Nashville: Thomas Nelson, 2002], 5).

42. One caveat I believe bears mentioning is that conversations about a couple's intimate life should happen with great care and propriety. Meaning, I would not counsel a woman alone in issues related to intimacy, but rather seek to engage either my wife or another female counselor. Similarly, I would not

Make time for sexual intimacy.

As you will see, these suggestions for change are not revolutionary or complex. They're simple and doable. One simple thing couples can try in order to rebuild sexual intimacy (or any kind of intimacy, really) is to make time for each other. A date night is not going to solve all your marital intimacy problems, but carving out special time for uninterrupted and unhurried conversation can go a long way toward cultivating intimacy.

C. J. Mahaney, in his helpful book *Sex, Romance and the Glory of God,* memorably reminds husbands in particular, "Before you touch her body, touch her heart and mind."[43] Husbands must remember that intimacy in marriage is something that requires an investment of time. In a similar vein, Matt Chandler writes to wives, "Your husband is not seeking just sexual willingness from you but sexual eagerness."[44]

Talk to your spouse.

Part of what carving out time for your relationship does is create space to talk. In an age where we can be chained to our phones and devices, there is something quietly revolutionary about simply talking face-to-face with your spouse. Tim Savage points out, "Perhaps the best way to create vibrant sexual intimacy is to excel at verbal communication. . . . This is a common theme in the Song of Solomon. For a poem designed as a tribute to erotic love, we are amazed how little we see of the movements beneath the sheets and how much we are allowed to eavesdrop on the verbal interaction of the two lovers. The husband and the wife seem to know that successful lovemaking is 10% perspiration and 90% conversation."[45]

The Song of Solomon is interpreted in a variety of ways, but what is undeniably true, whatever your interpretation, is the role of language and communication to convey love and intimacy. As Solomon and his bride speak to one another, you quickly realize this conversation is passionate, intimate, sensual, and provocative. There is freedom and generosity in how they speak to one another. Their praise is effusive; their lovemaking anything but stale or boring. There is a thoughtfulness and beauty that attends their complements of one another. As Simone Weil, the French philosopher wrote, "Attention is the purest form of generosity."[46]

I remember a recent conference I attended where a well-known speaker commented about the role of conversation in his marriage. While not denying the

---

encourage a female counselor to counsel a husband alone on issues related to intimacy. This is where a "two is better than one" approach is best for your personal integrity as well as the counsel for the couple.

43. C. J. Mahaney, *Sex, Romance, and the Glory of God* (Wheaton, IL: Crossway 2004), 58.

44. Chandler, *The Mingling of Souls*, 136.

45. Savage, *No Ordinary Marriage*, 115.

46. https://www.brainpickings.org/2015/08/19/simone-weil-attention-gravity-and-grace/.

pleasures of sex with his wife, he related how good it was simply to talk and enjoy his wife's company. A bit tongue-in-cheek, he shared that in some ways their talking with one another was better than sex . . . that's how enjoyable, deep, and meaningful their time together was. Duane Garrett writes, "Many homes would be happier if men and women would simply speak of their love for one another a little more often."[47]

For couples needing some prompts for conversation, David Powlison offers three questions to prime the pump:[48]

1. What are your burdens?
2. What are your joys?
3. What's your purpose?

Powlison offers helpful questions underneath these three starter questions that they can investigate on their own. He summarizes his intent with these three: "What happens when you start asking and answering these three simple questions? You start to talk about what's really happening—your joys, your burdens, and your direction. I guarantee you that those conversations will bring about the conditions that make two people one. When two people sorrow together, rejoice together, and join together in a life task, the result is intimacy and closeness."[49] Additionally, I give couples questions to have a more pointed conversation about their intimate life. They can work on these together in the privacy of their relationship, and discuss with you any problems they bump into:

- Do you and your spouse view your sexual intimacy as an overall part of the way you glorify God through your marriage?
- How often do you initiate sexual intimacy with your spouse?
- When was the last time you and your spouse were able to get away for an overnight trip?
- Have you and your spouse had a conversation recently about your sex life?
- What would be one thing you could do to improve your sex life?
- What is one thing you could stop doing to improve your sex life?
- What obstacles, roadblocks, or sins are hindering you from having a meaningful intimate life with your spouse?

---

47. Duane Garrett, *Proverbs, Ecclesiastes, Song of Solomon*, New American Commentary (Nashville: Broadman, 1993), 379.
48. David Powlison, *Renewing Marital Intimacy: Closing the Gap Between You and Your Spouse* (Greensboro, NC: New Growth, 2008), 18–19.
49. Ibid., 19.

- What are ways you are introducing variety and spontaneity into your lovemaking?[50]
- Do you engage in nonsexual, affectionate touch with your spouse?

Be quick to forgive.

A variety of reasons were discussed that can contribute to intimacy struggles in marriage. One issue that bears special mention here is the practice of forgiveness. A lack of forgiveness leads to a spirit of bitterness; both will kill marital intimacy. It should not be assumed that a wife is the one to whom this admonition is given. Some mistakenly believe that a wife will be more prone to become unforgiving, and thus sexually unavailable or cold to her husband. I have seen a number of husbands hold a grudge or maintain an unforgiving spirit toward their wives which has, in turn, affected their desire for intimacy.

One area where a spirit of bitterness can arise with husbands relates to who initiates sex. Generalizations in marriage can be misleading, but in my experience a majority of husbands feel they initiate more often than their wives. After being rejected, a husband can become embittered with his wife for her apparent lack of interest. Brad Hambrick writes of the balance of who should initiate, "Both husband and wife should regularly initiate sex. The ratio does not have to be precisely 50–50, but it also shouldn't be 80–20. Both initiating sex and responding affirmatively to the initiation of the other are unique ways to love each other. You each should be able to bless the other with both responses: pursuing and responding. This maintains a balance in confidence and voice for both of you."[51]

Husbands and wives should keep short tabs on sin. Where does confession need to take place? David Powlison writes, "Start with an honest assessment of your heart, so you know what is getting in the way of intimacy with God and your spouse. Are you lazy? Preoccupied? Filled with resentment? Fearful of being hurt? Finding out why there is distance in your relationship is crucial so you can know where you need to repent and where you need God's help."[52] When husband and wife commit to a daily habit of confessing sin and forgiving each other, a positive implication will be a stronger relationship of honesty, security, and trust. When those elements are present in a marital relationship, physical intimacy can thrive and flourish.

---

50. Brad Hambrick has an excellent article on various kinds of marital sex: http://bradhambrick.com/eight-no-six-kinds-of-marital-sex/. Brad writes of his post, "The list is not exhaustive or technical, so as the two of you discuss the list feel free to add to it and change the titles. The purpose of the list is not to help you study for a matching quiz, but to give you expanded vocabulary and concepts for communicating about sex."

51. Brad Hambrick, "Initiating and Declining Sex in Marriage Need Not Be Awkward or Upsetting," April 25, 2014. http://bradhambrick.com/initiating-and-declining-sex-in-marriage-need-not-be-awkward-or-upsetting/.

52. Powlison, *Renewing Marital Intimacy*, 13.

Cultivate nonsexual, affectionate touch.

A practical way couples can rebuild marital intimacy is through cultivating nonsexual, affectionate touch: sitting close to one another on the couch, hugging, holding hands, loving kisses and caresses. I counseled one couple who struggled with a variety of issues, one of which was their intimate life. The wife complained about how every time her husband wanted sex, he would begin to rub her feet. What began as something enjoyable became a dread to her because it signaled the fact that he wanted something from her.

For some couples who have experienced a bit of a drought in their sex life, engaging in sexual intercourse can seem like a bridge too far. Help them get there by encouraging them to simply embrace and touch one another. Affectionate embraces from a spouse can communicate deeply of care and love in marriage without the encumbrance or burden that every touch signals one spouse's desire for sex.[53]

Enjoy sex now because it's temporary.

Whenever I officiate a wedding, I remind couples of two things: marriage is temporary, and thus, sex is temporary. I don't say this to be a killjoy, but to introduce a bit of reality and levity into the ceremony. For most couples at the altar, sex is at the forefront of their minds (or at least the husbands'). It is good to remember that sex doesn't make a marriage. Is it good? Absolutely! But is it the ultimate thing to pursue in marriage? Absolutely not. Sex, like all of God's gifts to us, is not an end to itself but is intended to point to the Giver of the gifts. Tim and Kathy explain how sex relates to our eternal future,

> Sex is glorious not only because it reflects the joy of the Trinity, but also because it points to the eternal delight of soul that we will have in heaven, in our loving relationships with God and one another. Romans 7:1ff tells us that the best marriages are pointers to the deep, intimately fulfilling, and final union we will have with Christ in love. No wonder, as some have said, that sex between a man and a woman can be a sort of embodied, out of body experience. It's the most ecstatic, breathtaking, daring, scarcely-to-be-imagined look at the glory that is our future.[54]

---

53. If the affection and physical touch naturally lead to sex, that is obviously a positive and not to be discouraged. What I hope to encourage couples who have had a dry spell in their sex lives is to simply ease into being near one another, being affectionate with one another.

54. Keller, *The Meaning of Marriage*, 236.

Sex in marriage, as Lewis writes in *The Screwtape Letters*, functions as "shafts of glory" where every "pleasure [becomes] a channel of adoration."[55] When couples are equipped with this viewpoint, it has the potential to lift their gaze to Christ. Matt Chandler sums it up well: "Married sex *can* draw you closer to God and your spouse, and one of the ways it does that is by pointing away from sex and toward the gospel of Jesus Christ. Sex is good, but it's not built for eternity. It won't be around forever. Neither will marriage for that matter. No, marriage and sex are good, but Jesus is better. He is better than everything in life. He is better than life itself. He *is* life."[56]

Counselor Fieldnotes

Counseling is a place where people have awkward conversations. It is never comfortable talking of things about which we feel shame, guilt, confusion, or ignorance. But isn't this concoction of experiences what couples bring to counseling about sex, romance, and intimacy (which are awkward enough without struggles)? As a counselor, you get to be God's ambassador to weary, burdened souls in the midst of this awkwardness—even sexual awkwardness.

What is the first part of being an ambassador? Conversation—listening, honor, and vocabulary. What is missing for most couples who experience difficulties with intimacy? Conversation—listening well to what is most important to their partner, honoring one another (remaining other-minded) during the exhilaration of their deepest passions, and vocabulary to talk about something that was taboo and off-limits until they said, "I do," and about which they likely learned their initial language in a middle school locker room or on the internet.

In this chapter, Jonathan has equipped you to have honest, informed, mature conversations that help couples learn to talk maturely about sex so they can engage playfully in the gift God intended them to enjoy as husband and wife. Our goal in counseling is often to help a couple, by God's grace, reach a level of maturity at which they can play well together; a healthy sex life is not something a couple works at (discipline) as much as plays toward (delight). Like the rest of the Christian life, we are teaching a maturity that liberates rather than confines.

---

55. C. S. Lewis, *The Screwtape Letters* (New York: Macmillan, 1951), 102.
56. Chandler, *The Mingling of Souls*, 142.

Whether your work with a given couple is preparatory (premarital) or restorative (post-betrayal), counseling on matters of sexuality requires what I consider the most fundamental skill of counseling—the ability, perhaps willingness, to be comfortable being uncomfortable. Do not assume that because you've read, or even mastered, the content of this chapter that counseling will be comfortable. Be willing to incarnate the wisdom and maturity of Christ into the awkwardness of sexual confusion, sexual brokenness, and sexual betrayal.

If, as a church, we are unwilling to meaningfully enter these difficult conversations, then the world will be happy to fill our silence and will continue to own the subject of sexuality. Thank you for equipping yourself to be a redemptive voice in the life of many couples on behalf of Christ.

Brad Hambrick, Pastor of Counseling, The Summit Church

RESOURCES

Daniel Akin, *God on Sex: The Creator's Ideas About Love, Intimacy, and Marriage*

Christopher Ash, *Married for God: Making Your Marriage the Best It Can Be* (ch. 4)

Joel R. Beeke, *Friends and Lovers: Cultivating Companionship and Intimacy in Marriage*

Denny Burk, *What Is the Meaning of Sex?* (ch. 4)

Matt Chandler, *The Mingling of Souls: God's Design for Love, Marriage, Sex & Redemption* (ch. 5)

Linda Dillow and Dr. Juli Slattery, *Passion Pursuit: What Kind of Love Are You Making?* (10-week DVD series and accompanying workbook for women)

Brad Hambrick, "Common Challenges to a Healthy Marital Sex Life," http://bradhambrick.com/common-challenges-to-a-healthy-marital-sex-life/

Timothy and Kathy Keller, *The Meaning of Marriage: Facing the Complexities of Commitment with the Wisdom of God* (ch. 8)

Scott Mehl, "Sexual Struggles in Marriage," https://biblicalcounseling.com/2017/04/sexual-struggles-marriage/

Margaret Kim Peterson and Dwight N. Peterson, *Are You Waiting for "The One"? Cultivating Realistic, Positive Expectations for Christian Marriage* (ch. 6)

David Powlison, *Renewing Marital Intimacy: Closing the Gap Between You and Your Spouse*

Tim Savage, *No Ordinary Marriage: Together for God's Glory* (ch. 8)

R. C. Sproul, *The Intimate Marriage: A Practical Guide to Building a Great Marriage* (ch. 5)

Walter Wangerin, *As for Me and My House: Crafting Your Marriage to Last* (ch. 13)

Chapter 16

IN-LAWS OR OUTLAWS?

Perhaps the most difficult of all relationships to deal with is the in-law relationship.

JAY ADAMS

That is why a man leaves his father and mother and is united to his wife, and they become one flesh.

GENESIS 2:24

When I attended The Master's College (now The Master's University), I remember my counseling professors telling us that the big three issues we would face in marriage counseling were: sex, finances, and in-laws. The first two made sense to me, but the latter seemed out of place. Problems with in-laws? Really? What about communication, decision-making, or raising children? In-laws?

Little did I know that one of my first marriage counseling cases would revolve around a conflict with in-laws. Problems with in-laws often trigger other issues with which couples need assistance within marriage, like communication, conflict resolution, and decision-making. Studies tells us that ensuring that couples enjoy a good relationship with their respective in-laws is important to marital health. Jim Daly at Focus on the Family quotes such research, writing, "According to a newly-released study, men who are on good terms with their wives' parents are more likely to enjoy a long-lasting marriage than those who struggle to get along with their in-laws."[1]

---

1. Jim Daly, "How Your Relationship with Your In-Laws Impacts Your Marriage," 2013. *Focus on*

Research professor and psychologist Terri Orbuch conducted a frequently-cited study on in-law relationships. Orbuch followed 373 couples who were newlyweds in 1986. She studied the responses of men and women in terms of how close they felt to their in-laws on a sliding scale. After twenty-six years, Orbuch came to two fascinating conclusions: when a man reported a close relationship to his wife's parents, the risk of divorce decreased by 20 percent; however, when women reported a close relationship to her husband's parents the risk of divorce rose by 20 percent.[2]

Orbuch explains, "Close in-law ties between a husband and his wife's parents are reinforcing to women and connect him to her. When a husband gets close to his wife's parents, this says to her: 'Your family is important to me because I care about you. I want to feel closer to them because it makes me feel closer to you.' And of course, that makes us as women feel really good."[3] Conversely, Orbuch noted that when a woman gets close to her mother-in-law, a variety of issues can emerge. One of which is the husband feeling that his mother and wife are aligning to get him to change something about himself. Orbuch notes, "This closeness can result in a unified front against the husband and, as you might imagine, is apt to infuriate him."

Additionally, when a mother-in-law feels a closeness to her daughter-in-law, there can be a "greater sense of access and ability to cross boundaries and meddle, which can seem threatening, particularly if a woman feels that her in-laws are interfering with her identity as a wife and mother."[4] All in all, Orbuch's study noted that in-law relationships are a significant area of stress for marriages.[5]

In light of biblical truth, then, how do we make sense of Orbuch's observations? A few orienting principles will be helpful in any marriage counseling situation where in-laws feature as the primary suspect.

- *Principle 1*: The biblical plan for marriage requires three things: leaving, cleaving, and a weaving.

---

the Family: http://www.focusonthefamily.com/marriage/communication-and-conflict/inlaw-relationships/how-your-relationship-with-your-in-laws-impacts-your-marriage.

2. Ian Kerner, "In-Laws Can Help—Or Hurt—Your Marriage," December 13, 2012. http://www.cnn.com/2012/12/13/health/kerner-inlaws/index.html.

3. Ibid.

4. Ibid. Orbuch notes further, "If women are close to their in-laws, especially early in marriage, this interferes with or prevents them from forming a unified and strong bond with their husband. Also, since women are constantly analyzing and trying to improve their relationships, they often take what their in-laws say as personal and can't set the clear boundaries."

5. In most writing on the topic of in-law relationships, mothers-in-law are singled out for particular attention. From my vantage point, this is largely due to the issues Orbuch notes in her studies as well as others. However, that should not obscure the fact that fathers-in-law present challenges for married couples as well.

- *Principle 2*: In-laws are not the *cause* of your marriage problems. They only reveal what is inside your heart.
- *Principle 3*: In-laws are not the enemy of your marriage.
- *Principle 4*: God desires unity between husband and wife, and thus, the primary relationship in marriage is with your spouse.
- *Principle 5*: Loving and pursuing your spouse does not have to happen to the exclusion of your in-laws.

Leaving, cleaving, and a weaving

A frequent aphorism in marriage is, "When you get married, you not only marry your spouse, you marry their family." While the statement makes some sense when taken in context, it's not biblical. When a husband and wife marry one another, they make only one covenant—with God, not to their in-laws. Counselors must be biblically clear: the primary relationship that is to be nourished and protected is the spousal relationship. Your husband or wife is your number one God-given priority in life.

Many couples you will see in marriage counseling have received some sort of premarital counseling; others have not. When issues arise surrounding in-laws, I will inquire if there was any sort of premarital counseling because this issue is typically covered.[6] Like other issues couples struggle with, you will have the opportunity as a pastor-counselor to both teach and remind.

Couples must be reminded of God's plan for marriage, which is laid out clearly without exception in Genesis 1–2. Adams concludes, "the most important prerequisite for a proper relationship with in-laws is a careful, intelligent, and prayerful application of the command found in Genesis 2:24."[7]

All biblical marriages should follow this pattern found in Genesis. Husband and wife leave their parents and cleave (unite) to their new spouse and become one flesh. Many couples have been taught to leave and cleave, but there is a third word here that often goes unaddressed: becoming one flesh. The word I like to use with couples is that of *weaving* their life together. Couples need to understand that cleaving to each other is not simply a one-time act performed at the marriage ceremony but a lifetime of growing together as a one-flesh couple. Even secular

---

6. Wayne Mack has an excellent section of teaching and homework in his book *Preparing for Marriage God's Way* (Phillipsburg, NJ: P&R, 2013), 75–85. While primarily designed for premarital counseling, this would work well in a marriage counseling session as well. Mack includes a sample letter, which could be written on behalf of a spouse to their parents, explaining the leaving and cleaving principle of marriage.

7. Jay Adams, *Critical Stages of Biblical Counseling* (Stanley, NC: Timeless Texts, 2002), 69.

marriage counselors recognize the problem when couples don't leave, cleave, and weave their lives together: "There's a reason why conflict with the in-laws is so common: it touches upon one of marriage's most important tasks: Establishing and maintaining the sense of 'we-ness.'"[8]

In *Preparing for Marriage*, two kinds of cords are severed in the leaving/cleaving process:

- *Severing the cord of dependency*: This means choosing not to rely on parents for material or emotional support.
- *Severing the cord of allegiance*: Before the wedding day, a person's most significant relationships are with their mother and father, but during that ceremony their priorities change.[9]

Jay Adams states, "Parents must never try to 'buy' the right to call the shots in their children's marriage."[10] If a couple is financially dependent on their parents, they should seek to become financially independent as soon as is wisely possible. From student loans to car payments, it is good for newly married couples to seek to establish financial independence.

This leaving, cleaving, and weaving does not mean that husband and wife no longer need to honor and respect their parents (Eph. 6:2). This transition from living under parental authority moves the husband and wife into a different sphere of relationship and relating.[11] Husbands and wives are called to honor their in-laws, but no longer is their relationship a relationship of obedience.[12] Likewise, parents of children should not seek to exercise authority over their married adult

8. John Gottman, *The Seven Principles for Making Marriage Work*, quoted in Craig Diestelkamp, "Establishing a Sense of 'We-ness' through the Holidays," December 14, 2017. *Live at Peace Ministries*: http://liveatpeace.org/establishing-a-sense-of-we-ness-through-the-holidays/.

9. David Boehi et al. *Preparing for Marriage*, ed. Dennis Rainey (Ventura, CA: Gospel Light, 1997), 96.

10. Adams, *Critical Stages of Biblical Counseling*, 70. If a couple is financially dependent on their parents, they should seek to become financially independent as soon as is wisely possible. Adams goes on to speak of the issue of financial loans from parents to their children. He advocates two prongs of attack: (1) repay the loan as soon as possible and (2) come to an understanding that the loan will not interfere with the authority structure of their home and marriage.

11. When there are extenuating circumstances (e.g. a married couple living with their parents or depending on their parents for financial purposes), it complicates matters significantly. This is why the biblical model is to be followed. When couples are dependent on their parents for their financial or living situation, it can present difficulty because it confuses the leaving/cleaving principle. Seasoned counselor Wayne Mack states plainly, "Children must leave behind an inordinate dependency on their parents when they get married . . . as children get older, they learn to do more and more things for themselves and become less dependent" (Wayne Mack, *In-Laws: Married with Parents* [Phillipsburg, NJ: P&R, 2009], 13).

12. A notable exception would be if a spouse works for a parent. Here again, even in the best of situations, I've seen this lead to problematic outcomes due to the confusion of roles and responsibilities.

children. Jimmy and Karen Evans write, "Regardless of how parents or in-laws gain authority in a child's marriage, it is always wrong and damaging to a marriage. . . . Parents should never try to exercise authority over their grown children, and children should never allow it."[13]

In-laws are not the cause of your marriage problems.

"But you haven't met my mother-in-law!" This frequent response is understandable, but as we learned in chapter two, external circumstances do not *cause* or *make* one to sin. Yes, in-laws can be a significant pressure point and trial for couples, both young and old, but that does not negate the truth of Jesus's teaching: "What comes out of a person is what defiles them. For it is from within, out of a person's heart, that evil thoughts come—sexual immorality, theft, murder, adultery, greed, malice, deceit, lewdness, envy, slander, arrogance and folly. All these evils come from inside and defile a person" (Mark 7:20–23).

The Bible teaches us that external circumstances and people can actually grow our faith and be an instrument of God to sanctify us: "Consider it pure joy, my brothers and sisters, whenever you face trials of many kinds, because you know that the testing of your faith produces perseverance. Let perseverance finish its work so that you may be mature and complete, not lacking anything" (James 1:2–4).

When people have a biblical perspective of their hearts and their situations, you can move from blame-shifting and pointing the finger to finding a biblical solution. Listen, this is not an excuse for sinful behavior on the part of the in-laws, but in marriage counseling that is not your primary responsibility to address. The couple's heart and behavior are what is on display. It is our job to direct them, whether it is encouraging and sustaining them in a time of suffering with their in-laws or admonishing or instructing them on how to respond biblically to their in-laws.

In-laws are not the enemy of your marriage.

Recently I met with a couple, and the wife had a strong antipathy for her father-in-law. She found him to be loud, obnoxious, and downright rude. She dreaded family gatherings and holidays. When she spoke of him, I could see how difficult it was for her to be around him. I asked her, "Sam, is your father-in-law the biggest enemy you and Mark face in marriage?" Sam responded quickly, "Absolutely! He's destroying our marriage!"

Gently, I guided both Mark and Sam to what Paul wrote in Ephesians 6: "Our struggle is not against flesh and blood, but against the rulers, against the

---

13. Jimmy and Karen Evans, *Marriage on the Rock: God's Design for Your Dream Marriage* (Ventura, CA: Regal, 2007), 262.

authorities, against the powers of this dark world and against the spiritual forces of evil in the heavenly realms" (Eph. 6:12).

Then we read what Peter wrote in 1 Peter, "Be alert and of sober mind. Your enemy the devil prowls around like a roaring lion looking for someone to devour" (1 Pet. 5:8).

Mark and Sam needed to be reminded that other people are not our primary enemies! Our struggle is against a powerful but defeated entity: Satan. He is a roaring lion—not a cute kitten—who wants nothing more than the demise of our marriages. He will seek to use and engage anything and everything at his disposal to wreak havoc on marriages. That power combined with our own sinful flesh and the corrupting influence of the world remind us of our absolute and total dependence on Jesus Christ.

Earlier in Ephesians, Paul brings all three of these potent enemies in marriage together: "You were dead in your transgressions and sins, in which you used to live when you followed the ways of this world and of the ruler of the kingdom of the air, the spirit who is now at work in those who are disobedient. All of us also lived among them at one time, gratifying the cravings of our flesh and following its desires and thoughts" (Eph. 2:1–3).

Joel Beeke writes, "Believers must fight a war on three fronts: the world, the flesh, and the devil. Soldiers on the frontline must always be alert, and how much more soldiers with invisible enemies!"[14] Couples must focus their prayer and attention on these issues, not meddling mothers-in-law or frustrating fathers-in-law.

The primary relationship in marriage is with your spouse.

Paul is clear in Philippians 2 that all of God's children should endeavor to have the mind of Christ. The mind of Christ is singular; he does not have multiple identities. What marks the mind of Christ? "Therefore if you have any encouragement from being united with Christ, if any comfort from his love, if any common sharing in the Spirit, if any tenderness and compassion, then make my joy complete by being like-minded, having the same love, being one in spirit and of one mind. Do nothing out of selfish ambition or vain conceit. Rather, in humility value others above yourselves, not looking to your own interests but each of you to the interests of the others. In your relationships with one another, have the same mindset as Christ Jesus" (Phil. 2:1–5).

The mind of Christ is marked by selflessness and humility. As husbands and wives become united with Christ, they will seek that same unity in their relationships. This unity is achieved; it does not just magically appear. Husbands and wives

---

14. Joel Beeke, "Through the Westminster Confession," May 2013. *Reformation 21*: http://www
.reformation21.org/confession/2013/05/chapter-173.php.

build a marital unity that embodies the unity they enjoy with Christ as they grow together in Christlikeness. This marital unity should affect every area of a husband and wife's relationship, including how they relate to their in-laws.

When people allow themselves to be put at odds over issues with their in-laws, they must do whatever it takes to address the fissure before it becomes a gaping chasm in their marriage. Small disagreements, perceived insults, and ill-spoken words are all tactics Satan uses to destroy a couple's unity. D. A. Carson writes about the fact that people cannot drift toward godliness; I believe the same argument can be made regarding unity: "People do not drift toward holiness. Apart from grace-driven effort, people do not gravitate toward godliness, prayer, obedience to Scripture, faith, and delight in the Lord. We drift toward compromise and call it tolerance; we drift toward disobedience and call it freedom; we drift toward superstition and call it faith. We cherish the indiscipline of lost self-control and call it relaxation; we slouch toward prayerlessness and delude ourselves into thinking we have escaped legalism; we slide toward godlessness and convince ourselves we have been liberated."[15]

Dealing with the small fissures in a marriage now, revealed by the pressure of the couple's in-laws, can hopefully prevent them from finding themselves in a deep chasm of marital disunity later on in the marriage.

Loving your spouse does not have to happen to the exclusion of your in-laws.

A frequent concern you will encounter in marriage counseling is one spouse who feels they must choose one side over the other. The conversation goes something like this, "Sally, you're putting me in a really tough spot here. I don't want to disappoint you, but I also know how much this Christmas holiday means to my mom and dad. How do I choose?" What this question implies is a lack of understanding of principle number one. In this scenario, the choice between his wife and his family is seen as having equal weight and importance, when in fact one is primary and the other is secondary.

A husband's top priority in marriage is his wife, and the reverse is equally true. "Aha! Gotcha!" says the wife, "I told you that you needed to prioritize me over your mom!" Here, the counselor can gently step in and remind the wife that being pleased and prioritized does not *have* to happen at the exclusion of her in-law's interests. How can that be, she might wonder? Here are some helpful, practical principles with which you can equip couples after the foundations listed above are covered.

---

15. D. A. Carson, *For the Love of God* (Wheaton, IL: Crossway, 2006), 23.

PRACTICAL SOLUTIONS FOR DEALING
WITH IN-LAW ISSUES

See your in-laws as God sees them.

The way in-laws are treated should not differ from how anyone else made in God's image should be treated. In-laws are not outlaws. In-laws are not a primary enemy or opponent. They are people to be loved and known. Therefore, love for them "must be sincere" (Rom. 12:9). They are people to be lived with in a peaceful manner (Rom. 12:18). If the in-laws are believers, Paul proclaims, "Let us do good to all people, especially to those who belong to the family of believers" (Gal. 6:10). Part of our calling as believers is to "make every effort to keep the unity of the Spirit through the bond of peace" (Eph. 4:3).

Help husbands and wives view their in-laws as image bearers of God. Encourage them to identify what is good. What is praiseworthy? (Cf. Phil. 4:8) Part of healing and restoring relationships is trying to see the other person's perspective. This can help build empathy on both sides of the marital equation. How can you encourage a wife to see her mother-in-law's frequent, albeit unwelcome suggestions? At first, they might seem like the suggestions of an interloper, but could it be that the mother-in-law simply wants to make herself available to help?[16] "Well, you don't know my mother-in-law," is the frequent reply. Yes, but God's Word tells us that biblical love is kind, trusting, and hopeful (cf. 1 Cor. 13:4–7).

When we love our in-laws and see them as God sees them, we need to move toward them in Christian love. We ask good questions and wait for wise answers. We seek to serve them and minister to them. We speak the truth in love. We confront when necessary. We seek forgiveness and repent when we are in the wrong! We seek to build them up and encourage their faith. If the in-laws are not believers, all the more opportunity to live a life worthy and commendable of the gospel.

Seek consensus, not compromise.

The definition of compromise is "a settlement of differences by mutual concessions." The problem with compromise in marriage is the subsequent definition of what those *mutual concessions* entail. Too often, one spouse desires that the other spouse make the concessions without offering anything on their own end. That is why I prefer the term *consensus*. Consensus is defined as, "general agreement

---

16. Jimmy and Karen Evans identify three scenarios regarding mothers-in-law that can help spouses understand potential conflicts a bit better:

Mother-in-law lacks other fulfilling relationships.

Mother-in-law's identity is wrapped up in her child.

Mother-in-law is adversarial with child's spouse. (Evans, *Marriage on the Rock*, 265–267.)

or concord; harmony." As we have seen earlier, unity, or harmony as it is defined here, is a biblical priority in marriage. A simple diagram I will use in marriage counseling illustrates the problems with compromise:

Fig. 1

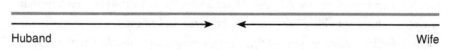

Husband   Wife

In figure one, husband and wife are on opposing ends of the spectrum. In certain counseling situations, husband and wife will be encouraged to each offer up "mutual concessions" to one another in order to meet in the middle. Unfortunately, as you can tell visually from the diagram, each spouse must give up equal amounts in order to meet in the middle. There is little room for error. Imagine this is a football field. Each spouse begins in their respective end zone and must travel at least fifty yards toward the middle. Let's say the husband is having a bad day and only makes it to the 49-yard line—there will be no opportunity for compromise because he is not meeting his wife in the middle. Let me offer an alternative I believe embodies marital consensus and love.

Fig. 2

Huband

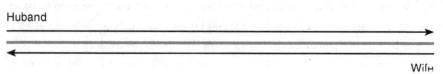

Wife

In figure two, husband and wife are on opposing ends of the spectrum but are encouraged to seek biblical unity. How is unity achieved? When we follow Christ's example of selflessness and sacrificial love. As a husband sees his wife, he endeavors to move 100 percent of the way toward his wife in love; similarly, a wife sees her husband and endeavors to move toward him 100 percent. In this scenario, each moves from their end zone to their spouse's end zone, and what they discover is that they now have much more room to make a decision that honors God and builds unity. Even if one spouse does not move 100 percent to the other, there is still a significantly greater opportunity to build consensus in this model as opposed to figure one.

A real-life counseling case can help us understand how this works practically. Pete and Haley were about two years into their marriage. Haley was extremely close to her parents, particularly her mother. They would talk on the phone every day, catching up on the day-to-day routines of life. At first, Pete didn't mind it so much, but sometimes he would come home from work and Haley would be on the phone with her mom. Other days, Haley's mom would actually be at the house hanging out. Because Pete had not said anything initially, Haley assumed it was not an issue.

After a long day at work, Pete had come home irritated and exasperated. Haley obliviously asked Pete to help her out with dinner. When he snapped back at her, Haley replied, "Someone's not in a good mood today" to which Pete retorted, "Why don't you just go over to your mom's house if I'm so hard to live with!" That opened up a can of worms, and Haley proceeded to ask Pete what he meant exactly. Needless to say, the conversation did not go well, as Pete unloaded his displeasure about Haley's relationship with her mom.

By the time they came into counseling, each of them had catastrophized the situation and completely misread the overall dynamic. Haley started off by saying Pete didn't want her to have a relationship with her mom anymore. Pete countered by saying Haley didn't make him a priority in their marriage. Now, if you take the compromise pathway with Pete and Haley, you might try to adjust expectations and reach a "compromise." Perhaps Haley only calls her mom three times a week? Or perhaps Pete agrees to a weekly dinner with Haley's parents in exchange for no calls with her family after 8:00 p.m.? Through compromise, you only address the surface level and you miss an opportunity to go deeper into the heart of the issue.

In a couple of sessions, I was able to help Pete and Haley see what was truly going on. Haley felt guilty and embarrassed that she had not asked Pete earlier in their marriage if her relationship with her mom bothered him. She had assumed he was fine with how often they talked, but after asking a few questions and listening, she realized Pete had tried to engage her before. If she had missed something like this, what else was she overlooking in her interactions with Pete?

Pete realized he wasn't really upset with Haley's mom or even how often they spoke on the phone or hung out. Deep inside, Pete was insecure and fearful of losing Haley. He shared with Haley and me that throughout his life, his friendships had been superficial because he had fair-weather friends. He brought that insecurity into marriage, and Pete began to realize he was actually upset by the prospect of losing intimacy with Haley.

In the consensus model, Pete and Haley were both encouraged to selflessly and sacrificially pursue the interests of their spouse first. Haley, knowing Pete's heart, was eager to move toward him in love. She had never *not* loved Pete, she simply had not known that what she was doing was failing to communicate love to him. Once she understood, she was fine cutting back on conversation with her mom. Conversely, as Pete acknowledged his own fears and insecurities to Haley, he found that such confession built intimacy. What he had thought was a weakness, God ended up using to bring them closer together. He told her in our final session, "You can talk to your mom as much as you want to. I know now that you do love me, and that you are committed to me."

What gets achieved in a compromise model is a quick fix. Rarely do such compromises end up working over the long haul. In a consensus model, there is more work to be done, but that work achieves a biblical goal of selfless love and embodied unity. Compromises work fine for "Where do we go to dinner?" scenarios; they do not work well where more substantive marital issues are on the line. Consensus engages the hearts of husbands and wives to fulfill their calling by looking out for their spouse's interests and by loving sacrificially. *Preparing for Marriage* sums it up well, "A 'oneness marriage' is the opposite of the world's 50/50 plan. It is a 100/100 plan in which both husband and wife set aside their own selfishness and experience true intimacy."[17]

Resolve to never speak ill of your spouse.

My wife, Jennifer, has many virtues, but one that has been eminently helpful to us in marriage is her resolve to never speak ill of me to her parents. I can honestly say that my wife has never in our marriage willfully sought to speak unkindly about me, not only to her parents but to anyone. Proverbs 11:13 states, "A gossip betrays a confidence, but a trustworthy person keeps a secret." Trust is an important element in any relationship, especially in marriage.

One of the ways marriage relationships break down is when one spouse confides in their parents about the faults of the other spouse. At first it might seem harmless, like a comment about how Rich never is home for dinner or an aside about how Liz parents the children. Before you know it, those conversations become a bit more involved, and more sensitive information is shared.

Husbands and wives need to agree to follow a pattern of communication that is informed by the Bible:

- Do I have my spouse's permission to share what I'm sharing?
- If I'm disappointed or hurt by my spouse, have I gone to God first and then them? (Cf. Matt. 18:15–17; Gal. 6:1–3)
- Is what I'm saying to my parents/in-laws building up my spouse or tearing them down? (Cf. Eph. 4:29)

---

17. Boehi et.al., *Preparing for Marriage*, 102.

Build new traditions, honor old ones.

When dealing with in-law issues, one common aspect ties them all together: time. How much time do you spend with each family on vacation? How much time do you spend with your extended family during the week? How do you divvy up time at the holidays? With whom do you spend Thanksgiving? Who gets Christmas? Who gets Easter? Who gets Arbor Day? Okay, maybe that's extreme, but you get the point. The amount of time you spend with parents is a frequent trigger for issues.

Again, as with any issue, we must approach it biblically. It's not enough to simply find a compromise at the expense of neglecting underlying heart issues. How a person spends their time is an important way in which they reveal what they value, love, and worship.

If husbands and wives are to leave, cleave, and weave their lives together, one of the ways they can practically do so is to build new traditions as a family. Often, during the busyness of holiday season, new families can be traveling so much from one place to the next that they miss an opportunity to weave their lives together. Marriage therapist Liz Higgins writes of the importance of forming new family traditions, "Finally, discuss ways in which you can establish your own family rituals when it comes to celebrating the holidays and insist that your in-laws respect them. Establishing your own family ritual creates shared meaning and builds a strong sense of 'we-ness.'"[18]

What would it look like if a spouse were to take aspects of their own family's tradition to build new ones together for their immediate family? Again, Higgins is helpful, "Acknowledge that your partner's family traditions are often just that: generational traditions that began years before you. If you bring a mindset of curiosity to your family gatherings this year, you may learn things about your partner and their family (and yourself!) that you never knew before."[19]

New traditions need to be built to help couples weave their lives together, but husbands and wives can honor old traditions as well. Yes, husbands and wives need to prioritize their relationship, but as we have said, that does not have to be mutually exclusive to honoring older, extended family traditions as well. In following the consensus model, how can husbands and wives find ways to honor their respective families?

What happens when there are overlapping desires and needs, e.g., both mothers want to spend Christmas Eve with you? Part of counseling will be to help

18. Liz Higgins, "How to Navigate the Holidays with Your In-Laws," December 23, 2016. *The Gottman Institute*: https://www.gottman.com/blog/how-navigate-holidays-with-your-in-laws/.
19. Ibid.

couples assess situations like this biblically. Here are a few questions you can use to help a couple think through their situation:

- Is your ultimate goal to please God in this situation?
- Have you and your spouse prayed and discussed the options?
- Are you both in agreement about how to move forward?
- How can you best communicate your decision to your parents in a way that brings harmony and unity?

Helping couples assess and prioritize requests on their time is one of the joys of pastoral counseling. What may seem at first like a minor issue is an actual opportunity to shepherd and guide couples to leave, cleave, and weave a family together for God's glory. God chooses the ordinary problems of life and marriage to sanctify both husband and wife and, as such, they are prime opportunities for both counseling and discipleship.

Utilize biblical tools for conflict resolution.

In more extreme cases of in-law situations, a more robust intervention may be necessary. As a counselor, you are well-positioned to function as a mediator between the couple and their parents. Utilizing biblical tools of conflict resolution is preferable to establishing or erecting boundaries to fence out the in-laws. Author Susan Thomas writes about a personal experience counseling a woman who was having problems with her in-laws:

> I remember a couple that adopted a boundaries mindset. The woman shared with me one day that she had read a book on the subject and that it was really guiding her in her relationships. She went on to describe that her life was like a piece of property with a fence around it. This was her domain given to her by God. She said she needed to make sure that everyone who came into that fenced in yard was right for her life. If people hurt her or she deemed them as toxic, then they were not allowed inside the fence. And, if someone inside the fence began to cause pain or behave in an ungodly way, they were escorted out of the fence.
>
> As I observed her life, I watched as she struggled with her in-laws and I eventually saw her lead her husband to cut them off for months with no communication until she was ready. Not long after, I watched some of her friendships deteriorate. She experienced conflict like we all do at some point. But, rather than work for peace and fight for resolution, she politely escorted

them one by one outside the fence of her life. She was very sad. And, the people around her were very sad.[20]

Thomas goes on to explain the problem when boundaries are used in this manner:

> While God-given boundaries are an important aspect of life, we must be aware of the danger of slipping into a boundary-driven mindset. In our attempt to protect ourselves, we may miss God's design for our relationships and His call on our lives.
>
> We are not to be boundary-driven in our relationships with others. We are to be love-driven! We are not to live in such a way that we demand people meet our expectations and then cut them off when they hurt or disappoint us. We are to love the people around us. We are to seek reconciliation rather than only self-protection.[21]

That is the key word: reconciliation! How can couples seek reconciliation when the relationship is broken? Is it to establish boundaries? Issue ultimatums? Draw lines in the sand? Or is it to biblically follow Scripture's command to reconcile broken relationships?[22] What is easy and comfortable is not always biblical, and what is biblical is not always easy and comfortable.

Counselor Fieldnotes

Relationships with parents and in-laws can be challenging for three broad reasons. First, if the relationship with parents were strained, filled with hurt, or nonexistent growing up, the relationship can continue to be a challenge now that the children are adults and married. Second, both the adult children *and* parents are still learning and growing. It's not uncommon for adult

---

20. Susan Thomas, "Am I Boundary-Driven or Love-Driven," July 2, 2012. *Association of Biblical Counselors*: https://christiancounseling.com/blog/uncategorized/am-i-boundary-driven-or-love-driven/.
21. Ibid.
22. There are some relationships with in-laws that will not be able to be reconciled, namely those where there is ongoing, habitual sin with no fruit of repentance (cf. Luke 17:3). See chapter four for a further discussion on the topic of forgiveness and reconciliation. In some cases where the conflicts between couple and in-laws are severe, I have encouraged them to pursue outside conciliation through a biblically-based organization.

children to begin to relate to their parents differently after they get married, and again after they become parents. They can have a growing realization that "my parents may actually know something and just want to help" versus "they just want to tell me what to do." Parents also need to learn how to see their children as adults, realizing that they can learn much from them, while encouraging a growing independence and flourishing apart from their "parenting." Third, a young husband or wife can still see and approach their relationship with their parents more from their experience as a child rather than from their experience as an adult living with Christ. Adult children can judge their parents for their lack of understanding of the gospel or for not being willing to "go deep" and talk about things beyond a superficial level.

As a result of these and other reasons, couples can take an "us versus them" attitude and justify their distance and boundaries based on past hurts and disappointments, their own pride and lack of love, or a lack of gospel perspective. Karen and I have found the need to shepherd couples through these various scenarios, helping them to see that God calls each of his children to be ministers of reconciliation, where Christlike love and forgiveness are at the heart of the relationship. God's call to pursue peace with parents and in-laws will be a pathway for both children and parents to experience the relationship each of them have longed for, but is only possible in Christ through the power of God.

Robert K. Cheong, PhD, Pastor of Care,
Sojourn Church, Louisville, Kentucky

RESOURCES

Jay Adams, *Solving Marriage Problems: Biblical Solutions for Christian Counselors*
Wayne Mack, *In-Laws: Married with Parents*

PART 3

CONCLUSION

Chapter 17

CARING FOR THE COUNSELOR

The expectation that we can be immersed in suffering and loss daily
and not be touched by it is as unrealistic as expecting to be able to
walk through water without getting wet.
RACHEL NAOMI REMEN

Come to me, all you who are weary and burdened, and I will give
you rest. Take my yoke upon you and learn from me, for I am gentle
and humble in heart, and you will find rest for your souls.
JESUS CHRIST, MATTHEW 11:28–29

If you have made it to the end of this book or have read through any of the
previous chapters, I hope you will not overlook this final chapter. At some point
in your counseling ministry, there will undoubtedly come a time when you come
face-to-face with the limitations of your humanity. You will have times when you
are overwhelmed and discouraged.[1] This is normal and natural. We are designed to
be fully present with those we care for, so it makes sense that we bear the burdens
of those we counsel. Paul wrote of having great sorrow and unceasing anguish in
his heart for the Jewish people (Rom. 9:2). He also wrote of the consistent pressure
he felt for all the churches he had planted and helped establish (2 Cor. 11:28).

---

1. Counselor Michael Emlet notes that those who do *not* feel some sort of emotional drain might
not be investing enough of their heart and soul into their counselees. https://www.ccef.org/resources/
video/help-i-am-emotionally-drained-counselor.

In this reality, how can we care for our own hearts during counseling? The apostle Peter writes about the need to be reminded of certain things in order to stimulate them toward godliness (2 Pet. 3:1).[2]

Dear friend and counselor, as you carry on this journey, may I offer you a few things by way of reminder to encourage and strengthen your soul?

10 THINGS TO REMEMBER IN MARRIAGE COUNSELING

1. Remember leaders like Moses.

In marriage counseling it can be helpful to remind oneself that Scripture is full of stories of leaders reaching the end of their ropes when it comes to ministry. Think about Moses for a moment. God's reluctant deliverer for the Israelites heads toward the Promised Land, which should have taken about forty days. On the way, he and the Israelites run into problem after problem. From worshipping a golden calf to complaining about the locally-sourced menu, we are reminded that ministry and leadership is hard work. One particular vignette gives an insight into the toil people can take on you,

> Moses heard the people of every family wailing at the entrance to their tents. The Lord became exceedingly angry, and Moses was troubled. He asked the Lord, "Why have you brought this trouble on your servant? What have I done to displease you that you put the burden of all these people on me? Did I conceive all these people? Did I give them birth? Why do you tell me to carry them in my arms, as a nurse carries an infant, to the land you promised on oath to their ancestors? Where can I get meat for all these people? They keep wailing to me, 'Give us meat to eat!' I cannot carry all these people by myself; the burden is too heavy for me. If this is how you are going to treat me, please go ahead and kill me—if I have found favor in your eyes—and do not let me face my own ruin."
>
> *Numbers 11:10–15*

Ever had days like this? Ever felt like this after a counseling session gone bad? Pastor, you are in good company. God knows the burdens of his leaders and cares about your well-being. Notice what God does in the next verse: "The Lord said to Moses: 'Bring me seventy of Israel's elders who are known to you as leaders and

---

2. The authors of the New Testament frequently exercise a ministry of reminder: 1 Cor. 4:17; 15:1; 2 Tim. 1:6; 2 Tim. 2:14; Tit. 3:1; 2 Pet. 1:12; Jude 1:5; finally, the Holy Spirit himself reminds us of the ministry of Jesus Christ (John 14:26).

officials among the people. Have them come to the tent of meeting, that they may stand there with you. I will come down and speak with you there, and I will take some of the power of the Spirit that is on you and put it on them. They will share the burden of the people with you so that you will not have to carry it alone'" (Num. 11:16–17).

We serve a God who is well-acquainted with human leaders. He knows we have limitations. He knows we cannot shoulder the burden alone. I believe that's exactly why he chose people like Moses, and why he chooses people like you—because you can't do it alone. You and I are utterly dependent on God for our strength. He does not leave his people alone!

2. Remember that the Word of God is sufficient to do the work of God.

It can be frustrating and disheartening when counseling does not seem to be making an impact on a couple's marriage. Week after week you pray and prepare for your sessions, and yet for every one step forward you take two steps back. Pastor, this is the long labor of marriage counseling. When our confidence is in our own abilities, we can be discouraged and disheartened at the lack of progress. Kara Bettis writes, "Christian counselors do not rely solely on their own intuition, training, and experience. They can internally pray for guidance with respect to what is most helpful for their counselees. It is comforting to know that, while I am responsible to get good training and keep up in my field, my client is ultimately in God's hands."[3]

It is at times like this that you must remind yourself that God's Word always impacts hearts. Isaiah writes that God's Word will "not return to me empty, but will accomplish what I desire and achieve the purpose for which I sent it" (Is. 55:11). Paul reminds us in 2 Corinthians 3:5, "Not that we are competent in ourselves to claim anything for ourselves, but our competence comes from God."

Our hope is in the efficacious work of the Word of God. Pastor, never doubt the power of God's Word to transform lives. It is both indispensable in our interpersonal ministry and our greatest hope for true heart change.

3. Remember that even the counselor sometimes needs counseling.

With counselors and therapists, the phrase compassion fatigue is often used to describe the emotional side effects of being deeply embedded in the lives of

---

3. Kara Bettis, "The 4 Great Challenges of Christian Counseling," February 2018. *Christianity Today*: https://www.christianitytoday.com/pastors/2018/february-web-exclusives/4-great-challenges-of-christian-counseling.html.

those they counsel. Defined formally, compassion fatigue is: "the 'cost of caring' for others in emotional and physical pain. It is characterized by deep physical and emotional exhaustion and a pronounced change in the helper's ability to feel empathy for their patients, their loved ones and their co-workers. It is marked by increased cynicism at work, a loss of enjoyment of our career, and eventually can transform into depression, secondary traumatic stress and stress-related illnesses. The most insidious aspect of compassion fatigue is that it attacks the very core of what brought us into this work: our empathy and compassion for others."[4]

Pastors who are involved in pastoral and counseling ministry should be cautious and wise when various symptoms of compassion fatigue manifest. Symptoms include:[5]

- cynical and critical at work/negative attitude
- irritable and impatient with coworkers
- fatigue: physical, mental, spiritual
- lack of productivity
- lack of satisfaction and fulfillment
- withdrawal
- sadness and worry
- sleep disturbance/nightmares
- addiction/workaholic
- detachment/isolation
- avoidance
- somatic complaints

If and when you begin to experience a combination of these issues, it could be helpful to pursue and receive counseling yourself. It should not surprise any of us that counselors need counseling. Often pastors and ministry leaders wait far too long to get counseling, thinking and believing they don't need it.

4. Remember that you are human and need rest.

Paul writes in Galatians, "Let us not become weary in doing good, for at the proper time we will reap a harvest if we do not give up" (Gal. 6:9). The verse is

---

4. http://www.compassionfatigue.org/pages/RunningOnEmpty.pdf. This definition is from a secular mental health point of view.

5. I'm indebted to the work of a fellow counselor and psychologist, Dr. Premala Jones, whose presentation on compassion fatigue at the Heartbeat International Conference in 2017 was helpful in preparing for this chapter. Dr. Jones is a member of Parkside Church and a member of our lay counseling team.

an apt reminder that weariness is an oft-ignored problem for many pastors. In ignoring the need for rest, we limit our abilities to truly labor and work for what is good.

I'm convinced that many pastors are overworked and under-rested. Think with me for a moment. The one day a week we are mandated by God to rest . . . pastors often *work*. Work and labor are not a result of the Fall, but overworking and under-resting are temptations humans have long battled. Regarding the temptation toward overwork, Tim Keller writes, "Thus Sabbath is about more than external rest of the body; it is about inner rest of the soul. We need rest from the anxiety and strain of our overwork, which is really an attempt to justify ourselves—to gain the money or the status or the reputation we think we have to have. Avoiding overwork requires deep rest in Christ's finished work for your salvation (Heb. 4:1–10). Only then will you be able to 'walk away' regularly from your vocational work and rest."[6]

One of the ways we can rest from the anxiety and strain of our work is to get regular sleep. Pastors can rest and sleep because we trust in a God who never sleeps and who never slumbers (Ps. 121:4). This is not just a reminder for our counselees; it is a reminder for us. Are you taking time to regularly sabbath and rest your mind, body, and spirit? Are you finding joy and happiness in everyday activities? Resting and sleeping are not an indulgence for most pastors, but a necessary discipline we engage in to provide the best level of care we can. Rae Bell, a research director for the Clergy Health Initiative at Duke Divinity School writes, "Clergy recognize the importance of caring for themselves, but doing so takes a back seat to fulfilling their vocational responsibilities, which are tantamount to caring for an entire community."[7]

5. Remember that you are not an island unto yourself.

I believe it was famous French general Charles de Gaulle who said, "The cemeteries of the world are full of indispensable men."[8] Pastors and counselors need to hear this word of reminder daily. You and I are ambassadors for Christ (2 Cor. 5:20), not ambassadors for self-sufficiency. We cannot do the work God has called us to without the help and support of the wider body of Christ. Paul reminds us of this in Romans 12:4–5, "Just as each of us has one body with many members, and

---

6. Tim Keller, "Wisdom and Sabbath Rest," http://qideas.org/articles/wisdom-and-sabbath-rest/.

7. "Clergy Health: Who Cares for the Caregivers?," June 28, 2012. *Duke Today*: https://today.duke.edu/2012/06/clergyhealth.

8. Steve Lohr, "One Day You're Indispensable, the Next Day . . ." January 17, 2009. *The New York Times*: https://www.nytimes.com/2009/01/18/weekinreview/18lohr.html.

these members do not all have the same function, so in Christ we, though many, form one body, and each member belongs to all the others."

Because counseling can be a fairly small enterprise (one-on-one meetings), we can begin to think of counseling as merely a dialogue between a few people. We can be forgetful that counseling is best when it's done as a trialogue—you—the counselees—and the Holy Spirit. We don't function in isolation but bear the priorities and presence of Jesus Christ to our counselees. Pastor David Gundersen reminds us, "I'm a member of the body of Christ, but I'm just a member. I'm not Christ, and I'm not the whole body. Sometimes, in extended ministry situations, I deceive myself into thinking that my role is far more transformative and indispensable than it really is. But momentary, temporal, passing opportunities remind me that I'm just God's servant for the moment, passing through people's lives and humbly offering them the little I have to offer as God orchestrates his vast network of faithful Christians to touch the world's many corners with his transforming grace."[9]

Pastors can proactively prevent some aspects of compassion fatigue by spreading the care to others so they can help shoulder the burden. When was the last time you shared ongoing counseling needs (albeit confidentially) with another colleague or trusted friend? When was the last time you sought out the help of another counselor or pastor? When was the last time you admitted to your counselee that you needed to research something or look something up before responding and answering a question?

6. Remember that your battle is not against flesh and blood.

In chapter two I mentioned that we are spiritually-embattled. Meaning, you and I exist in a world where there is a spiritual battle going on for the hearts, minds, and affections of those we lead and counsel. Paul reminds us, "For our struggle is not against flesh and blood, but against the rulers, against the authorities, against the powers of this dark world and against the spiritual forces of evil in the heavenly realms" (Eph. 6:12).

Sometimes when I'm counseling couples and they have recently experienced a victory in their marriage, I will remind them that spiritual growth in marriage does not mean Satan gives up on them. If anything, Satan will want to work overtime to trip up and tempt couples away from the path of marital harmony. If Satan is

9. David A. Gundersen, "Drops of Grace: The Limits and Opportunities of Momentary Ministry," February 20, 2017. https://davidagundersen.com/2017/02/20/drops-of-grace-the-limits-and-opportunities-of-momentary-ministry/.

eager to play the role of spoiler in marriage, then it should not surprise us that he would aim to attack us as counselors too.

Pastor and biblical counselor Dr. Paul Tautges lists twenty ways Satan seeks to destroy us;[10] I'll mention a few here that I have experienced personally, which you also might identity and resonate with:

He may try to cripple your effectiveness through confusion, discouragement, and despair (2 Cor. 4:8–9).

He may corrupt your mind and steer you away from the simplicity of Christ and his gospel (2 Cor. 11:3).

He may tempt you to deceive others in order to create or maintain the impression of being more spiritual (Acts 5:3; John 8:44).

He may tempt you to do evil (Matt. 4:1; 1 Thess. 3:5).

He is—at this moment—prowling about seeking to capture and destroy you, chiefly through pride (1 Pet. 5:6–8).

You and I could probably add many more things to this list. Remember then what God has commanded us in such times, and be encouraged, "Finally, be strong in the Lord and in his mighty power" (Eph. 6:10).

7. Remember that there are times you need to step away.

Throughout this book, hopefully you have recognized the fact that as a pastor, counselor, or ministry leader you are many things, but you are not a . . .

- savior
- redeemer
- miracle worker
- lawyer
- career advisor
- psychiatrist
- psychologist
- divorce attorney
- financial advisor
- doctor

Pastor, you are a counselor. There will be times in counseling couples when you realize that your abilities and gifting only go so far, and another individual's care and gifting is needed. Don't be afraid to voice this. This does not mean you're

---

10. Paul Tautges, "20 Ways Satan May Seek to Destroy You," February 13, 2012. *Counseling One Another*: http://counselingoneanother.com/2012/02/13/20-ways-satan-may-seek-to-destroy-you/.

a failure; if anything, it's a recognition of your finiteness as a human being. In chapter three I detailed several scenarios where I explained why and how counseling should end. Take heed to that; do not fall prey to the lie that you are the *one* thing this couple needs. The couple needs Jesus Christ and the hope that is offered through the gospel, not you!

8. Remember that you don't know how God will use your counsel.

When we must step away, we can still have confidence that God will use the message conveyed in counseling like a seed. I love how J. B. Phillips paraphrases the Parable of the Sower in Mark 4:13–20:

> The man who sows, sows the message. As for those who are by the roadside where the message is sown, as soon as they hear it Satan comes at once and takes away what has been sown in their minds. Similarly, the seed sown among the rocks represents those who hear the message without hesitation and accept it joyfully. But they have no real roots and do not last—when trouble or persecution arises because of the message, they give up their faith at once. Then there are the seeds which were sown among thorn-bushes. These are the people who hear the message, but the worries of this world and the false glamour of riches and all sorts of other ambitions creep in and choke the life out of what they have heard, and it produces no crop in their lives. As for the seed sown on good soil, this means the men who hear the message and accept it and do produce a crop—thirty, sixty, even a hundred times as much as they received.[11]

What I love about this parable is that the sower is largely in the background. His main role it seems is to sow the seed—the message of God. But look deeper at the parable from another angle. Each of the situations represented—the roadside, the rocks, the thornbushes, the good soil—all represent opportunities for a counselor to help and aid in the health and productivity of the seed. Sometimes a counselor's role is to fall on a seed and protect it so that Satan can't come away and pluck it out. Other times our role perhaps is to move rocks out of the way so a real and robust root system can grow and tap into something deep and rich. Or maybe our role is to trim back certain thornbushes that have choked out any hope of thriving and flourishing.

Whatever our role is, we seek by God's grace to speak truth in love and entrust

---

11. J. B. Phillips, trans., *The New Testament in Modern English* (New York: Macmillan, 1959), 76.

the results to God. David Gundersen has another good reminder for all of us in ministry: "I grow more and more confident that God raises up ministers and then retires them—with their lives and ministries passing far more quickly than they ever dreamed—so that the one constant factor in every Christian's transformation is God himself. He is the common denominator in all the operations of grace. He is the spring, the source, and the fountain. And if I get to dispense just one droplet of living water for one of his thirsty children who's quickly passing through my ministry, I will consider it a sacred honor and a privilege of grace to have been entrusted with such a stewardship."[12]

9. Remember to pay attention to your own marriage.

As I have written this book, there have been several times when Jen and I have benefitted from the counsel and input of others. Here and there we will half-jokingly say, "Hey, we need to get marriage counseling!" Marriage counselors should be honest about their own marital issues when appropriate and when helpful within the context of their own counseling. Guidelines against self-disclosure in professional settings are there for a reason, but in a Christian setting, wise self-disclosure can be a benefit. Counselors can empathize and love their counselees knowing that similar travails have afflicted their own marriages. Paul writes of the delight he had in sharing life with the believers in Thessalonica: "Because we loved you so much, we were delighted to share with you not only the gospel of God but our lives as well" (1 Thess. 2:8).

Pastors should pay attention to their own marriages especially in light of what I call the public-private margin. The public-private margin is the difference between one's private life at home and the public life they live in front of their congregation. In terms of ethics and behavior, I personally want that margin to be as slim as possible. The husband-father-pastor-counselor people see in public should be the husband-father-pastor-counselor my wife and children see in private.

A fellow friend and counselor once remarked that the reason he was still married was because he did marriage counseling. Years ago, I could not have understood how true that statement was, but after a decade of marriage counseling, I find his statement to be very true. So much of what I'm able to pass along in marriage counseling has been borne out of the crucible of my own marriage—more often than not learning from my many failures, shortcomings, and faults. The grace I need in my marriage is the same grace my counselees need. At the end of the day, I am more like the people I counsel than I am different.

---

12. Gundersen, "Drops of Grace," https://davidagundersen.com/2017/02/20/drops-of-grace-the-limits-and-opportunities-of-momentary-ministry/.

10. Remember that when listening to the full extent of evil and suffering, there is hope in Jesus Christ.

Counselors regularly sit and hear the full weight of the depravity of humanity. From the seemingly inconsequential frustration of a wife to the full-blown anger, rage, and abuse by a husband, counselors hear the full spectrum of evil in the world. Counselor Heather Gingrich of Denver Seminary writes, "If counselors are not grounded in the broader truth of God's love and care, and the reality that Christ came, died, and rose again precisely because of such human depravity, they can lose perspective and only see the darkness."[13]

I firmly believe that biblical counseling, as opposed to secular mental health, has the sturdier worldview and theology that is both capable of comprehending a world where such evils take place, but also capable of comprehending and worshipping a God who is sovereign over all. From the macro scale of human redemption to the microcosm of marriage, biblical counselors serve a God who is actively at work in both. We serve a God who is sovereign over evil and human suffering and who ultimately triumphs over it through his Son Jesus Christ. Praise be to God!

What other hope can we offer? What other system of counseling can offer a hope that actually moves and motivates marriage to exist for something larger and greater than personal fulfillment? We cannot give what we do not have. We must have this hope firmly planted in our hearts and souls as we counsel. May we consistently offer this hope in every session, in every meeting, in every encounter!

I pray that out of his glorious riches he may strengthen you with power through his Spirit in your inner being, so that Christ may dwell in your hearts through faith. And I pray that you, being rooted and established in love, may have power, together with all the Lord's holy people, to grasp how wide and long and high and deep is the love of Christ, and to know this love that surpasses knowledge—that you may be filled to the measure of all the fullness of God. Now to him who is able to do immeasurably more than all we ask or imagine, according to his power that is at work within us, to him be glory in the church and in Christ Jesus throughout all generations, for ever and ever! Amen.

EPHESIANS 3:16–21

---

13. Bettis, "The 4 Great Challenges of Christian Counseling," https://www.christianitytoday.com/pastors/2018/february-web-exclusives/4-great-challenges-of-christian-counseling.html.

Counselor Fieldnotes

Jonathan's chapter on caring for the counselor addresses the critical area of compassion fatigue. While this may be a newly identified concept for some, it has undoubtedly been experienced by many pastors, church leaders, and counselors as they cared for hurting and broken people within their congregations. Often mistaken for burnout, compassion fatigue differs in that the exposure to such intensity of emotion and pain impacts the empathetic counselor directly. In my private practice work, it is not uncommon for such pastors, church leaders, and counselors to present with symptoms of anxiety, depression, and feelings of being overwhelmed due to experiencing compassion fatigue.

These ten reminders provided by Jonathan are excellent ways to decrease the intrinsic risk of any counselor growing weary of doing good. Such risk is threatening not only individually but systemically as well. In other words, it does not just impact the individual counselor, but it has the potential to spread throughout the organization. If gone unchecked within a church or ministry, it can wreak havoc on an entire team. Jonathan's reminder list encourages counselors to be intentional, to personally recognize and respond to compassion fatigue. Additionally, the reminders listed help counselors to reserve the results of couple and marital reconciliation for the work of the Holy Spirit. Consequently, this will enable the counselors to remain emotionally healthy and biblically helpful in assisting the couples and their marriages.

Premala Tara Jones, PhD, Psychologist, University of Akron

RESOURCES

Kara Bettis, "The 4 Great Challenges of Christian Counseling," https://www.christianity today.com/pastors/2018/february-web-exclusives/4-great-challenges-of-christian -counseling.html

Christopher Ash, *Zeal without Burnout: Seven Keys to a Lifelong Ministry of Sustainable Sacrifice*

Brad Hambrick, *Burnout: Resting in God's Fairness*

Adam Mabry, *The Art of Rest: Faith to Hit Pause in a World that Never Stops*

David Murray, *Reset: Living a Grace-Paced Life in a Burnout Culture*

————, "Grace-Paced Living in a Burnout Culture," https://www.desiringgod.org/
    articles/grace-paced-living-in-a-burnout-culture
Shona and David Murray, *Refresh: Embracing a Grace-Paced Life in a World of Endless
    Demands*
J. I. Packer, *Weakness is the Way: Life with Christ Our Strength*
Joshua Waulk, "Too Tired To Care," http://biblicalcounselingcoalition.org/2016/06/29/
    too-tired-to-care/

ADDITIONAL RESOURCES

In addition to the resources I mentioned at the end of each chapter, here is a selection of resources.

Biblical Counseling Organizations

Christian Counseling and Education Foundation (CCEF): https://www.ccef.org
Association of Certified Biblical Counselors (ACBC): https://biblicalcounseling.com
Association of Biblical Counselors (ABC): https://christiancounseling.com
Biblical Counseling Coalition (BCC): https://www.biblicalcounselingcoalition.org
Institute for Biblical Counseling and Discipleship (IBCD): https://ibcd.org

Biblical Counseling Blogs

Care Leader: https://www.careleader.org
Paul David Tripp: https://www.paultripp.com
Faith Lafayette: https://blogs.faithlafayette.org/counseling
Tim Lane: http://timlane.org/blog
Robert Kellemen: http://www.rpmministries.org
Dave Dunham, https://pastordaveonline.org
Kevin Carson, https://pastorkevinsblog.com
Brad Hambrick, http://bradhambrick.com
Mark Shaw, http://www.histruthinlove.com
Paul Tautges, http://counselingoneanother.com

My Favorite Books on Marriage

Jay Adams, *Marriage, Divorce, and Remarriage in the Bible*
Christopher Ash, *Married for God: Making Your Marriage the Best It Can Be*
Alistair Begg, *Lasting Love: How to Avoid Marital Failure*
Bryan and Kathy Chapell, *Each for the Other: Marriage As It's Meant to Be*

Dave Harvey, *When Sinners Say, "I Do!": Discovering the Power of the Gospel for Marriage*

Timothy and Kathy Keller, *The Meaning of Marriage: Facing the Complexities of Commitment with the Wisdom of God*

Andreas Köstenberger, *God, Marriage, and Family: Rebuilding the Biblical Foundation,* 2nd ed.

Wayne A. Mack, *Strengthening Your Marriage*

Jim Newheiser, *Marriage, Divorce, Remarriage: Critical Questions and Answers*

Ray Ortlund, *Marriage and the Mystery of the Gospel*

Dwight and Margaret Peterson, *Are You Waiting for "The One"?: Cultivating Realistic, Positive Expectation for Christian Marriage*

John Piper, *This Momentary Marriage: A Parable of Permanence*

Tim Savage, *No Ordinary Marriage: Together for God's Glory*

Winston T. Smith, *Marriage Matters: Extraordinary Change through Ordinary Moments*

Gary Thomas, *Sacred Marriage: What if God Designed Marriage to Make Us Holy More Than to Make Us Happy?*

Paul David Tripp, *What Did You Expect? Redeeming the Realities of Marriage*

Walter Wangerin, *As for Me and My House: Crafting Your Marriage to Last*

Marriage Intensives and Small Group Curriculum

Winshape Retreat Center, https://marriage.winshape.org

Twelve Stones, http://twelvestones.org

Family Life, "Weekend to Remember," http://familylifeministries.org/weekend-to-remember

Paul David Tripp DVD, "What Did You Expect?" https://www.paultripp.com/products/wdye-dvd

Family Life, "The Art of Marriage," http://www.familylife.com/theartofmarriage

Premarital Counseling Resources

Ernie Baker, *Marry Wisely, Marry Well: A Blueprint for Personal Preparation*

Rob Green, *Tying the Knot: A Premarital Guide to a Strong and Lasting Marriage*

Brad Hambrick, *Gospel Centered Pre-Marital Mentoring Program*, http://bradhambrick.com/gcm/

John Henderson, *Catching Foxes: A Gospel-Guided Journey to Marriage*

Wayne A. Mack, *Preparing for Marriage God's Way: A Step-by-Step Guide for Marriage Success Before and After the Wedding*

Sean Perron and Spencer Harmon, *Letters to a Romantic on Engagement*

Margaret Kim Peterson and Dwight N. Peterson, *Are You Waiting for the One? Cultivating Realistic, Positive Expectations for Christian Marriage*

David Powlison and John Yenchko, *Pre-Engagement: Five Questions to Ask Yourselves*

Dennis Rainey, *Preparing for Marriage: The Complete Guide to Help You Discover God's Plan for a Lifetime of Love*